Maps *of* Sorrow

Migration and Music in the Construction of Pre-Colonial AfroAsia

Maps *of* Sorrow

Migration and Music in the Construction of Pre-Colonial AfroAsia

SUMANGALA DAMODARAN
and ARI SITAS

Tulika Books

Published by
Tulika Books
44 (first floor), Shahpur Jat, New Delhi 110 049, India
www.tulikabooks.in

First published in India in 2023

ISBN: 978-81-950559-9-9 (hardback)

Printed at Chaman Offset, Delhi 110 002

Contents

Maps and Figures

Acknowledgements

The ideas in this book were presented at several places in Delhi and Cape Town, and were developed through discussions with several people: many thanks to Madan Gopal Singh, Sazi Dlamini, Pritam Ghosal, Reza Khota, Mark Aranha, Luis Gimenez Amoros, to Ambedkar University and the India International Centre in Delhi, the Centre for African Studies at the University of Cape Town, Ciraj Rassool and the Centre for Humanities Research, University of the Western Cape. The journal *Critical Arts* published the paper that was first written and which formed the basis for the project 'Recentring AfroAsia: Musical and Human Migrations – 700–1500 AD', funded by the A.W. Mellon Foundation between 2016 and 2021. Special thanks to Saleem Badat for his faith that the project made sense. The work of several research scholars on the project has been quoted here: Shobha Talengala, Ayesha Sheth, Robert Nyamushosho, Nkosenathi Ernie Koela, Luis Gimenez Amoros, Kathyayini Dash, Mark Aranha, Valmont Layne, to name some, but the work of numerous others has been valuable. Sincere thanks to all the colleagues and students on the project for their collegiality and patience with what might have appeared as impossible ideas for smaller projects and performances.

Karen Press played a major role in gathering and organizing sources and meticulously going through and helping us organize two drafts of the book. Robert Nyamushosho helped with maps and Mark Aranha with musical transcriptions.

Our sincere gratitude to Indu Chandrasekhar for her faith that the book will be completed and getting things going in record time, as always. Thanks to H. Basantarani for her meticulous editing and patience with our delays.

Introduction

In November 2020, the AfroAsian Ensemble based in the multi-country Re-centring AfroAsia (RAA) Project[1] inaugurated a performance titled *A Sea-drift of Songs*. Seven of the eleven compositions involved sounds that were deemed to have ancient roots in AfroAsia. We were able to do so through the work undertaken between 2016 and 2020 by a range of researchers, post-doctoral fellows, and doctoral and master's students of the RAA Project, an international collaborative project initiated by the reflections and hypotheses contained in this book. The ensemble that performed *A Sea-drift of Songs* was drawn from India, Turkey, Spain, Ethiopia, Tanzania, Zimbabwe, eSwatini and South Africa. It attempted to reconstruct a range of narrative songs imagined to have been sung by freed slave women after the fall of Baghdad in the thirteenth century, now stranded on an island in the AfroAsian seas that link Africa, Arabia and India. Indeed, slave women or women in servitude played a major role in the construction of musicality in the years between 700 and 1500 CE. They were from everywhere, and although for a while Baghdadi elites favoured lighter-skinned performers, the majority were Africans from the region of sub-Saharan Africa, then called Zanj.

The overall narrative of the performance took a number of creative shortcuts. One such was to use the wondrous and fabulist account set down in the tenth century by Captain Buzurg ibn Shariyār, *The Book of the Wonders of India* (Buzurg, n.d.), in which he tells stories (or records descriptions by other captains and voyagers) of extraordinary creatures on land and sea, and extraordinary tales of life and death that can be connected to verifiable settings and places.[2]

Key for us was his tale of an African encounter in the land of Sofala, in what is now northern Mozambique. The king of Sofala ruled over an area that was the 'gateway' to the lands of gold around which Great Zimbabwe emerged, and later, the kingdom of Mwene Mutapa or Monomatapa. Its gold, ivory, copper and iron were to be found all the way to Baghdad, Cairo, Khambat (Cambay), Kochin, the Indonesian island worlds and China. In Buzurg's tale, harsh winds and seas forced the landing of a ship carrying Arabian merchants on the Sofala coast. The shipwrecked passengers and crew feared the worst as fables of cannibalism were prevalent in sailors' lore. But they were welcomed by the king and his retinue; they were housed, fed and helped to rebuild their large dhow, and were hosted there until the monsoon winds returned to allow safe passage. Instead of showing gratitude, however, the captain and his men abducted the king and scores of other people, chained them up in the hold, and transported them to be sold in the slave market at Basra.

Ten years later, the captain's dhow met a similar fate near Sofala. It was once again wrecked and beached, and those on board now really feared the worst, certain that they would be recognized and killed. To their bigger shock, they found that the king they had abducted and enslaved reigned supreme. Instead of killing them, however, he forgave them and described how he had worked hard while in captivity, how he had been manumitted, and how he had travelled up the Nile, through Habesh, the Great Lakes Region and the Congo, fearing that he would arrive home to find he had been usurped. But he was not – he regained his role as king. And he returned having learnt about the world from sages, warriors and commoners throughout the known world.

Seafarers have left behind outrageous stories about the Indian Ocean, the Arabian Sea and what would be better called, from our perspective, the AfroAsian seas, from Sinbad the Sailor of *The Arabian Nights* to our dear Captain Buzurg. There is also a contemporary turn towards this region in literature, a desire to revisit ancient lands that flourished before the Portuguese claimed to have discovered the world: works by Naguib Mahfouz (1959), Tariq Ali (1993, 1998), Amitav Ghosh (1992), Zakes Mda (2013), Kamila Shamsie (2014), Yvonne Odhiambo-Owuor (2019) – and the list is growing.

There are oral stories within each cultural formation of Africa, as Jan Vansina (1985) alerted us to, that harbour traces of the real: we were surprised by how much elders from the Venda community retold of the past when our AfroAsia project visited areas in southern Africa that might have been the Mapungubwe kingdom. They responded with aplomb, taking us further back than the rise of Mapungubwe in the eleventh century CE. We were told how the two Karanga brothers and their followers crossed the Limpopo River, and how they usurped power from the Khoi through cunning and force. How their magical trumpets bellowed their foes to sleep, allowing them to skewer each one to death and thus avoid doing battle with them. How then they intermingled with the Khoi. How their stories are sculpted in the enormous ceremonial drums (3 x 2 metres) which we are busy reconstructing in the context of the RAA Project.

Creating *A Sea-drift of Songs*, like writing this book, was no easy task, as an array of characters threatened to overwhelm us. The more musical participants in the journey – performers and composers – each had their own doctoral and post-doctoral routes and cultural formations demanding attention. Research on eastern Africa brought forth stories of the journeys of the *ngoma* drum, and the people who drummed and danced to it along the coastlines of Southeast Asia, from the Indus Valley to Indonesia. Scholars from those coastlines followed seafarers and fishing communities that claimed distant origins (in Greece and Africa) and poetry that spoke of longing, separation and travel, passed down by nomadic communities that traced pathways into Sassanid and Abbasid lands. Women in the south of Zanzibar traced Shirazi origins. Archaeologists from Dar es Salaam University started diving to find the remnants of Pliny's citadel off the island of Mafia. Artists were studying astrological maps and also narratives and drawings of gigantic birds that could lift elephants sky-high and drop them to their death. In short, besides the written record, we encountered oral stories, ways of playing music and orature claiming antiquity that demanded careful attention.

The RAA Project that we have nurtured since 2016 has thus had a serious performative side over and above its archaeological, historical and sociological work. So it was unavoidable to have a mix of research and flights of imagination in the output of the project's members. This started in 2018, when the senior scholars in the project crafted an eleventh-century love story, *Ife and Bilal*. It brought together the worlds of Kerala and Ethiopia, with Arab traders playing at intermediation. There were also performances by the Indian ensemble Chaar Yaar led by Madan Gopal Singh, which retold the travels of the lament, and its elements in Sufi and Bhakti traditions from the eleventh to the eighteenth century. And there was the Insurrections Ensemble's *Threads of Sorrow* production, hinting at the roots of slavery in the AfroAsian seas.[3]

A Sea-drift of Songs was a kind of turning point. What has followed it is work by some of the RAA musicians and artists on the true, tragic story of Gabriel, a sixteenth-century Beta Israel Ethiopian, abducted and sold as a slave to Muslims in Arabia and India, then converted to Christianity by the Portuguese Jesuits in Goa, escaping their hold on him to return to a Muslim world and then again to Goa, constantly switching faiths to survive until the Inquisition convicted him of apostasy and sentenced him to labour in the galleys. Other RAA Project researchers followed the 1414 journey of three giraffes from Kenya's Malindi to Bengal, and then, thanks to Zheng He, one giraffe's further journey to Emperor Yongle's court. This resulted in a plurimedial production, *Giraffe Humming*, which is an imaginative reconstruction of the journey of the giraffes.

What we are presenting in this book is under threat of becoming *passé* as researchers and senior students expand the boundaries of this AfroAsian effort. Its original hypothesis was that the polycentric world of the pre-fifteenth century involved systems, processes and interactions that were interconnected and traversed great distances. That instead of sociology's concept of 'traditional' society, the world was very much about forms of urbanity and agrarian change, and full of the movement of people, influences and ideas. It was also punctuated by the movement of symbolic forms like music, crafting long-distance acuities and constellations that were kinetic but also sedentary and canonized. It was a complex system with dignified and impressive civilizational hues, but also one of hardship and sorrow, of classes and castes, of racial and ethnic derogations, and of bondage, servitude and slavery.

The book begins with a chapter by Ari Sitas in which he constructs a fictional character, Garai, who traverses the known world in different periods, from Mapungubwe in southern Africa to the distant worlds of northern Africa, southern Spain and India, and back to southern Africa. Originally inspired by Zakes Mda's novel, *The Sculptors of Mapungubwe* (2013), the narrative of Garai's journey offers a way of presenting the empirical research that has been done on the spaces and places he encounters. The second chapter, drafted by Ari Sitas with the help of Sumangala Damodaran, traces the historical and theoretical consequences of this research, stretching historical materialism and historical sociology in new ways. The third chapter, drafted by Sumangala Damodaran with the help of Ari Sitas, traces the methodological difficulties and breakthroughs such research entails. The fourth chapter, drafted by Sumangala Damodaran with the assistance of Mark Aranha for musical transcriptions, goes to the heart of the musical argument, demonstrating the aesthetic constellations that preoccupied the elites and commoners of the time.

Our readers must remember: this is the beginning of a much longer journey.

Notes

[1] Between 2016 and 2021, a multi-institutional and multi-country project titled 'Recentring AfroAsia: Musical and Human Migrations – 700–1500 AD' conducted research exploring pre-colonial links between different parts of AfroAsia, using music as an entry point to understand connections. With support from the A.W. Mellon Foundation and based at the University of Cape Town, South Africa, the project included universities in India, South Africa, Ethiopia, Tanzania and China. The project supported 90 students at graduate and post-doctoral levels from eighteen countries, more than forty senior research scholars, and produced about a hundred research papers and seventeen artistic and musical performances. The authors of this book were the international co-directors of the project, and the book presents the overarching arguments that have come out of the project. From June 2022, the project has been continued with support from the National Institute of Humanities and Social Sciences, South Africa.

[2] According to a *Wikipedia* entry (https://en.wikipedia.org/wiki/Al-Ramhormuzi), 'it is now believed that Buzurg is probably a purely fictional personage. Apart from the attribution of this book to him, his existence is otherwise unattested. The attribution apparently dates from the thirteenth century, long after he allegedly lived. Recent research has shown that the book was more probably written in Cairo during the second half of the tenth century, by a scholar called Abū 'ImrānMūsā ibn Rabāḥ al-Awsī al-Sīrāfī' (Ducène 2015).

[3] www.insurrectionsensemble.com

CHAPTER ONE

Of Chata and Garai

Beginnings of a Journey

Chata, the protagonist of Zakes Mda's *Sculptors of Mapungubwe* (2013), defiant sculptor and traveller whose *mbisili* art troubled the kingdom (it was deviant, it was disliked, it was threatening something undefined), provides an imaginative beginning for this journey. It is a story of creativity, of a different relationship to nature, of the impulsive need to travel to where these mirrors and goods come from and to learn from seafaring, of being abducted as a slave near Mogadishu, of returning through the Congo, of using gold for beauty rather than power; and it raises the contemporary issue of the role of art. Mda's is a sensitive reconstruction of the ancient kingdom and its woes, and even if fiction often trumps research, it is believable. Well, almost believable.

Let us rename our Chata Garai, to keep the stories distinct.

At first our project's Garai, like Chata, had to be of the years between 1075 and 1290, the years of Mapungubwe's emergence and reign which reached its peak in the late thirteenth century. He too would be a mix of a Leopard Kopje community (Shona-Karanga cluster, a sub-branch of the Shona people) and the !Kung. He could not have been a gold miner – gold, like copper, was mined further north; it came from southern Zimbabwe.[1] Indeed Shadreck Chirikure (2015) provides a vivid description of metallurgical work in and around the citadel, so there is no point in repeating it here, save to say that there was plenty around.

Let us place him in front of a mirror, the commodity that so fascinated Chata in the novel – he would have worn a cotton or bark thread tunic spun there; spinning whorls were very much part of the traded stuff brought in and were put to good use, and later, locally manufactured (Huffman 1988:

677; see also Huffman 2000). He would have had strong arms and hips from metal-working activity, with quite rough fingers. He would have had extra leather clothing for the colder months and a leather bag. He would have had copper and ivory bangles, and perhaps a gold earring or leglets. He would have worn a colourful necklace made of shell beads (ostrich or freshwater mussel) and glass beads (opaque, transparent and translucent brownish black, red, blue-green, yellow, light green or cobalt blue) all the way from Cairo (Saitowitz 1996; Wood 2011). He would have had a knife (Huffman 2005), a carved stick or a spear, and perhaps a bow and arrows. He would have had a gourd of home-brew and his special little bag filled with healing pastes and plants, slag, chisels and crucibles.

This is a far cry from the portraiture that has animated colonial anthropology about Garai's kin. Part of this effort to research and write about it is to bring Africa out of that colonial snare and into a worldly conversation outside the dioramas of tribal life. People, as is obvious, are both predictable and outrageously creative – they leave traces in very obvious places, near water sources and where flora and fauna are amenable to coexistence; but they also spend endless hours creating sonorities out of stretched-out skins, extruding metal wire, carving out and bending wood, all in the service of something beyond the notions of use value or exchange value.

Let us make Garai musical then: there would have been winds and strings aplenty. (Mda mentions the timbila; archaeologists further north believe that the mbira was available [Nyamushosho and Chirikure 2019], but let us stick to what is more certain.) Wind instruments made from horns or carved baobab or bamboo-like reeds (Blench 2012a, 2012b), or an ivory horn (Fagan and Kirkman 1967) would have been handy and common. A bow strung with animal intestine or extruded iron or copper would have also been possible (Camp and Nettl 1955). It is our misfortune that most such instruments were biodegradable. But that would do.

The homestead had to be his father's, as he would still be an unmarried man if he were to dare travel. The home would be a grass-thatched rondavel hut (known also as a *gota*) made of plastered poles and adobe walls erected on a thickly compacted and gravelled floor. His rondavel would be to the side of the paternal barrack and close to his maternal barrack. If he was an iron or metal worker, his father would have been one too – a member of one of the knowledge and craft clans that had a special relationship to the royal court. Metal workers were a revered cult whose members were mostly men. There would also have been a toolshed and a workshop, probably at the centre of the homestead (Hall 1998: 97–98). There would have been a cattle enclosure, and a space for a local donkey or two and perhaps chickens. To be able to leave, he must have had a brother or brothers to shoulder the burdens of absence, because we would have to make him travel.

There, on the precipitous hill in the distance, the royal court and the ruling elite would hold sway, and he would know that for about a fifth of the way to the coast he would still be subject to Mapungubwe's rule; other, smaller hills would have similar patterns of hierarchy – the chiefs and headmen at the top, the commoners below. According to Huffman (1988: 679),

> these important residences [were] similar to elite hilltop settlements some distance away from Mapungubwe: for example, Little Muck, 13 km away; Mmangwa, 40 km to the west; Mapela Hill, 85 km north-west; and Macena Hill, 96 km north-east. They [were] invariably near low-lying Mapungubwe-phase villages which were still organized around central cattle byres, for example at Mtetengwe. These different kinds of settlement provide the best archaeological evidence for a three-tiered political hierarchy: the low-lying sites were probably inhabited by commoners; the small hilltop sites were probably occupied by district leaders; and the capital at Mapungubwe would have been the supreme authority. (Also see Huffman 2000)

It would have taken about a month to reach the ocean, or ten days by boat if the flow of the river was adequately strong – that is, through the summer months when rain was plentiful. But such a journey had to follow pathways away from the river itself along its shallow or non-navigable parts, and often because of the presence of wild and predatory animals. And yet those months when the water was high would have been hot and humid, so the trip would have been better endured in the dryer months; but then again, it would have had to avoid the sorghum-harvesting months because arms like his would have been needed then. It would have been spring – remembering that the four seasons so clear in the Cape are less so as we approach the Lowveld and the tropics. There would be only summering and wintering along the Limpopo River.

The pathways towards the ocean would have traversed another polity of sedentary agriculturalists whose patterns of organization and command would have been familiar to Garai and his kin. They would have been the pre-Ndwandwe clans intermixed with the eMbo people who had migrated from Kenya four centuries earlier. Many people would have been involved in the patterns of trade between Mapungubwe and Sofala.

The historical periods our project seeks to cover would have needed three Garais. There is a vivid summary of those periods of emergence in Martin Hall's work (1987: 91–116). The first one would have been at the beginnings of Mapungubwe, in a space of urbane settlement ('rurban', in the words of Pearson [1998]), but without the grandeur of the thirteenth century. His people, the Leopard Kopje community, would have moved to the Shashi Limpopo Basin and displaced the centrality of the Zhizo people whose epicentre would have been Schroda. The Garai I people, or the residents of the hill whose urban settlement has been named K2 (Bambadyanalo), were the precursors of Mapungubwe, situated a kilometre or so away (Fagan 1984: 529; Hall 1987: 117; Huffman 1988: 671). It was estimated that the immediate settlement would have numbered about 1,500 people (Huffman 2005: 17).

The Shashi/Limpopo area has middling rainfall and, according to Huffman (1988: 669),

> the broken sandstone ridges provide cultivable soils and mixed woodland; the warm temperature and relatively low rainfall generate sweet savanna grasses; and the Shashi and Limpopo Rivers ensure a more-or-less permanent water supply. In addition, the Mopani woodland between the two rivers is prime elephant country, and ivory would have been easily available: even today this area is rich in elephant. Furthermore, the rivers that drain the western gold reefs of Zimbabwe flow into the Shashi and Limpopo near their confluence; and so it would have been possible to pan for alluvial gold.

But Garai I would have had a major task to please our narrative: in the first period he would have had to take us further up the map to witness the rise of Baghdad after the suppression of one of the most vigorous slave rebellions in history, whose flames were kept going by the majority of African slaves (the Zanj) for ten years (869–879 CE). He would have taken us to southern Spain following another African (Al-Tabari 1992), the manumitted slave Ziryab who set up the music schools of al-Andalus. He would have observed the growing inter-regional relations between eastern and southern Africa. He would have given us a glimpse of the transition from a world of connections between Ethiopia, eastern Africa, the Mediterranean and Southeast Asia to one punctuated by the spread of Islam and the growth of Muslim trading networks (Bathily 1988: 734; also Anfray 1995).

Here, iron would have been moved to India with the cycles of the monsoon, and increasingly, gold to the Muslim world at large and to Khambat in Gujarat, undergirding their rising power. At all destinations raw materials

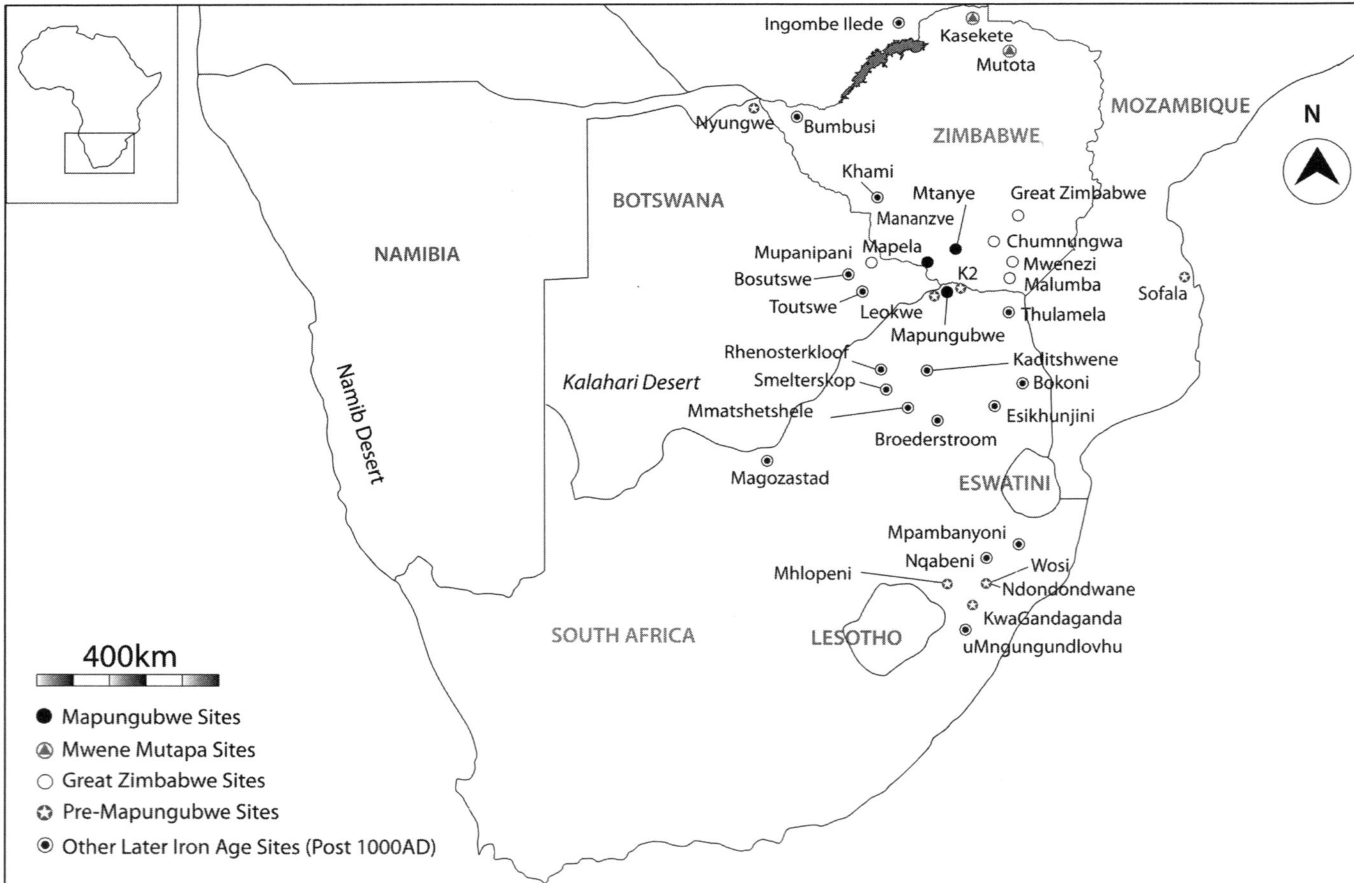

Map 1.1 The Mapungubwe, Great Zimbabwe and Sofala Triangle
Source: Map constructed by Robert Nyamushosho, Archaeology Department, University of Cape Town, 2020

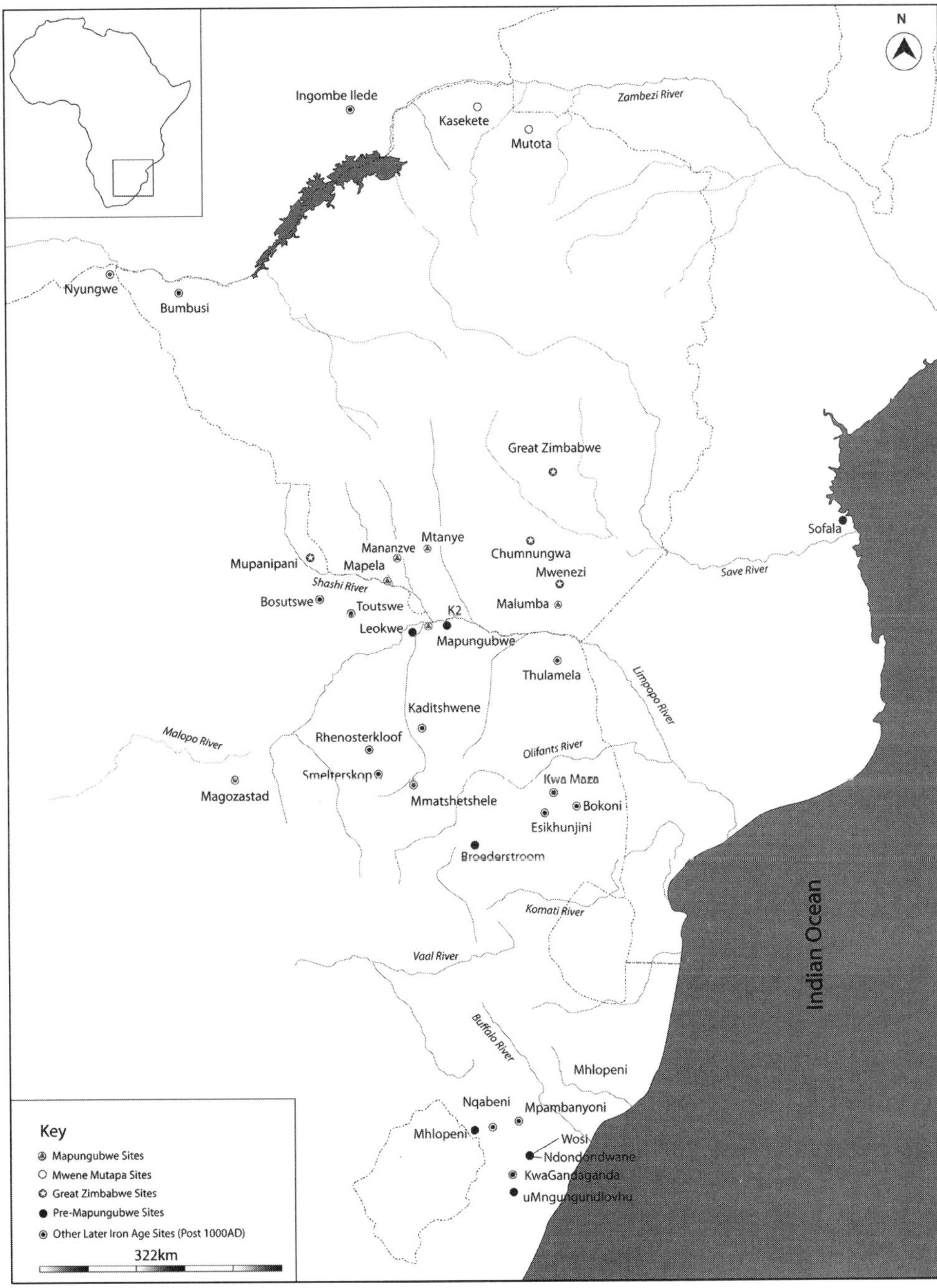

Map 1.2 The Mapungubwe, Great Zimbabwe and Sofala Triangle in a wider context
Source: Map constructed by Robert Nyamushosho, Archaeology Department, University of Cape Town, 2020.

like flax, cotton, gum and indigo, subsistence products, luxuries for the home from spices to slaves, and luxury goods from ivory to pearls were traded. The remarkable trust relationships involved in far-flung trade, the drafts, the bills of exchange, the promissory notes, were all being initiated.

Our Garai II would have lived in the new agglomeration of power. By his time, gold was being locally manufactured at Mapungubwe. The golden rhinoceros and the sceptre found in elite graves on the hill of Mapungubwe signified the emergence of the metal as a status symbol. This was also a time of transition to what archaeologists call the Zimbabwean era. According to Huffman (1988: 678),

> the spatial organization of the Zimbabwe Culture differed in several ways from the Bantu Cattle pattern: the king lived inside a stone enclosure on a hill above the court, not at the base of the hill; elites were buried in hills rather than in the byre; royal wives lived in their own area rather than with the king; and important men maintained prestigious residences on the outskirts of the capitals.

The population of the capital of Mapungubwe would have reached 5,000 people by then (Huffman 2005: 40–41). By the time of Garai II's involvement, the coastline of eastern Africa and its islands were punctuated by significant urban formations: Mogadishu, Barawa, Malindi, Mombasa, Kilwa and Sofala; Pate, Pemba and Kizimkazi in Zanzibar (Kusimba 2004; Masao and Mutoro 1988), with the last becoming a major hub of transshipment of people and goods. By then, the very ships would have grown larger, although navigation would have still been dependent on the 'sidereal rose' (Tibbets 1971; Tolmacheva 1980).

The third Garai would have stood in the ruins of Mapungubwe, knowing that further north his distant kin in Great Zimbabwe and their distant kin in Ing'ombeIlede reigned with vigour. The Zambezi River would by then have eclipsed the Limpopo. We will return to this world and the transition from Great Zimbabwe to Mwene Mutapa when we deal with Sofala in the pages that follow.

Great Zimbabwe, architecturally, politically and spiritually, marked a highpoint in Zambezia. We are aware that however impressive its Acropolis was, its granite boulders and stone walls, which started to evolve into an epicentre by the eleventh century, it was the enormous settlement around it that gave it its urban form. As new archaeological digs reveal, too, it was a network of further productive and metal-processing settlements that provided for a more spread-out political economy of trade and survival. Somehow the rise and decline of Mapungubwe and Great Zimbabwe coincided with the rise of all this – the great enclosure with its high and thickset walls, its conical tower, leading inwards to smaller enclosures housing, our archaeologists insist, the ruling elite of the time. The gold and copper ornaments found there, traces of exotic objects from China, Persia and Syria, abounded (for example, a jade teapot, porcelain, celadon, glass beads, Arabian glass). Its rulers were not only wielding political power, but functioned as an epicentre of trade as well. We could have Garai walk north there, and wander up to the eastern side of what is now the Democratic Republic of the Congo.

What if Garai III walked south? He would have been witness to the consolidation of what we call Mzansi these days (southern Africa) after three centuries of decisive migrations. Unlike the Shona-Karanga people of his ancestors, there would be in what are now the North-West and Mpumalanga provinces the other tree of ethnic clusters, nudging south Venda, Sotho, Tsonga, Nguni and Inhambane. And everywhere, the Khoi (!Kung), the ones who did not intermingle with the so-called Bantu people, had become itinerant pastoralists herding their Afrikander cattle south, east and west. He would have been crossing over, according to Ngcongco (1984: 386), 'the origin of the major cultural traditions that are so characteristic of the Bantu-speakers living in the region, the Sotho/Tswana and the Nguni'. By about 1500 some of these traditions were taking shape, to be inherited by the main ethnic groups known in the nineteenth century. It would have been impressive to realize how the customs and mores of Greater Zimbabwe and the Highveld further south, bride-wealth and political organization, resembled one another.

He would have traversed wondrous terrain: there would have been trees, shrubs and climbers furnishing fruit, or elements that could have been brewed into a beverage of note! No fewer than 63 varieties of fruit trees proliferated from Mapungubwe to the southernmost corner of the Tsonga or Venda domains. There would have been mosquitoes and the odd infestation of tsetse flies. But the veld and its woodlands would have been resplendent with edible animal life – bushpigs, impala and waterbuck, grouse and fowls, and unless he was alert, there was a range of animals about that would have gnawed his innards – crocodiles and hyenas at one extreme, leopards or lions at the other.

It would have been a wondrous space of birds, too: hoopoes, stilts, chinspots, cuckoos, bustards, innumerable doves, honeyguides, sunbirds, storks and the peculiar hornbills. And, of course, there would have been the rhino, the elephant and the giraffe. And somehow, the settlements, the villages and all these natural energies coexisted in a fragile equilibrium between the people and the fauna and flora of the area.

What would have surprised him was that around what is named Phalaborwa these days, there was as much copper production as there was all the way up in Ing'ombeIlende. And it was a rich seam that was mined, finding its way down the Olifants River (of more recent times) which Vasco da Gama called the 'river of copper' in 1498, according to Ngcongco (1984)! And as he was heading further south, the salt works near present-day Tzaneen and the metal works and smithies of the Venda would have made him curious. Would Mapungubwe's ritual songs of metal work resemble these? Would he have been allowed to display his skills and learn theirs?

And then, among the various strands of Nguni people – the Hlubi, on the eastern side of Ukahlamba/Drakensberg, with their rectangular homes, as opposed to the endless domain of circles in the vast expanse from Zambezia to the northern parts of contemporary Drakensberg. And pressing on down through the subtropical terrain later to be called Zululand, he would not have failed to notice how the Khoi left an indelible mark on all Nguni and Sotho dialects (Ngcongco [1984] claims 14–20 per cent of their vocabulary!). He would have also noticed that their cattle were of a different lineage and breed – the Sanga breed. But the intermingling of Xhosa and Tswana, and to a lesser extent Zulu, with Khoi genetic material would have been invisible to him. He would have met the independent, itinerant and pastoralist Khoi for sure by the time he reached the south. They had been on the move since the fourteenth century:

> The Khoikhoi expanded southwards and south-eastwards from the high veld, travelling along rivers wherever possible. Once they reached the Vaal/Orange confluence, one section followed the Orange downstream and expanded into Namaqualand and Namibia, where they reached Sandwich Harbour before 1677. Another branch headed south along the rivers from the confluence, crossed the Sneeuwberge and split into two branches: one travelled eastwards and inland from the coast to Natal, the other went westwards to reach the superb pastures of the Cape area. (Ibid.: 388)

What could he have learnt from the south, given that much splendour was to the north and the enticing world of wondrous exotica was to the east? The bias of our project does not allow him to move west to find the intensity of the ascending kingdom of the Congo, or further on, how his distant kin, the Herero, intermingled with the Khoi in the harshest landscape. Indeed, what could he have learnt?

For one, that there was an intensity of transactions that was localized. Goods moved between small and expansive polities: raw materials, processed goods, earth's resilient bounty, luxuries, but there is no record of slaves. There was communication – the languages evolving were also dialects of larger units, and there was movement of people and cattle (disaffected individuals, brides and their bride-wealth) across borders. And Shadreck Chirikure (2020) is right: there was agency and choice about what moved and why. People accepted a lot of bling from afar, but they were very selective about it.

We shall explore in the next chapter why the emphasis on such local agencies is important.

We made Garai musical, though, and gave him a bow – that guaranteed instant acceptance from the entire gamut of formations, including the Khoi, who shared subtle variations in the bow's construction. But in walking great distances, the bow and his voice met untold imaginary dangers and comforts, from the hyena to the extravagant birds of the landscape. And he must have carried deep within him the sense of fissure from prior homes, as all migrating people do. He would have known how class structures determine a deep segregation between rituals for the self-selected 'some' and rituals for all. Each separate sphere had its 'musics', and there were the gatherings, the rites of passage, ranging from ecstatic possession to what would be called in the future a *giya*, a military dance.

There would have been, then, the songs and dances linked to age-sets, but also, at a deeper level of *ubuciko* (the skills acquired through age-sets), the music, rhythms and songs of the more esoteric knowledge hubs: of healing, metal-working, composing, rain-making and many more, as Thokozani Mhlambi has argued in his work (Mhlambi 2017).

The period under discussion witnessed major changes and shifts based on control of land and people, long-distance trade and an endogenous pattern of development, and the development of urban forms which, as Graham Connah insists in his second edition of *African Civilizations: An Archaeological Perspective*,

> were not aspects of a single process; not all cities were capitals of significant states and not all states had large static centres of population. Nevertheless, they were both important manifestations of pre-colonial complex societies, and it is sometimes difficult to discuss them in isolation . . . urban centres also showed

> considerable variety: some were densely populated for long periods, some only briefly occupied, some completely mobile, some with transient residence from season to season and year to year, and some with dispersed settlement covering enormous areas. (Connah 2001: 353–54).

In short, we are weaving a story that claims that another past *was* possible: it is not hard to imagine a world with different forms of beauty, sorrow and ugliness. But in stating this, two meanings are intended at once: firstly, we are loosening up and liberating what has been trapped in the demeaning category of the 'traditional'. Secondly, what was emergent in that other time was a potential that was never to be realized, because of the entanglement brought about by European foraging, settlement and later colonization.

In turning the clock back to the seventh century and moving slowly forward to the fifteenth, we are recovering both meanings. The former involves an assertion: there were societies in emergence and decline with their own complexities and rhythms. The latter gives rise to a sense of mourning about a range of potentialities that were never brought into being. If we could for one moment free ourselves from the Hegelian and the Comtean teleologies, the plenitude of all parts of the planet could be brought into conversation: Africa was always in the world and the world in Africa, and, as Catherine Coquery-Vidrovich and Henri Moniot have argued (1974: 349), Africa was a continent that 'never lived in isolation'.

As demanded of our imaginative journey, though, we have to follow Garai I, II and III down to Sofala and the Indian Ocean.

Sofala

Each Garai – Garai I, Garai II and Garai III – would have reached a different Sofala, even if the journey remained the same from the Zimbabwean highlands to the tropical coastline. In his first two incarnations, he could have easily chosen another route: perhaps to follow the pathways of the Limpopo River down to where it meets the Indian Ocean. That would have been closer to the Inhambane port, which had been a thriving one even before Arab traders established their dominance there. According to Maylin Newitt's history of Mozambique (2017), Persian and later Muslim traders had been active there, trading in pearls and in ambergris. It was also a place of cotton production, primarily by the Tsonga locals, until Garai's Karanga people invaded and took over activities there in the eleventh century, and spread them to Sofala too.

According to Richard Hall,

> gold had certainly been a stimulus in the surge of activity which created Zimbabwe. The Indian Ocean port of Sofala was reached by a twenty day journey, down from the plateau and due east across the coastal lowlands. At the coast the merchants waited with Syrian glassware, Persian and Chinese bowls, beads, cowrie shells, spoons and bells. The dhows, arriving on the monsoon, also brought cargoes of bright-coloured cloth, known as Khambaya, from the great Indian port of Cambay. For centuries such goods had been an irresistible lure for the people of the interior. (Hall 1998: 94)

For Garai to reach Sofala, though, he needed to nudge further north and then decisively east and follow the Buzi River pathways, to face the port where it meets the larger Phungwe River forming an ever-changing floodplain which, with its regular flooding, was in the end to swallow up Sofala as time marched on. On the road, he would have come across men walking in file, toiling down the paths to the sea, balancing baskets of goods on their heads, stretchers on their shoulders or with oxen dragging heavier loads, intoning some rhythmical tune for each step. They would have been accompanied by armed men and later, as the Mwene Mutapa kingdom was to be famous for, warrior women.

On arrival, Garai I could have been absorbed by the activities there and made into a sedentary intermediary in the tentative port of that time – he could have served as an easy link to the trade in gold and ivory (Masao and Mutoro 1988). Garai II, like many others, could have helped create the Swahili language that undergirded the dhow culture of the ocean which linked Sofala, Kilwa, Zanzibar and Madagascar (Matveiev 1984; Sutton 2002), and which brazenly, thanks to south Indian and Gujarati traders, reached Calicut, Surat and Basra (Chami 1998; LaViolette 2008). He could also have embraced Islam, but like all locals retain ancestral rituals and rites of spirit possession and exorcism he knew from home. Garai III would have been faced with the larger port – a vassal to two powers, Kilwa on the ocean side and the Mwene Mutapa kingdom in the highlands.

All three Garais would have been in awe of the bustle in the port and the vastness of the ocean, but they would have also been aware of the hardship of it all; the work being done, the haulage and cartage, the bargaining over goods, over gold dust or rods that he would have carried as a reliable source of exchange, the ivory stacks, the leather goods, and all the stuff that was to head uphill; and by the time of Garai II and Garai III, the presence of human chattel. He would have walked through yards where men were fixing sails and crafts, preparing the dhows for their next voyage.

The masters there would have asked of course what he was 'good for'. It would not have helped if he elaborated in complex ways his *izikathelo*, or the virtues of his craft; instead, he would immediately have shown the ironsmiths that he could smelt, pattern and pound. He could have shown strength and a proclivity for hard labour and endurance; he could have shown musical technique with his bow and ivory-carved horn (and perhaps even a flute). He would have been impressed by the xylophones, the timbilas made mostly of remnants of mangrove pole. He would have noticed the discomfort of some Arabs in regard to music, brew and dance.

Garai III would have arrived at a Sofala firmly under the control of the Shona hinterland. The Muslim trading class that came to dominate the space by the thirteenth century paid tribute to the paramount chief or king inland, to ensure that the supply of gold, ivory, iron and slaves continued. It would have been a busy harbour still. He would have noticed that there were two kinds of Muslim, light-skinned ones (Shirazis and Arabs) and dark-skinned ones, Garai-likes of prior centuries. All would be speaking Swahili. The *ngoma* traditions of rhythm, dance and song would have been preserved in the rituals of the latter.

He would have noticed that there were two urban formations boxed into one – and here I am stealing Michael Pearson's (1998) concepts – a *foreland* facing the trading sea and the timber works of the mangrove coast, and an *umland* facing the agrarian surroundings through which the town was fed, with its fruit plantations and coconut groves and sorghum fields, with its yams and cattle.

Garai I's world would have been the world described by the fabulist Buzurg; his *Book of the Wonders of India* includes four alleged sightings of Sofala in the tenth century (Buzurg n.d.: 25–29). Instead of a place of cannibals as it was feared, it turned out to be a fine place with a fine king. Whom they abducted to sell into slavery!

Daylight returned; the king and his companions were put together with the other slaves, whose number amounted to about two hundred heads; he was treated no differently from his fellow captives. The king said not a word, he did not open his mouth. He made as if we were unknown to him and we did not know him. On their arrival in Oman, the slaves were sold and the king with them.

Alas, whom did they find when they returned a decade later? The very same king, still in power, having been manumitted in Baghdad, having crossed over to Egypt, having sailed up the Nile to Nubia, having crossed Abyssinia, having experienced hardships through savannah and rainforest to reach home. And he did not put them to the knife or serve them in a pot. He forgave them!

The undertow of slavery is ever-present in Buzurg's account, which, however exaggerated in his description of dhows that could hold more than 200 slaves to make a point, continues unabated even after the Zanj rebellion of 869 CE in Baghdad (Al-Tabari 1992; Talhami 1977). Al-Tabari's account is written 90or so years after that conflagration. In WaqWaq (Madagascar), Buzurg's characters brazenly tell stories of

> constantly cheating the people of the country, stealing their children, buying some of them from others with *pagnes*, dates and other small items, we did so well that the ship was soon loaded with a hundred slaves, big and small. . . . On the ship, some of them were chained by the feet, others tied up; the children remained free (Buzurg n.d.: 16).

There were also slaves of different hue:

> the most beautiful slaves that we had ever seen in our lives, and the happiest; they sang, they gambolled, frolicked, teased each other. Their bodies were plump, and soft to the touch like cream; so nimble, so lively that they seemed ready to fly off in an instant. Only their heads were small, and below their flanks you could see a kind of wing or fin like those that tortoises have. (Ibid.: 23–24)

They were bought, they were lovable and entertaining, but in the open seas, 'with one bound, threw themselves overboard like a cloud of grasshoppers' (ibid.: 24).

But in Garai I's encounters with sailors, carters, captains and merchants, the worlds of the fabulous that made up the dhow cultures of the sea must have instilled both fear and wonder in him. Stories of gigantic crayfish, crabs, fish, birds, snakes, enormous ants the size of cats, flying scorpions hurtling through the air like sparrows, fish with human features, so obviously there near Zeila in the land of the Abyssinians, where there is a fish that has the exact face of Adam and his body and hands. Or worse, the fish Zhaloum that has the face of a man and sex organs that are human, both male and female, whose skin is thicker than the elephant's and made for good and sturdy shoes.

What of cannibals everywhere: not only in Zindj's (Zanj's) lands but also in Fansuour, Lameri, Kalah, Qaqola, Sanf, where they cut the human flesh into strips, dry it in various ways and serve it as dessert with good wine? Or what of the islands thronging with sex-starved women, a thousand to a man, who make you instruments of pleasure until you die of exhaustion? Or, in Kumr (also called WaqWaq), the big trees with gourds that have human features and voices that speak as they are shaken? Or the lands near Somalia, where the Zindjs abduct you and castrate you to parade your parts in public and excite envy? What of charmers of snakes and crocodiles, and diviners, sages and scoundrels, pirates and Christians? What of storms and monster waves, magic stones and cliffs, and elephants of all kinds and sizes employed in all professions? What of the markets of the Djinns in Kashmir?

But also fabulous places like Serendib/Ceylon, with its teeming cities and markets, a place which also sports horror:

> on the mountainside there is an enormous tree of copper and bronze, bristling with thorns like thick needles or skewers. And facing the tree stands a big idol with the face of a Black, whose eyes are topazes. Each year, the people of the country celebrate a feast day before this idol. They go there, climb the mountain, and whoever wishes approaches his Lord, drinks, sings, prostrates himself several times before the idol, then throws himself from the top of the mountain onto the bronze tree, whose spikes tear him to pieces. (Ibid.: 11)

There, too, is where the shipwrecked merchants were served 'a dish containing pieces of cooked meat, with heads, hands and feet just like the heads, hands and feet of young boys' (ibid.: 26).

Or further still, majestic China where in the king's garden in 'Khanfou', twenty *jerib* in extent, they would see 'narcissus, stocks, anemones, roses and a thousand species of flowers' and were 'astonished to find gathered together in one single garden, at the same moment, all the flowers of summer and winter' where everything that you see, trees and flowers, 'is made of silk' (ibid.: 73).

But then the sailors were bound to ask him, too, about the truth of cannibalism and whether here in the land of the Zindjs they could be shown these birds that either 'seize a beast in their beaks or claws, carry it up into the air, let it drop to earth to kill it and break it open, then land on it and devour it' or 'seize elephants and tear them apart' to eat them (ibid.: 99). And how far were the deserts where the gold was mined, and where were the anthills with ants the size of cats?

Setting foot on the dhow would have been an overwhelming experience for Garai III. He would have benefitted from the poet and navigator Ahmad Ibn Majid's description of how to get to the places he arrived at in his *First*

Navigational Poem (*As Sufaliyya*, the poem of Sofala), an astronomical guide to the route from Surat or Calicut to Sofala (Ibn Majid 1470). This poem, which wove together a combination of astronomy, mathematical calculation and captains' lore, was written as a manual for navigators, and takes us with some detail from Somalia down the coastline past Zanzibar, Kilwa and Madagascar. It is also said that some of Zheng He's fleet wandered there in 1422, but no account of this journey has been forthcoming (M. Huan 1970: 1–33).

Beyond the lands described by Ibn Majid there was a place of mists and foul weather, of savage islands and, in the fabulous lore that Buzurg had recorded six centuries earlier, gigantic birds that could lift elephants into the air and hurl them to their death. A later rendition of Ibn Majid's poem (1506) has him confirm that the Franks had voyaged through those mists. He also confirms that there were people on the coastline, people of a redder hue, all the way to where the land turned towards another vast expanse of ocean (Ibn Majid 1470).

Garai III would leave the lands of 'Muna-Musavi' and its reign over 'Zabnavi' (Ibn Majid 1470: Folio 94), and Sofala with its sand dunes and coconut groves, skip past the dangerous Sulanyat reef, and head past the (Tanzanian) coastline with its Muslim populations ruled by 'infidels'; he would reach Kilwa, 'the royal' in Ibn Majid's words, twist past Kwale and Charka, sail past Inkanjunda Island and along another long coast with scattered villages to reach Zanzibar, 'the great island', the 'pretty', 'neat' and 'welcoming place' of vibrant trade.

If we are to believe Alan Villiers (1969), who sailed in dhows in the 1930s in AfroAsia and especially along the Arabian and African coastlines, little had changed by then in the nature of the crafts, the zhambooks or sambooks that still traded through the open seas. But the largest zhambook he sailed in does not tally with what Buzurg and others described in the tenth century and artists depicted in the twelfth. The numbers on board, 'merchants, officers, sailors and other people of diverse nationalities, amounted to twelve hundred' (Buzurg n.d.: 42). Then there were his claims that anything up to two hundred slaves were held 'below', whereas the zhambook Villiers sailed in could accommodate a maximum of eighty people on the deck and a few women in the hold. The illustration included in the Buzurg volume (admittedly drawn three centuries later) showed a three-tiered vessel; it seems that the large ones were very large indeed. Unfortunately, Abdul Sheriff, in his great discussion of monsoons and dhows, does not specify details about the size of the vessels, but he seems to side with Buzurg rather than Villiers (Sheriff 2010).

But what Villiers (1969) emphasizes as an ancient custom was the presence of music, song and dance. There were designated musicians on board, employed to play for the crew and lead them in song – songs with lyrics like 'Oh Allah, help us with our work/fill the great sail with wind' would have been there from times long gone. The presence of work songs, of songs of hardship and longing, must have been age-old. For this musical aspect of the dhow voyages Garai I, Garai II and Garai III would have been game: the *ngoma*, with its song, drumming and dance, was of his soul, sinew and bone. Below deck, the slaves sang too. And when they were not allowed to do so, they whispered.

We shall return to their singing and their songs when we reach Basra.

Zanzibar

Zanzibar would have been hot, humid, fair and, as Buzurg said, 'neat'. It would have sported plenty of dhows in its natural harbours, but its main port (where the capital city, Stone Town, is now) would have hosted vessels from all over the AfroAsian seas. They would be anchored there surrounded by a bustling posse of local boats of various sizes moving people and goods around. The port faced west towards the African mainland, but this was a day or two away, difficult to reach with dugout canoes – and thus offering some safety from irate indigenes disturbed by the raids for slaves and the hunts for skins and ivory.

Admittedly, Garai I would have needed heaps of help to comprehend what was being said or indicated on the island. He had the safety provided to him by his (by now) half-load of gold. And he would have been under the good protection of the sea captain who received the other half of his gold in exchange for passage and provisions. It would not have been hard to surmise that the captain thought through the politics as well – keeping the Karanga of the Sofala outpost happy was good for business. But understanding what was being said would have been a challenge. The occasional common word had survived migrations up and down the coastline, even in Swahili (Matveiev 1984). The predominance of Arabic, Farsi and Gujarati in the port would have been quite an ordeal for Garai I. The settlements of the Omani had begun in earnest by the year 750 CE; the Shirazis and the Gujaratis followed suit thereafter.

Garai II would have had it easier. He would have come across a sturdy class of settlers with a mix of Swahili and Arabic speech and a cosmopolitan material culture. Richard Hall describes how they would have been eating 'from Chinese floral-pattern plates, as well as oriental stoneware and opaque white porcelain . . . they would have possessed fine pottery and glass goblets from Persia, phials containing attar of rose, many household ornaments and brass oil-lamps. . . . Their combs were made of tortoise shell, cosmetics were kept in carved copper bowls' (Hall 1998: 31). The mirrors that fascinated Garai in Mapungubwe would have been in plentiful supply. Although his people were reluctant to accept crockery from China or India and preferred the indigenous black and red vessels that were of important ritual provenance, mirrors, glass and scimitars were more than enticing.

He would have been informed that this opulence was nothing in comparison to what could be found at Kilwa (Wilkinson 1981), the citadel that Ibn Battuta ([1958]1994) praised as one of the finest in the world, with the exquisite stonemasonry of its mosques and stately homes. We leave the descriptions of this citadel to Abdul Sheriff (2010) and even to the original account by Ibn Battuta, because it would have delayed this narrative somewhat. All we need here is to know that both Garai II and Garai III would have had a good view of what these littoral and trading societies amounted to.

To be balanced in this account, we need to make a further point: although gold would have made Garai I acceptable in the world of material things, there was a spiritual side to this bustle that may have eluded us. He had to know by then that the Qur'an was an important book and that Arabic was its navigating tool. So, the Zanzibar interregnum that held him idle for three months before the sails were spread out once more against the wind, learning to speak Swahili and Arabic, was a survival-linked 'must'.

It would not demand a degree in anthropology to sense that beneath the veneer of poise, moderation, rectitude and devotion lurked subterranean spiritual upheaval. Not only were the African ways of keeping ancestral lines close ever-present, but rituals, including rituals of spirit possession, were also at hand. The island was full of restless and evil spirits with their colonizing habits of possession, too. And so it was that healers (usually women) who back home would have been called *izangoma* would now combine the old and the new in their exorcisms, and in the music that made exorcism possible. Such evil spirits were known to have been brought by foreigners (as they are to this day): the WaqWaq, the Abyssinians and the Omanis. Garai had new things to learn, and for sure the potions he had carried with him from home would be severely tested.

The other turbulence he would have experienced was sexual, and came at a price – well-manicured concubines for the rich, prostitutes for the common man of various cultural rankings. For the common man, Habeshi women occupied the top rank, Nubian women second place and Zanj women, third. For the rich, the lighter the skin, the better. For the more seasoned trader or captain or even sailor, there was also a trend to cohabitation, that is, the taking of a local 'wife'. Their children would come to populate the islands far and near.

It is into this liminal stage that we have to introduce an unrequited love story – heteronormative of course, because we lack the evidence of other preferences in the literature on Mapungubwe, Sofala and Zanzibar. (In Baghdad, we could have told another story: there, polymorphous sexuality thrived for a while.) In our story of Garai, the reason for the delay in sailing out of port also had something to do with precious human cargo. A prized woman from the Abyssinian highlands and her entourage of two were destined to reach Gujarat for a marriage with an Abyssinian commander of fearsome Mamluk battalions. But to have women on board who were not chattel demanded conversions of space: a special cabin had to be constructed or set aside so that they could be pampered and looked after out of sight of a guffawing crew.

We could imagine that such was the excitement that even the captain could have been confused by daydreams of abduction or elopement. Rumours abounded that the women were quite beautiful. How the captain or his informers came to witness such beauty was difficult to fathom, because in all their public outings they hid well behind their veils. We could also imagine that Garai had them breeze past him three times, and only a fertile imagination could construct a face or a knee or a waistline underneath all that *khambaya* cloth and silk. But as the story demands, his heart missed a beat when his lucky moment arrived – at the spice market, near the piles of pepper, turmeric and vanilla pods, the woman closest to Garai broke out into relentless sneezes that disturbed her veil until it slipped right off. The Muziris trader in command of the spice racks would have turned and asked, 'did you see her?' with a glint in his eyes, or 'did you see that?' with a frown. The trader's attitude matters little; we introduced him to boast a bit about our knowledge of the worlds of markets. To boast further: of course, if it was Garai II or III we were considering the trader would have been from Calicut, because the hub of trade moved up the Kerala coastline.

What is more to the point is that past the spice market stood the huts of the slaves, in an enclosure of mangrove poles guarded by Nubian strongmen.

The talk of the town was that inside the enclosure there were serious practices of selection and separation taking place. The slaves had to be divided up according to talent and possible specialization. Those with strong lungs were chosen for pearl-diving, those with enduring strength for the salt pans and reclamation works at Basra, those with musical skills for the training schools of Basra, warrior types for the Mamluk regiments, children for household chores, nimble fingers for craft work, and so on. Garai had to nudge his way towards the enclosure because in the thatched central space he was to be a judge of musical talent, thanks to his captain's good word about his ability. It was there that he touched for the first time the Abyssinian mazenqo with its mewing sound, the sorrowful sarangi and, of course, the strumming oud.[2]

It was on his way back from the enclosure that evening that he was ambushed and captured by pirate brigands, and before he knew it, he had been tied up and carted onto a hefty dhow. He could smell smoke as the brigands set everything afire at the port and on as many ships as they could reach within the hour. He was bundled and splayed under a thick net of ropes. There were two such clusters, one for men and one for women, and to his surprise he was close enough to touch elbows through the net with the Habeshi woman of his dreams. The ordeal of the journey to Basra is left to the imagination - thirty days of unimaginable horror. But after the first two days, as all captives do, singing starts, calls are responded to, music endures. She turned to him without a veil and sang along. They sang in any language they knew, as words no longer mattered, only the music did.

Ethiopia

If Garai presents us with the complexity of a triple identity because of historical change, the Habeshi woman, whom we will call Martha, and her retinue not only mirror such a complexity but add a dilemma about where her aristocratic lineages lie! It was a time of great upheaval there too: the first dynasty gets usurped by an irreligious rebel queen, the second emerges by suppressing the first and second, and the third emerges by suppressing the suppressors, claiming lineage to the first, and it would be obvious that much of an aristocratic lineage gets put to the knife, their landholdings usurped, and what was a quasi-feudal opulence turned to dust (Pankhurst 1998). To add to our problems, we are less interested in the aristocratic Martha than in her attendant, Mariam. It is Mariam we are concerned with since we decided that it was her veil that dropped in the marketplace, it was her face that enchanted Garai. For our purposes, we shouldn't care much about Martha (although her 'story' – that is, the story of the dynastic lineage of which she would have been a member – is better documented; see Pankhurst 1998) because she either did not survive the piratical assault or managed to obtain a passage to Gujarat.

Let us try and imagine how Mariam was put into servitude to a lady. Her father had land, as a mid-level peasant who paid tribute to the landed gentry – a small piece of land but quite enough to allow him to oscillate between subsistence, supplying the market and having enough for the tax he would have to pay. Let us imagine three sons and two daughters. The first son would be a future peasant, a small-scale landowner, so agrarian life like his father's would be his lot. The second would be enlisted in the military; with good fortune he could rise to some high position and it was not unknown for soldiers to be allotted land after having performed good service. The third would be offered to the monastic orders where life would be austere but immensely secure and, depending on talent and virtuosity, powerful. It is obvious that for a young woman, the father's favourite being in service quite young to female gentry would be a way out of family hardship and possibly up the class ladder; education and refinement would be her lot. The remaining daughter's life would be all about the household and domestic chores, just like her mother's (Pankhurst 1998).

Like Garai's, let us make Mariam's homestead musical. It is easy to say the word musical, but immediately we realize that the clashes over music-making could become a living hell. If the father was a village-level musician and played the krar, as many did, the strings of this harp-like instrument would be of animal intestine, extruded from goat or sheep, and perfected for use by the women of the household. It is not unreasonable to think that Mariam could have learnt to play the krar, although women were not supposed to play musical instruments in public; they could sing in accompaniment to the krar and the mazenqo on special occasions. They would all look down on the music of the more 'animist' south, with its call-and-response and dance rituals.

The monastic brother would be totally contemptuous of the 'devil's instrument', tormented that his loved ones indulged in base practices like that, but prohibited because of his family's status from touching and playing the begena, the 'angelic instrument' of the kingdom (Betreyohannes 2010).[3] He could become a master chanter, a virtuoso of the liturgical chant that Saint Yared had composed as a music of ecstasy, devotion and longing in the seventh century; this was a chanting craft reserved for men, the envy of Christendom.

This intimate struggle over the divine and the secular, over class and other distinctions, is relevant because it would also mark the relationship between Mariam in servitude and her keeper, Martha. Admiration of the girl's voice and disdain for the culture that produced it could easily be imagined. The gentry and the court would oscillate between two musics, the epic and heroic that accompanied military displays (and was later identified by Al-Farabi in his *Grand Book of Music* or *Great Book of Music* or *Great Treatise of Music* as an Abyssinian mode, the *sudud*) and the liturgical (Al-Farabi 2016: 543–47).

It has been said that the origin of the deepest religious emotion in Christendom and Islam, the melismatic intonation that Yared perfected in the liturgy and that the Prophet accepted as the *azaan* call, has deep Ethiopian roots (Betreyohannes 2010). Both Yared and Bilal, the Christian saint and the first muezzin of the Prophet, had common musical roots. But all that was the domain of male voices and would keep us away from the task at hand: our concern is to get the various women down from the highlands, through the inhospitable terrain of the Danakil with its cluster of slave-raiding fiefdoms, to Zeila, by now firmly in Muslim hands. From there, they would have to hop on to a dhow and slide down the map, out of the Red Sea to reach Zanzibar.

The Marthas' ancestors would recall a time when Ethiopian ships would cross such seas all the way to Muziris or Khambat along the western coastline of India, during the height of Aksumite power. That age was over – the age of shifting alliances with Byzantium and the Sassanids, and, depending on the teller, with Palestine and Rome. However filial the relationship might be with the rising Arabian powers since 615 CE, the coastline was in Muslim hands. An overland route to, let us say, Mombasa would be blocked by the Oromo and Galla who were nudging their way inland, pushed by the chaos of slave-raiding closer to the coast. The Christian pathways towards Alexandria, whose bishops ordained the Ethiopian bishops, would also be difficult and would take us off course. The Abbasids would by 815 CE have reached the Mediterranean, beat back Byzantium, ransacked Cyprus and taken half the population into slavery.

Martha and Mariam I would have undertaken the journey during a serious decline of Aksumite power (Crummy 1999). Martha and Mariam II would have travelled during a time of significant Christian revival, in the heyday of the Zangwe dynasty (1137–1270). This followed a period of serious decline in the influence of the religious and monastic orders, when the rebel queen Judit or Gudit shunned them and eliminated much of the later so-called Solomonic line of the gentry. But during the Zangwe period, what with the emphasis on church-building and excavation and the strengthening of the monastic orders, we can even imagine Mariam's brother en route to Jerusalem with the full support of Saladin (who had liberated it from Frankish Christendom) to occupy a place in liturgy and ritual. Saladin allowed the continuance of Christian ecclesiastical practices in Jerusalem, as long as they were not linked to the Roman Catholic Church.

Martha and Mariam III would be under the Solomonic dynasty's sway, with a serious consolidation of power around the Amharic core of the imperium, where Mariam's brothers would be at the core of military and monastic power. Perhaps they would have tired of the roving dynastic court which, eschewing roots in any one urban formation, moved its thousands of members, with armaments and all, from province to province. The codification of rule and law by then would have found its parchment in the Fetha Nagast (which, by the way, endorsed slavery – Anonymous 2009). What would have preoccupied refined women would be the tales of wonder, the very literature that was becoming a must for the dynastic line – fabulous tales with a religious twist like the 'Harp of Mary', alluding to divine musicality, song cycles such as 'The Harp of Glory – An Alphabetic Hymn of Praise for the Ever-Blessed Virgin Mary' (Anonymous 2010), a sung poem of extreme emotion, but also the tales of Eksander/Alexander, the Ethiopian saint, with their accounts of wondrous lands from the country of the Brahmin to the lands of Agog and Magog, to the infamous cities of Contrivance.

Our fine ladies would have travelled to Zanzibar in a relatively comfortable way on the back of a system of connections (camels, horses, carts and daises) that transported them and other tradeable goods like ivory, gold and silver to the coast, together with other slaves – a forced diaspora of people, two women for every man, of whom one in three were of Habeshi lines.

Baghdad

The idea that Garai and Mariam could have met in Basra should be deleted. On disembarking they would have been separated. A meeting later in Baghdad would have been possible for Garai and Mariam I and II, but it would have been a chance meeting, a million to one chance that could take place through authorial fiat. By their third incarnation, Baghdad would have been sacked and wrecked by the Mongols some time before.

Basra was a thriving urban formation and an extended slave camp. Most Zanj slaves were processed there through its traders and its 'display houses'. So, Garai I's fate in a display house would be a moment of crisis – would he be drafted into the craft businesses as an assistant, enlisted as a soldier in the military core, sent to work on the plantations, or put to work in the entertainment world of Baghdad, whose hierarchies were plenty and whose complications were plentiful? It is to an inn-keeper that we will send him, because like the Zanj women he would have rhythm, and by now would have mastered aspects of the oud and even a range of flutes from his exposure to them in Zanzibar.

Garai presented a risk to the seller: a price for him could hit rock bottom unless he had a special talent of sorts (Talib and Samir 1988: 716). Mariam could fetch a better price just because of her looks. There would be a downward pressure on prices anyway, because the slave traders wanted to pay low and sell high. The market for Abyssinian women was better in Aden or Zabid, but that would have presupposed a Nile journey to Egypt and beyond.

Zanj women received the worst descriptions in the traders' market catalogues (ibid.: 15), but Abyssinians would also be considered useless for singing and dancing, even though they could be slender and soft! Despite the above prejudices, the fact that they had some knowledge of music helped. Although accurate numbers are hard to come by, Baghdad had plenty of dark divas even though Caswell (2011) informs us that the dominant Al Mawsili school had a preference for lighter-skinned ones! Through our authorial choice, Garai did not have to go to the salt pans, the plantations or the reclamation works. And as he had not been castrated, he could not be sold as a eunuch. Mariam did not have to go into domestic service or prostitution. The fact that Mariam I could sing and could understand what an oud was, or its smaller cousin the mizhar (Caswell 2011: 2), would have elicited some smiles. She was to be sent to the famous training schools of Basra to be 'developed' as a *qaina*, a singing slave woman, for Baghdad. The traditions and nature of such compositions and singing will be the subject of the fourth chapter; suffice it here to state the following: if she was taught the finer arts of music, poetry, repartee and the art of love, she would fetch a good price. Of course, the market at that time for lighter-skinned women was better; and those trained in Medina coming from new sources of slavery – Slav, Turkish, Andalusian or Cypriot – could fetch close to 1,000 dinars. The job of the slaver was said to be onerous because price was related to sex, age, physical condition, abilities and race. It was rumoured that a concubine with musical talent and good looks could fetch no less than 13,000 dinars.

It is important to add a note on race here. Despite the teachings of the Qur'an (Talib and Samir 1988: 711) and the Prophet's castigation of race thinking, and even the historical fact that his most devoted followers were manumitted Ethiopian slaves, despite the long history of Ethiopian, Nubian and Zanj people even in pre-Islamic times as warriors, poets and craftsmen (ibid.: 707), racist ideas proliferated. It was the famous Black Crows like Antara, Khutaif and Sulayk who formed the pantheon of Arabic poetry in what is now Iraq (ibid.: 714), conquered from the Persians, where the highest concentration of Black slaves was to be found.[4] The dominant notion of race was one based on climatic determinism, which was very much in vogue with philosophers and held sway all the way to Ibn Khaldun's time as the basis for defining the inferiority of the Black. Talib and Samir (1988) quote from one of the manuals for slave traders about the Zanj women:

> their defaults are innumerable, the darker the uglier; they are not up to much. . . . Dancing and beating the rhythm are engrained in their nature. And since their manner of speech is unintelligible, they are given to blowing (musical instruments) and dancing. It is said: were the Zanj to fall from heaven they would beat the rhythm on falling. (Ibid.: 716)

In the mid-700s, Baghdad was a small settlement about 80 kilometres away from where the Sassanids ruled, with hardly more than a few hundred inhabitants. By the time we are describing, it was a thriving consequence of the Abbasid revolution (Kennedy 2004: 35); and by the time of Garai II, it would be close to riotous ruin.

At the time of Garai I's arrival in the early ninth century, it would be a city of the order of a million or two (depending on the source). Ronald Segal notes that in the years that followed Garai's stay, it would measure nine to ten kilometres, 'much larger than imperial Rome had been, and roughly equal to the area that Paris would eventually cover only by the close of the nineteenth century' (Segal 2003: 25). Of course, it would be a city of wonders, contrivances, music, poetry and wine (Mirelman 2009), a multicultural and metropolitan society. Garai would have entered through the Basra gate in the south, and wondered at the circular geometry of the city's design (Le Strange 1983: 88). Its founder, Mansur, paid brilliant attention to form and geometry, nuzzling the design towards the Tigris River and sorting out the canal system so that the Euphrates River could become useful, too. Mansur would have faced the Golden Palace with its resplendent mosque (ibid.: 36).

His grandson Harun Al-Rashid would have a court that was wealthy and cultured (ibid.: 115).

Garai II would encounter a fractious place controlled by military men (Saljuk Turks) and reviving from internal strife and riots, the most famous of which would have been the 'Revolt of the Naked', of the poor and the working masses, which was brutally suppressed (for a description, see Clot 1989). He would have met with a general intolerance of things festive or musical. And if we timed him well, he could have witnessed the deterioration that happened under Ma'mun's reign, full of intrigues and rebellions (Kennedy 2004: 164). It was a long period of catastrophes (Abu-Lughod 1991) – famine in 1057, floods in 1069 and 1077, riots in 1088.

Garai III would have been shipped away from Baghdad, a struggling place as the Mongolian horsemen and their auxiliaries put most of the people to the knife. He would have been sent west towards Cairo, or east towards Sindh.

In Garai we have a proud man from the African South, facing a world of servitude and of demeaning categories. Garai II's language skills would be good, too good for the inn-keeper and his customers' needs. He would hear and tell stories, and he would know that at the heart of the city there was a world of pious and industrious men whose wisdom was legendary, a world of engineers and philosophers who at best would tolerate a Sufi incantation now and then, but debate whether Sufi ecstatic dance was a sacrilege or a capitulation to the carnal. He would be sent to them for supplies of wine. He would have to walk past the Hall of Poets, the Booksellers' Market and the Butchers' Market on the way (Le Strange 1983).

By now, Baghdad itself had emerged as a vibrant city, a stone's throw from Ctesiphon and the ruins of the Sassanids (Fabrizi 2015). Its energy was incomparable:

> . . . into the bazaars of the city came porcelain, silk and musk from China; spices, minerals and dyes from India and the Malay Archipelago; rubies, lapis lazuli, fabrics and slaves from the lands of the Turks in Central Asia; honey, wax, furs and white slaves from Scandinavia and Russia; ivory, gold dust and Black slaves from Eastern Africa . . . rice, grain and linen from Egypt; glass, metal ware and fruits from Syria; brocade, pearls and weapons from Arabia; silks, perfumes and vegetables from Persia. (G.D. Sawa 1989: 3)

It was a cosmopolitan and multicultural centre, a centre of science and translation. Nestorians and Syriac Christians were translating the Greek classics; Persians, the wonderful poetry of the Sassanids; Indians, the texts of literature, mathematics and astronomy. And 'musicians, music theorists and music litterateurs were from a variety of ethnic backgrounds, colours and creeds. . . . The music product was a conglomeration of musical styles (Near Eastern, Arabic, Persian and Byzantine), whereas music theory first blindly copied Greek models, then assimilated and moulded these models' (ibid.: 7).

This is the story of Baghdad, a high point of philosophical reflection in the ninth century. The city's refined aesthetic tastes and vibrant ethos came not only from its own inhabitants, but from a constant movement of musicians and travellers who brought with them knowledge and experience from faraway lands. Thus, while art, both as philosophy and as practice, is known to have flowered especially during the Abbasid era, its energy was never about self-combustion (Farmer 1929).

In the first period, Garai could have found in Baghdad, at the House of Wisdom, the marvellous book of 850 CE, the *Book of Ingenious Devices* by the brothers Ahmad and Hasan Ibn Shakir. Among the hundred or so devices whose construction they describe is the design for a music organ that plays itself – an automaton trained to play various songs by means of encoded pins on a rotating cylinder. The second Garai would have found another scientist-engineer's book, that of Ibn al-Razzaz al-Jazari, whose *Book of Knowledge of Ingenious Mechanical Devices* includes descriptions and diagrams for construction of a perpetual flute and a water-clock with drummers, cymbalists and trumpeters who play every hour. It has other wonderful and very 'useful' devices, such as a mechanical slave girl to pour the drinks.

All this more than pleased Harun Al-Rashid, the legendary caliph of the Abbasids. It was said that the ruler's mind was devoted to the House of Wisdom, but his heart was with the music and poetry flourishing at the time. But even there his heart was to be broken in two, torn between the two powerhouses of music and slaving Ishaq Al-Mawsili and Ibrahim ibn Al-Mahdi, whose retinues included some of the most formidable slave-women musicians of the day.

It seems that since Ishaq's father's time, the Al-Mawsili centres of servitude and music had cultivated a preference for lighter-skinned women in performances, whereas his opponent, Al-Mahdi, was more broadminded than that. Ishaq, like his father Ibrahim, was a great musician, composer and poet, but also like his father, he partnered with other slave traders and profited greatly from the trade. And even though the latter had placed a free Black woman who was once a slave in command, the legendary Ulaya, bought for 100,000 dinars and then manumitted (Caswell 2011: 6), the scales of prestige were tipped towards the Mawsili side with the genius of Arib, who had more than a thousand songs in her composition repertoire (Caswell 2011; Gordon 2004).

Could Garai I have heard them? Indeed he could have, as the inns were populated by the patrons of the upper-class *majlis* (performing arts salons). They would demand of the 'lesser' women of the inns some of the songs they had heard at court, and often in a drunken stupor belt them out themselves. Garai would have come across the outrageous poet of the time, Abu Nuwas, whose homo- and hetero-erotic verses thrilled and frightened all and sundry. Although he would frequent the most famous of such haunts, Ibn Ramin's, with legendary singing and free-loving women like Sallama, Sada and Rubaya, Abu Nuwas would also seek out the even lower-caste venues run by Christians and Jews – a poet who could scandalize the elites and drag himself through drinking houses flirting with debasement. And how he would use his Persian descent to laugh at Arabs and their Bedouin tent mentality (Caswell 2011).

But in the main, there was a distance between the high and the low, in a very elite-conscious caliphate (ibid.: 44; G.D. Sawa 1985). The city experienced an explosion of energy that lasted more or less three-quarters of a century before it was stifled (Caswell 2011: 48). Garai I would find himself among a lesser stock of musicians: Persians, Khorasanis and people from 'Hind', talking of other times and distant places reached by caravan or boat. When not entertaining the upper-class clientele they would be telling other stories, especially the tales of Khusrow and Shirin and their unrequited love that were by then an expanding song-poem of note; or tales about the fate of Khusrow's daughters who rebelled against their slave condition so much that their defiance saw them not flogged but manumitted and married off to princely men; and other stories culled from epics that were heard on the Silk Roads all the way to China.

By contrast, Mariam I would have the opportunity to rise in the ranks of the *qiyan* (the singing slave women), and enter a world of sex, refinement and compositional craft. In Basra, she would have learnt how to be a proper Abbasid *qaina*, a courtesan with artistic graces, how to discuss literature, how to be flirtatious, and how and when to offer sexual favours. But most importantly, how to perform and compose songs. Would this be a better life than the one endured by the other slave women, the *jawari,* who served time in domestic labour? Would the *qiyan* have had it better than the so-called free women who had to wear the prescribed *hijab*? Would their existence, being privately owned for public pleasure (Caswell 2011), bring with it dignity?

But in our story, we will have to send her west to join another emergent powerhouse of sound and merriment in al-Andalus and Cordoba, to serve the legendary Ziryab. Mariam II will not be sent to Baghdad because the prohibitions on music and musicians and 'slave girls' will be on the rise (G.D. Sawa 1985). And Cordoba will be in trouble, too, as the frontiers between Moor and Frank were shifting at this time and the tolerance levels for the lavish world of craft were under severe strain. Cairo would have been a better bet (Abu-Lughod 1971). Mariam III could be sent once again to southern Spain, only to join the Moslem exodus to Morocco, to travel southwards with Andalusian music or to Cairo, which was by then a stronghold of the Mamluks. She could have met Othello there, still in chains. She would have looked for but not found the legendary descriptions of the wondrous automata in the Ethiopian Christian Chronicle of Alexander, the Ethiopian saint: inside the Citadel of Contrivance, whose walls were of adamantine stone, and of brass and of iron, and whose foundations were of lead – a dead city which God had exterminated because of the people's greed and 'their lascivious dances and fornications' – there was this giant musical device 'with wheels and pulleys, and levers', accompanied by an innumerable host of cunning contrivances that made figures of men and women of brass who danced to perpetuity. Alexander's men were captivated by the singing of songs to the sound of the drum and the flutes and the pipes and the organ that were most wondrous to listen to. The machine was a figure in the form of a man; 'vain things' they were for Alexander, 'which were moved from beneath by levers and wheels' (Pankhurst 1992: 246).

Cordoba

Mariam I would have taken a year to reach Cordoba if she was added to the cartage of people and goods on the overland route that skirted the African coastline to the Mediterranean Sea. Setting out from Baghdad to Syria could be done by barge on the Euphrates all the way to Raqqa; in other words, by following the grain barges to and from that entrepôt or following the land route via Anbar and Hit, then again reaching Raqqa. Then on to Aleppo, and from Aleppo to Damascus – the mix of dry steppe and desert and fertile strips in Palestine would then give way to the desert of Sinai and then the great Nile delta. Ifriqiyah could be reached by boat or via coastline by-ways (Kennedy 2004).

Although the journey to Cordoba would be long, she and the other slave women kept good company even though their feelings could only be expressed in poor Arabic. They were well protected because they were rather pricey chattel, and even better protected by armed men because the whole Umayyad domain in North Africa was undergoing ruptures and disturbances. It seemed the Berber chieftaincies were resentful of Arab control and tribute. The traders knew that on the other side, in al-Andalus, their arrival was eagerly anticipated (Talbi 1988).

It will be obvious to any discerning reader that long journeys lead to introspection: greed is always mixed up with hope, and despite the hardships there has to be an 'over there' of redemption. And yet, there had to be always a pressing sense of loss for Mariam I, who could have lived in aristocratic comfort in Sindh or Al-Hind even though the military life of her madam would have had its own uncertainties. She was a different person now – her training in Basra opened up an Arabic world, but her trainers were not in any rush to convert her to Islam. It was better that way, she heard, because if she turned devout on them it would disturb their dinar-filled dreams (Talib 1988). And especially during such long days of travel, with so many tongues spoken on the way over, and above love, hope and redemption, there had to be a sense of nostalgia for home and a longing for someone to speak to her in Amharic.

There had to also be the sensual arts that Abyssinian women were supposedly known for, the forbidden things that would mould her into an upper-class courtesan (Caswell 2011). So, her sense of love and redemption had to negotiate this as well, and her role as an object of love, lust and constant sexual predation (Gordon and Hain, eds 2017). Furthermore, she was also an artist now; four years of strict training had created competencies in her not only of voice but also across a range of instruments, moods and *maqāms*, and with a turn for good and appropriate phrasing in her attacks on songs her own and those of other people – she had an acoustic skill of note. We could imagine her taking in all forms of new sounds on the way, wherever they set up camp.

Finally, the sense of being so close to and yet so far from places that cluttered her youthful imagination must have irked her, too. They skirted the Holy Lands and Jerusalem and the place where Moses parted the sea, and there in the distance was Mount Sinai; they could behold ahead the grandeur and marshes of the Nile on which, in better times, she could have sailed upstream so both the river and she could reach their birthplace. And somewhere in those stories would be Eksander, Solomon and Sheba (Pankhurst 1992).

After the crossing of the Roman or Rum Sea to reach Cordoba, this Jewish/Christian place with a Muslim heart (Shannon 2007; Shiloah 1991) and by all accounts a thriving culture, she would have been amazed by the first enormous city she was to visit. Baghdad, she had skirted and indeed that would have been the largest place she had ever seen; Raqqa, Aleppo, Damascus, Alexandria, Karawaya were large enough; but Cordoba was the largest by far on the European land mass (Talbi 1988).

The singing girls from the east were very welcome in the palaces of Cordoba (Farmer 1929) and it must have been a surprise for them to find that the leading light of culture, energy and music there was none other than Ziryab, a Black manumitted slave from Baghdad. It is known that the music of Baghdad moved, through human jealousy among the leading musicians, to North Africa, al-Andalus and Cordoba. It was alleged that Ishaq al-Mawsili, the son of the famed Ibrahim, had ordered one of the principal carriers of the music, Abu-l-Hasan Ali-ibn Nafi, or Ziryab as he came to be known, out of Baghdad after Ziryab's petulant debut in Harun Al-Rashid's court. In most sources about Ziryab, we encounter a genius, supposedly of African descent, a master musician and theoretician who had the courage to disagree with his mentors (Damodaran and Sitas 2016).

Ziryab's move to al-Andalus was not unique: it was part of a process of migration of intellectuals and artists, and part of the larger movements of Arab and Berber people into areas of southern Europe, particularly the Iberian peninsula, in the ninth century, after the setting up of the Umayyad dynasty in al-Andalus as well as in northern Africa in the early eighth century (Chejne 1974). There, the multicultural musical tradition that became known as the 'Andalusian School' was developed, which in turn reflected strong connections to Baghdad and later, with the coming of the Roma, influences from India as well (Wright 1992).

Notable among the creative networks of the time were four slave-women singers – Qamar, trained in Baghdad, and Qalam, Fadl and Alam-al-Ajfa, trained in Medina. Qalam was of Basque Christian origin, captured at a young age and sent to Medina to train as a musician. She was also a famed dancer, a calligrapher and a reciter of Arabic poetry. She was later purchased for the Umayyad caliph at Cordoba and brought back to Spain. Two male singers from the ninth century, Alun and Zarqun, pre-dated Ziryab and were among the first to travel to al-Andalus from the east (Chejne 1974; Davila 2009).

Ziryab was something of a 'complete aesthete'; it appears that he established a school of fashion and a school of culinary arts in Cordoba, in addition to his infrastructure for musical instruction and development. Ibn Khaldun wrote rather positively about him in *The Muqaddimah*:

> The Mawsilis had a young [apprentice] servant, by name Ziryab, who had learned from them how to sing. He learned so well that they became jealous of him and sent him away to the West. He [the ruler Al-Hakam] honoured him greatly. He rode out to welcome him. He showered him with gifts, fiefs, and allowances. He gave him a place in his dynasty as one of his boon companions. The musical heritage Ziryab left in Spain was transmitted down to the time of the *Reyes de taifas.* In Sevilla, [the craft of singing] was highly developed. After [Sevilla] had lost its affluence, [the craft of singing] was transplanted from there to the coast of Ifriqiyah and the Maghrib. It spread over the cities there. A sprinkling of it is still left there, despite retrogression in the civilization of the region and the decreasing power of its dynasties. (Ibn Khaldun 2004: 137)

Ziryab had indeed been trained by Ibrahim Al-Mawsili and was in fierce competition with the legendary Ishaq, the scion of the musical family we have already mentioned. And Cordoba's aristocracy held on tight to their dilettante, larger-than-life man, because they were not to be outdone by the Abbasids. The story of the slave women of Cordoba is well documented. Ziryab (Neubauer 2001) had about thirty-eight of them in his immediate circle, mostly from the rival school of Medina. Through their devotion he was to innovate in sound, in instrumentation, and could be at the heart of a flurry of artistic achievements until his death.

We will never know whether Mariam I was conscious of how important her composing and performing work was in the service of Ziryab. It is almost certain that he would have told her how lucky she was to be in his service, rather than in that lair of uncouth patronage and mediocrity in Baghdad, with its duplicity and callousness on issues of race and privilege. Here, he would have continued, even the Jewish and Christian composers were more generous and more open to the sounds that came from near and far. All these Ifrique Muslims knew about the begena and the krar, of which dozens of varieties were being manufactured in his school. And it would have come to pass that in Ziryab's drunken shadow and buoyed by his gargantuan energy, the slave women would have led an easier life. Mariam I was to die there. She was no longer called Mariam; from the time of her days in the training school in Basra she had been called Ghizlan.

A bizarre episode is recorded in which Ziryab's relation to two of his slave assistants, Ghizlan and Hunayda, speaks directly to our story:

> It was said of him that the *jinn* used to teach him at night one song from a *nawba.* He used to rise quickly from sleep and call his two female slave-singers, Ghizlan and Hunayda, who took up their 'uds', and he took his. Then he communicated to them what was taught in his sleep, and he wrote the poetry for them and hastened back to his bed. When he arose in the morning, he remembered neither poem nor melody, nor did he know who made him forget that because of his intoxicated state, since he was only grasping [the music] in his inebriation. Those female singers of his informed him of what he had communicated to them, and he ordered them to sing it for him, and when they did that, he memorized the information. Then he took his 'ud' and corrected the composition of the song, and completed for them what they had omitted in it. And so they were called 'Ziryab's two (song-)holders' (*masikatayn*). Afterwards, they went into the palace to teach [the song to] the singing girls, and thus they made this information about their master known there and verified about him. (Davila 2009: 132)

Mariam II would have been trained through a post-Ziryab canon. The new instruments that were crafted in Cordoba, including the five-string lute and the six-string qithara, would have travelled all over northern Africa and the eastern Mediterranean, and reached Khorasan and beyond following the trade routes. What also moved were haunting forms of poetry crafted by Andalusian women which were a far cry from the erotic and elegiac forms popular in Baghdad. Mariam II would have been taken towards Granada rather than Cordoba, which had deteriorated and its old grandeur been shattered after the 1066 massacre of the Jews and the Reconquista by the Christian forces. Passing by Palestine's holy places would have irked her in a special way had her brother been there, chanting away in Ethiopian style in Jerusalem under Saladin's protection.

By the time she reached the Nile her journey would have come to an end, because the news would have filtered through that the Almohadi aristocracy in Granada had put a stop to matters corporeal like music, and even had doubts about Sufi devotional song and dance. The dream of splendour and money, of the good life, was being transformed. She would have been ushered to Cairo to at least bring in some money, as the inns there needed *jawari* singers rather than *qiyan*, and the Mamluks now in control there, having been slaves themselves, were more tolerant of the corporeal joys of men, even though they were brought up under fierce military discipline.

Mariam III would have experienced deep confusion. She could have been sent to Granada but would have been without training in any school in Basra or Baghdad, which would have been struggling to recover a century and a half after the Mongols had razed it to the ground. She would have been a slave, period, and as such, her life in Granada would have revolved around domestic chores or outright prostitution. Her musical ear would have picked up the major chasm between the music of the Christians and the devotional laments and panegyrics of the Almohadi. The former had expunged all traces of the latter's melisma and minor notes, while the latter had banished the erotic. And then she would have had to flee to Fez or be integrated into the victorious Christendom. She could have followed the darker-skinned nomadic people, the Roma, in their desperate attempt to keep their autonomy. She could have used the confusion of the time to reach Egypt and face the stand-off between the Ottomans and the Mamluks. Perchance she could have met Othello, still in bondage, dreaming of joining the Venetian Franks (although Shakespeare does not record any such meeting in Othello's soliloquies); she could have followed the Nile back 'home' or made it to Port Said, where Ibn Majid would cart her off to Calicut as there were many Habeshis there.

Khambat

We abandoned Garai I in the lower-class haunts of Baghdad, hanging out with *jawari* singers and musicians from Khorasan and Al-Hind. We have to find a way, let us say, by the year 860 CE, to get him out of there – nine years before the murmurings of slaves, and especially the Zanj, would turn into one of the most violent rebellions ever (Segal 2003). And when the inns were shut tight in the heart of Abbasid power, it was the fate not only of the few hundred brilliant performers of the upper classes, but also of the few thousand who subsisted in the political economies of leisure for the lower rungs of society, that hung in the balance.

There was later a period of glasnost and revival, the time of Al-Farabi and his networks, ninety years on; but in the main, the years we are concerned with were ones of hardship. The innkeepers would have run faster than their slaves. It would be obvious that our Farsi friend who led the travelling group would not advocate anything definite because he knew the sway of Abbasid power had reached the Indus River and Balochistan. It would have been people from the other side of the river, from Al-Hind, who could argue that the Jains and Banias in his place of origin would be more merciful to music. The Brahmins would be merciful too, but only towards a certain type of music.

Khambat, our travelling troupe agreed, would be one of the safest of places. Garai I, having met Khambat merchants in Sofala, would say that they had introduced him to the best type of cloth and to a peculiar new food which we neglected to mention – rice. Of course, some harsh words would have been exchanged with the Persian friend, because his superior attitude to the Abbasids could not offer a safe alternative in the vast lands that stretched away from Baghdad in the east. What the Persian leader guaranteed, though, was that the places were not hostile to travelling bands of performers as long as they respected the norms of the imam and the biases of each village. So, the *jawari*, the man from Al-Hind and Garai I had to pretend they were his slaves, and that they were returning from a pilgrimage.

The Persian did boss the way to Khambat, which took 250 days, first to the south and then through untold hardships to Al-Hind. They followed the route to Ahvaz, from there to Shiraz, from there to Bandar Abbas, from there to Chahabar and then to Sindh. At Ahvaz there were major markets and work possibilities, and endless sugarcane fields where he hired his slaves out for seasonal sugar work whilst they performed; and thanks to the Turkish *jawari*, they could bring new shadow puppet stories to add to the local Saye-Bazi (a local puppetry tradition) forms. Our Persian friend, knowing the language, starred at storytelling, and in their expanding renditions of the Shirin and Khusrow story. The man from Al-Hind mourned on his sarangi, and Garai blew his lungs away and sang in tune (Beeman 2002; Nettl 1992; Zonis 1973).

In Shiraz, they also bought fruit, especially grapes, dried them in the sun and sold them further on; in Bandar Abbas, they fixed dhows and cleaned the warehouses at the port; in Chahabar, they got into a fight with Rajasthani travelling musicians moving west; and then, without warning, Sindh and the grand delta of the Indus River appeared, inviting exclamations but also comparisons with the Euphrates and Tigris. On the western side of the river Garai found settlements of his own Zanj, playing peculiar chord instruments and orating poems about distant seas. They were neither free nor bonded – they were there as labourers servicing the Abyssinian troops. Crossing the river, Garai found more Zanj in Khambat, hanging out with Shirazi and Bania traders loading cargo for Kilwa, Sofala and the lands of gold. He was aghast in the jewellers' market when he saw what Karanga gold was worth.

The Persian friend stayed behind, he did not dare cross the Indus, that's where the world stopped. His friend from Al-Hind promised to take him to Kashmir to show him the legendary market of Djinns. He dispatched the three *jawari* women to the Somnath Temple further inland. Garai could not believe the opulence of that temple, with its hundreds of musicians and dancing girls and with an equal number of barbers. He was left with the jewellers, and agreed to accompany a trading expedition to far-off China as the musician on board.

So, Garai I was in Khambat, looking at the ocean, longing to get home. There were another two Garais to deal with – they too needed to get home. The length of the journey from Baghdad to Khambat would not have altered, 250 days or thereabouts. Garai II could not have been part of a band of travelling players; he would have had to find his own way, but the road to the west would seem more tortuous than the eastern road. The grand Mamluk battalions had taken Egypt and there was a great tension between the Turkish forces, the Berbers and the armies made up of Zanj warriors. The turbulence was moving east too, and it was heard that such battalions had overrun the heart of Al-Hind, taking control of Delhi (Waterson 2007).

Garai II met them on his way out of the Basra gate, and volunteered to be part of their wind and drum contingents in exchange for food. Although many looked like him, they did not speak Swahili or any of the other languages he knew, from Shona to Tswana or Nguni. He realized that these were forces who had been raised since childhood as warriors, and spoke only Arabic. He heard that after the Zanj rebellion all the Zanj, even the ones serving in Abbasid regiments, had been slaughtered. The Abbasids had decided to cultivate military monsters without mothers, fathers or kin: womb-to-cutlass warriors. He marched ahead of them next to the banners, blowing or drumming, day in, day out, until they reached Sindh and crossed the Indus River (Waterson 2007). There he stared at the expanse of water in amazement, and when he asked about Khambat, he was told that they were not to cross towards Khambat (Hall 1998: 50, 62). The river had changed its course and on the other side there was now a white desert of salt, a vast expanse of barren nothing, a space of devastation, so they had to move up and then east to a place called Rajasthan. (Garai III would have had it easier; the brigands would have turned towards Khambat, avoiding Basra.) Garai II was fortunate in that the Sindh side of the river had a few thousand of his kind; he met them helping the armies set up camp. He revelled in their late-night rituals and music, where they danced hard and spoke to ancestors long gone. They helped him cross in a small sailing boat to reach Khambat.

Both Garais would end up in the jewellers' street, where people would understand where he had come from. The Banias were keen to meet him because they wanted more information about Sofala and beyond. It was always easy to find an Arab translator to help with communication. Garai II would have marvelled at the complex madness of it all: the multitude of Jains who wouldn't hurt a mosquito, the word was *ahimsa*; the elaborate network of temples and festivals; the violence of caste: Brahmins perfecting the complex order and within that, musicians in defined *jatis* (castes). And next to all that the Sidis with their Zanj and Swahili musical codas, their bows and *ngoma* rituals, freed from slavery but living outside the caste system as polluted low-lifes (Lodhi 2008).

It is claimed that much of the thirteenth century owed its musical finesse and thinking to people like our Garai II. The two grand books of music we are aware of, Al-Farabi's *Great Book of Music* and Sarangadeva's *Sangita-Ratnakara* (Sarangadeva 1951), were based on the practices of the musicians of the time whose compositions and performances they had experienced, and Sarangadeva's book on its author's very own practice as well.

Garai II's period was particularly inventive as regards music on what is now the Indian subcontinent. It is ironic that as the Islamic expanse from Baghdad to Sindh was becoming obsessively anti-musical, the Muslim parts of north India and especially the Delhi Sultanate were more than encouraging musical development and the enhancement and innovation in Hindu music and dance. And so were the Hindu principalities and courts, and so were the devotional schools expanding and reflecting on such repertoires. We will have to wait for Garai III for a bridge to occur between the high and the low, thanks to the Sufi movement in the case of Islam and the Bhakti movement in the case of Hindu craft, allowing for bridges too between what was considered folk and classical music (Massey and Massey 1993).

The first Garai would find a Dravidian coastline with a large presence of Jews, Christians and Muslims – there would be Black and White Jews and many Habeshis around. The second Garai would find a Malayalam-speaking littoral in Kochi, very much a cosmopolitan foreland with an aristocracy of Brahmin landowners and a revised but stricter caste order. The third would reach Calicut, by then a remarkable centre of trade and trans-shipment of goods from China, Indonesia and Japan (Damodaran and Sitas 2016). But by then the city and kingdom of Vijayanagara, with the most fascinating urban vibrancy, would have deeply impacted the coastline that nourished it (Mahalingam 1951; Sastry 1955).

What would have surprised Garai I and Garai II further was the discovery that the legendary musical story of love, of pain and redemption, that had spread from Persia to all parts of the known world, the story of Khusrow and Shirin in its manifold versions, made canonical in the Delhi Sultanate (Massey and Massey 1993; Trivedi 2012) following the grand works of Persian poets like Nizami (2012) and Ferdowsi (2007), and popularized by travelling musicians, had traces of reality in Kochi. There was a Sassanid king, there was a Syriac and Christian Shirin, and most of the Kerala Christians were there as a result of her initiative at a time of great persecution (Baum 2004).

What would be evident is that further north, in Malabar, slaving had been going on for a while and slaves would be part of the plantation labour force. We could have made Garai II or III the slave Kappiri, who was beheaded by his masters, inaugurating a spirit ritual with its music and dances; or perchance Garai III could have witnessed its existence and drawn meanings from it because of his prior exposure to spirit rituals in Africa.

Calicut was vividly described by the Chinese scribe on Zheng He's great expeditions into the AfroAsian Ocean, Ma Huan (1970), who, a few years before Garai III's arrival, remarked on its beauty, governance and cosmopolitanism.

We have a duty, though, to send the Garais back home. We have to leave this coastline and return them via Madagascar to Sofala. What is of vital concern is to get Ibn Majid's ship to Calicut, to load up for his last journey to Sofala.

Both Garai II and Garai III would have to work very hard to obtain a passage from Khambat or Calicut home to Zanj. To do so, they would both have to be involved in the loading of the ships with textiles and glassware, with wondrous and ornate metals and pearl, and navigate south to load up with varieties of spices and artefacts – at Kochi or Calicut in the time of Garai II, Calicut in that of Garai III. From there, at the right time, they could sail out towards Madagascar (WaqWaq) and the lands of the southern Zanj. And while Garai III would be at the dock, embarking, Mariam III would be on the ship, disembarking. Would they have recognized each other after so many trying years?

All three Garais would encounter a verdant south which would bring back memories of the Sofala coastline they had left. They would be bewildered by the extent of the spice plantations and the mountains of peppercorn around them, thrilled by the Onam festival for the legendary King Mahabali with its harvest rituals, elephant processions swaying to the rhythm of temple drums, ornate boat races and flowers everywhere. Garai II, who lived during the greatness of the Zimbabwe kingdom, would recall the first fruit festivals of his erstwhile kingdom, the drumming and the collective memory of ancestors ancient and recent.

Notes

[1] From the Mberengwa area (Mount Buhwa) and Gwanda Greenstone Belt, as well as from north-eastern Botswana in the Vumba and Tati Greenstone Belts. But Mapungubwe would have been a gold and copper processing and trading hub.

[2] The mazenqo or masenqo is a single-string instrument with a square resonator made of wood and stretched over with rawhide. The string is made of horsehair and tuned with a wooden peg.

[3] The begena is an Ethiopian ten-string instrument, very close to the Mediterranean lyre.

[4] References to Black Crows are there in early pre-Islamic Arab poetry, in the stories around Ziryab, and continue to be cited even by Roma Flamenco singers like La Caita. See chapter 4.

CHAPTER TWO

Recentring AfroAsia

Another World Was Possible

Federico García Lorca's sublime search faced east: he was in search of the 'deep song', the '*cantejondo*'. This 'black sound', as he said, which 'climbs up inside you, from the soles of the feet . . . [such a] mysterious power which everyone senses and no philosopher explains'. It was to be sought

> in the primitive musical systems of India, a stammer, an emission, higher and lower pitch, of the voice, a marvellous buccal undulation, that breaks out of the echoing prison of the tempered scale, will not suffer the cold rigid pentagram of our modern music and makes the hermetic flowers of semitones, open in a thousand petals. (Lorca 1922: 4)

We often return to this impressive paragraph, trying to ignore the word 'primitive' and nonetheless attempt to extract a possible mapping for our search.

Of course, Lorca knew a lot about music, about Granada and al-Andalus, about the flamenco and the *duende*, and his duets with the singer La Argentinita (he on the piano, she in song) from the 1920s and 1930s are widely available now, skirting around such expressivity (Lorca and La Argentinita 1994). We too have been on the road leading away from the tempered scale to find our way of opening hermetic flowers into a thousand petals. The difference is that we are facing from the east and south, from the planetary spaces where such 'buccal undulations' would be very much at home. Why is the task so hard, then? How do we reconstruct voicings out of so much stammer and emission?

Our contention is that if we listen carefully in AfroAsia for soundscapes and their associational clusters, although instrumentation, arrangements and notations differ, there was and is a familiarity between them that is uncanny. There appears to be a common *aesthetic constellation* that defined and defines musicality. This, we will demonstrate in the pages to come.

We argue that this constellation was a creation of human interactions of the *longue durée* of 700–1500 CE, a product of long-distance trade and travel in a world that, in the words of Janet Abu-Lughod (1991), was quite vibrant 'before European hegemony'.

It would have been easier to start our story with the entanglements that occurred during the foraging by a number of European powers starting in the sixteenth and seventeenth centuries, because the sources for this period are more accessible to us linguistically. We could have sketched out how, at a point in time, you could have a piano playing and composing for the emperor in China, and an orchestra of eunuchs with white wigs performing inside the forbidden city as Ignatius Sambo (a freed Black slave from Guinea) was composing music for the emerging bourgeoisie in England, while guitars were being traded for ivory and slaves between the Portuguese, the Lunda and the Ethiopian court.We could be looking at the arts and songs of slave rebellions and pirates' shanties in Madagascar, or at the earth-shattering events that produced genocides and revolutions (the American, the French, the Haitian), and identifying emergent forms. We chose not to do so, choosing instead the more difficult path.

We shall attempt to show how aesthetic constellations emerge, and how they have to be understood in a translocal sense. They were linked to large-scale movements in society that created unique aesthetic acuities, which in turn allowed for aesthetic forms to travel and make themselves available to people who, deeply embedded in their own social spaces, could draw on these forms to innovate, imitate and create new constellations in turn. So, we argue that the experiences and actions of subaltern people and classes as historical agents have profound implications for aesthetic forms, from their most public to their most hermetic manifestations in musical composition or performance. We followed a mythical Garai in all his incarnations in chapter one; now we have to turn to what made all that possible.

The Andrew Sherratt Legacy

What made our work easier was our encounter with the late Andrew Sherratt and his work that encouraged us not to lose the 'bigger picture', which was one of animated inter-societal relations and a restlessness of movement: of people, of goods, of financial transactions, of ideas and philosophies, of art and, as in our case, music.[1]

It allowed us not to miss the far-flung interconnections and polarizations of prior worlds, although we were only concerned with a tiny portion of the large swathes of time Sherratt tried to interconnect. He was indeed a daring archaeologist, providing the clues for how to do this through scholarship focused on long-distance interactions from 1800 BCE to 1500 CE. His work has been particularly revolutionary. Unlike most in his profession, he dared to 'think big', and his work opened up spaces and provided a landscape for studying and understanding the past. His dialogue with world systems thinking and his search to establish long-distance connections between far-flung regions of the planet, tracing trade routes and patterns of interaction, is only now beginning to be absorbed by the social sciences.

We are fortunate to have had internet access to his ArchAtlas Project, which traced visually for all to see the dynamics of long-distance transactions, and demonstrated how interconnected the world was between 3000 BCE and 1500 CE (Sherratt 2004). It did this by leaping 500 years in each of its frames; wherever the lines on the maps intersected, there was to be found an urban hub of profound significance. The representation of this evolving world revealed the known transactions in material and symbolic goods, and it was a decisive step in providing us with a relational conception of emergence. We have been working to extend this through our own research, adding elements on the so-called Far East and its connections to the Americas, the Indian Ocean's relationship to Africa, and what we could glean about movements within Africa and to a lesser extent within the Americas.

The two maps in Figures 2.1 and 2.2, of trade routes in the eleventh century CE and fifteenth century CE respectively, explicate what the ArchAtlas Project suggests. There is an undoubted thickening of interactions during those five centuries.

The main point is simple: that the world was punctuated by a long-distance dynamic of trade and interaction, and that the simplistic categories of 'pre-'anything or 'traditional' obscure more than they reveal. In this world, China was always a major hub of activity. And with this the centrality of the Holy Lands, the Crusades, Venice and Ghent shrinks somewhat.

The more complicated story is to be found in Sherratt's detailed and ambitious focus on the implications of sedentary agriculture and, within that, the 'secondary products revolution' (for example, wool) and how trade

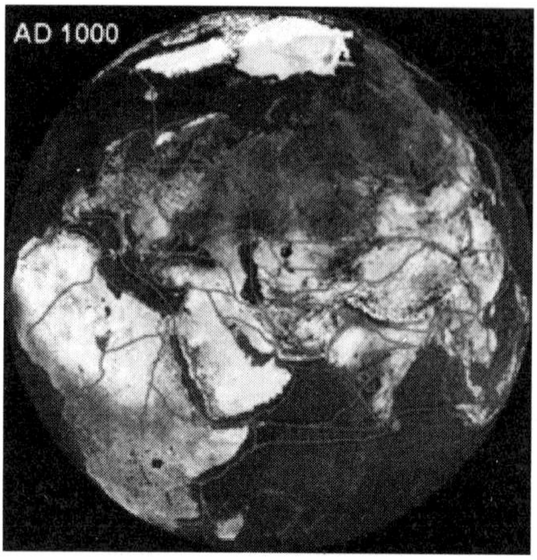

Figure 2.1 Long-distance trade connections, 1000 CE. (*Source*: *ArchAtlas*, Version 5.0, https://www.archatlas.org/, accessed 7 June 2021.)

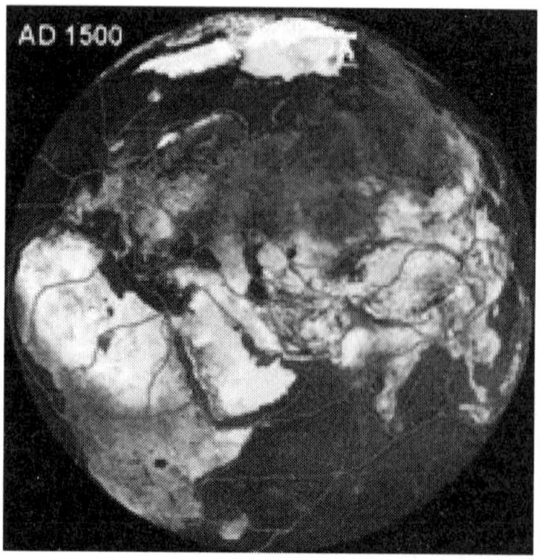

Figure 2.2 Long-distance trade connections, 1500 CE. (*Source*: *ArchAtlas*, Version 5.0, https://www.archatlas.org/, accessed 7 June 2021.)

in these products created new cores and peripheries, new urban formations, new energies and intensities; and how the system spread like a floral calyx (his preferred metaphor) to engulf the globe (Sherratt 1981). This work was extended to include symbolic and hallucinogenic goods, and in his piece, 'Envisioning Global Change: A Long-Term Perspective', he introduces the more than useful concept of a 'hegemonic regime of value'. In his words,

> the outward growth of an urban system can be described as the expansion of a hegemonic regime of value, in which new consumption practices are promoted. Its typical commodities are metalwork, textiles and psychotropic consumables such as alcoholic drinks, packaged within a system of beliefs and practices within which they have a coherent ideological role. (Sherratt 2000: 123)

Baghdad was such an epicentre of value in 1000 CE; cities in China, including Beijing, were to follow by 1500 CE.

These urban-to-urban contestations around 'value', the relationship between such centres as producing and consuming enclaves, the relationship in turn between them and the rural hinterlands, the 'umlands' (Pearson 1998) that fed them, the regimes of extracting rural surplus and their relationship to nature, forests and other sentient beings, pose a profound challenge to the received narratives inspired by an orthodox 'materialist conception of history'. There is no time to dwell on this here in a sustained way; suffice it to state that we are well served by remarkable environmental histories that have been rehearsed in the past two decades. Since China remains a subtext here, a good starting point would be Mark Elvin's *The Retreat of the Elephant: An Environmental History of China* (2010) and Timothy Brook's discussion of the link between the Little Ice Age and Chinese statehood in *The Troubled Empire: China in the Yuan and the Ming Dynasties* (2010), underlining how the Little Ice Age, in combination with population growth, had a devastating effect on forests by the eighteenth century (Williams 2007).

Here, of course, we have to understand a broader ecosystem within which human societies have created livelihoods, gender relations, communicative processes and hegemonic regimes of value. All emerging formations which could be explored from the eighth century CE to the contemporary era involved profound tensions within such systems and their biodiversity. Nature itself, of which human systems are but a part, is often rebellious in its own right, and its intergalactic dynamics and planetary ructions can overpower eco- and social systems with immense consequences (Radkau 2008; Richards 2005). If we were to write the natural history of the planet, as Karl Marx often aspired to do, we would be tracing how the Little Ice Age and its concomitant high drought and flood intensities, the Black Death, smallpox, plagues and famines, ENSO (El Niño-Southern Oscillation) effects sealing the fate of tropical humanity, the proliferation and destruction of sentient beings and plants, mutant viruses and so on, have affected and infected social systems.

On this count alone, there are hints at major devastations in the twelfth and thirteenth centuries in Ethiopia, in northern and coastal India, in Egypt and Byzantium, and in China. There are also hints that the Black Death could have reached the southern parts of Africa, and both intense climatic change and nutritional challenges could have interacted with power to usher in economic and political centralization. These challenges could be related, finally, to the decline of the Great Zimbabwe polity, but the empirical evidence being collected and archaeological work being done are accumulating too slowly for our impatient need to narrate.[2]

In turn, social systems have been very capable in their own right of transforming ecosystems in important ways. We should be tracing how human migrations and settlements, hunter-gatherers and pastoral nomads have created environmental strains and shocks. The real drama would relate to the emergence of settled and sedentary agriculture, which, in clearing out lands, in slashing and burning, in powering up demographic inclines, caused enormous ecosystem adjustments. We need to consider how hegemonic powers attempted to create and systematize legitimate regimes of natural plunder, and at the same time immunize their domains from the risks and disasters that might be intricately linked to their efforts.

Both the simple interaction with the Sherratt-inspired maps and the more complex analysis of emerging relational worlds of accumulation and trade highlight the serious need to revisit the tentative sketches provided in Marx's *Grundrisse* (1974) about pre-capitalist formations and, given the plethora of insights offered by the landscape just described, revolutionize our understanding of the evolution of modes of production, exchange and social formation. This time we must develop new rigour, not in the arcane and scholastic way that Althusser and his protégés searched *Capital* for more scientific concepts to turn historical materialism into a 'science', but through the remarkable new scholarship of the past twenty years. What is of the essence, too, is to revisit the seemingly flawed ideas in western sociology about oriental despotism, and in Chinese and Indian scholarship about the concept of the Asiatic mode of production. Sherratt's work on the plausibility of prior world systems, the secondary products revolution, the idea of a calyx-like emergence of centres and peripheries, and the rise of urbanity and 'hegemonic regimes of value' which are also concerned with the symbolic, has provided us with a serious starting point.

Of Ibn Khaldun and Marx

The floral metaphor is enticing but imprecise – it is hard to capture emergence and pathways, social organization and its armies and traders, if the image is one of seeds, growth, decay, flourishing and spread; the argument is in danger of turning its apertures into vents with its air leaking out. And yet it is enticing because it does away with simplistic notions of progress from hunter-gathering to the post-industrial present. Our search for more rigour in our conceptualization of emergence and movement took us to the sources of the time, which proved rewarding in terms of thick description but poorer in theory. Who stood out heads and shoulders above all was Ibn Khaldun.

Syed Farid Alatas (2013) has been punting Ibn Khaldun's importance as a historical sociologist for the last two decades, especially his take on dynastic state formation and its decline. He not only outlines Ibn Khaldun's importance as a theorist but also shows how the medieval historian's theory, with some melding with Marxian notions of modes of production and exchange, can arrive at an explication of the rise of the Sassanids and the Ottomans, and also of their decline.

Ibn Khaldun sees the effervescence of *asabiyyah* (social solidarity) in the consolidation of dynastic power as central to an emerging power, an epicentre of power and hegemony, but at the same time, the same success leads to its opposite: an enslavement to luxury which results in a loss of the very *asabiyyah* that got them there in the first place, and a consequent waning and demise (Alatas 2013: 14, 17). Ibn Khaldun's analyses in his 1377 magnum opus, the *Maqaddimah* (Ibn Khaldun 2004), throw some light as well on the musical accomplishments in the vast expanse that constituted the Islamic *umma*. As was noted while following Garai and Mariam in chapter one, there was some racist commentary about sub-Saharan Africans in Ibn Khaldun's work, emphasizing their propensity to frivolity, rhythm and dancing, and some terse description of the musical crudeness of 'Desert Arabs'. We will return to the musical side of Ibn Khaldun's *oeuvre* later.

For now, Lorca's floral metaphor and Andrew Sherratt's extension of it, with their implications of flourishing, decay and regeneration, fit well with a Khaldunian approach of rise and decline, and both converge on the importance of the 'urban' or urbanity. For the Tunisian cosmopolitan thinker of the fourteenth and early fifteenth centuries, it was a sign of agglomeration of crafts and luxury and therefore signified the beginning of the end, a sign of decay – the move away from the nomadic and the 'tribal' is a withering away, a lameness. For Sherratt, it is the enticing energy point that radiates the results of manufacturing and of aesthetic and material value. In both thinkers, there is a need to look at such forms of emergence and interconnection carefully, breaking from the demeaning narratives of the 'traditional'.

Hard as it was to clear our brains of deeply ingrained ways of thinking about the past and open them to a different way of explicating emergence, the euphoria was short-lived. Recent scholarship demands standpoints and taking sides in debates: whether production trumps trade or trade trumps production; whether the Aligarh School or maritime historians are right in India; whether revisionist or Africanist archaeologists are right about the east coast of Africa; whether one stands with the work of the 'Great Divergence' historians (Buck 1999; Pomeranz 2000; Pomeranz and Topik 2012; Wong 1997) or against them. All this noise is necessary, because the relationships need explication to arrive at the centripetal and centrifugal forces that facilitated change and the forces that blocked it.

Immediately, the idea of AfroAsia brings with it not just the Indian Ocean and its monsoon cycles, but also endogenous debates about all this. For a long time, Indian archaeologists and historians mirrored European accounts of the period under scrutiny. The emphases were on the early or late medieval period, and produced powerful work centred around the Aligarh School which, however critical of the sociological canon, has eschewed work on long-distance relations.

To give an idea of the necessity of all this, enter Irfan Habib, the eminent Marxist historian of the Mughal period in India (Patnaik 2000). He refuses to name what existed outside Europe, and specifically India, as 'feudalism', and he is uncomfortable with the idea of an 'Asiatic mode of production'.[3] In rejecting the linear idea of the development of modes of production, he has to account for why medieval India, during the period from 1200 to 1750, with an expansive monetary sector, did not 'succeed' without the intermediation of colonialism (Habib 1995).

This notion of 'success', he rejects as well:

> . . . to admirers of British rule, generally, it seemed that the fault lay with certain inherent weaknesses in Indian society. The influence of an 'enervating' climate, the heritage of 'Oriental despotism' and recurring cycles of anarchy (inhibiting the accumulation and investment of capital), primitive techniques and ignorance, the rigidities of the caste system, the prevailing system of resignation as opposed to enterprise, all created conditions in which nothing but a subsistence economy could function. From such wretched beginnings, the British could not, whatever they did, lift the Indian economy to European levels. (Ibid.:180)

He therefore argues that

> . . . our principal conclusion with regard to the extent of capitalistic development within Mughal India may now be summarized. We find that in both agricultural and non-agricultural production, production for the market formed a very large sector. In agriculture, there existed *khud-kasht* cultivation, based on hired labour, representing an advance, in form, toward capitalist farming. In handicrafts, merchant capital had developed considerably and had brought artisans under control through forms of the putting-out system. But the manufactory as an established form was yet largely outside of the sphere of commodity production. In other words, capital was by and large merchant capital, and though the economy was fairly monetized, domestic industry still predominated. (Ibid.: 231)

Habib feels compelled to partly defend Marx, because Marx did indeed recognize the contradictory nature of British colonialism – both destructive and regenerating. Whereas the first was intended, the second was not: Britain, like the bourgeoisie in general, 'created these material conditions of a new world in the same way as geological revolutions have created the surface of the earth' (ibid.: 3). Habib does not want to depart from an understanding of a mode of production which for him, however 'monetized', is a pre-capitalist social formation. According to him, a rushed departure from Marx's attempt to understand the two elements of 'the village community' and 'Oriental despotism' in order to understand surplus extraction would be a mistake, however wrong might have been their initial formulation, based on the scanty sources available during his lifetime. Whereas Andre Gunder Frank (1998), whom we will be discussing later, would visit India to point to urban formations and trade, Habib would point to agrarian relations of exploitation. For Frank it would be a partial view, as the Mughals were not the entirety of India, and any avoidance of consideration of overland long-distance trade and seaborne and thus maritime relations would miss the target.

By contrast, the work of historians like K.N. Chaudhuri (1991) on 'Asia before Europe' with its emphasis on trade and trade relations, Sanjay Subramaniam (1990a, 1990b, 1993) and Muffazar Alam with Sanjay Subramaniam (2007) emphasize much of that in assessing India's role in 'early modernity'. The emphasis is on the ways in which Asia was part and parcel of the entanglement that came to constitute modernity. Although their work focuses on a period about two centuries later than what our own work is trying to disentangle and re-entangle, it does touch on the prior times, thus standing in contrast to the Aligarh School's more 'national' emphasis.

It is at this point that one mourns the self-destruction of maritime China. There was the early fifteenth century period, with Zheng He's stewardship over the Pacific Ocean and Indian Ocean (some say the Atlantic as well), the accounts of his enormous fleet carrying thousands of armed men, scribes and traders, collectors and astronomers, opening up in the course of his voyages trade links and bodies of knowledge. There was this great opportunity for the world to be described and accounted for to eternity. The mourning is not about the change of policy by the Chinese emperor and his retinues, not about the destruction of these impressive fleets, but about the destruction of his very archive. Historians have often hoped that somehow there was a Plan B, and somewhere the real archive or parts of it were hidden or saved by some generous soul. Alas, such an archive has not been found, a real Rosetta Stone was put to the flames of ignorance. What we have left is a slimmer volume from one of Zheng He's trusted followers, Ma Huan (1970), his indispensable text *The Overall Survey of the Ocean's Shores* dating from 1433, which, however vital and detailed, increases the yearning for a Zheng He mothership of an archive.

Apart from observations on the African coastline and parts of the Arabian world, there are vivid accounts in Ma Huan's work of south India, including Calicut with its remarkable cosmopolitanism (of course, part of the enthusiasm of the author came from the fact that there were tens of thousands of Muslims to be found there, a bias that he shared with Zheng He). There are hints to be found of a wealthy 'hinterland', but no detailed account of the rising Vijayanagara flourishing away from the coastline. Once one delves (as we will be doing shortly) into the enormity, the economic, social and cultural emergence of this Hindu kingdom with its merchant and craft guilds and its complex social organization, Calicut itself becomes a kind of hinterland instead, a small inlet and outlet for goods, people and ideas. In Calicut, one could find the musical echoes of past Jewish, Persian, African (mostly Habeshi) soundscapes, even though Ma Huan's survey singles out the very Carnatic veena. Yet to deal with the emergence of a codified and emergent 'Carnatic' music, one has to move decisively inland to trace how it was incubated in contrast to all the 'impure' sounds around it produced by Vijayanagara's rising elites.

Across the ocean, the debates by archaeologists and historians of southern Africa echo the very concerns that their Indian counterparts have articulated. Sofala could be read as the coastline's Calicut, and Mapungubwe or Great Zimbabwe as its Vijayanagara (Delius 2007; Tiley-Nel, ed. 2011). The archaeologists Huffman (2000, 2005, 2007) and Chirikure (2015, 2020) focus on their rise and decline. Both are conscious and critical of colonial myths about Africa's backwardness and inability to produce such civilizational markers without external intervention. Both want to assert internal energies and agency of local clans and polities. Yet, Huffman (2005) situates such energy as a consequence of Africa's immersion in the world's trading networks. Chirikure (2020) disagrees, emphasizing rather the internal dynamics of agency and differing and discriminatory choices about what forms such an immersion should take. Whereas Huffman celebrates the urban and monumental achievements of such southern African polities, Chirikure is against monumentalism and looks for more horizontal narratives of emergence: in his view, both polities are in horizontal relationship to mining clusters and settlements and a range of 'ruralities'.

The point of our work, though, is that a synthesis between the contrasting schools is possible, and theoretically and empirically more productive. There is no way that the movement of symbolic goods like music can be understood without paying attention to overland pathways and maritime routes of trade, pilgrimage and interaction. But the creativity unleashed by all this cannot be fathomed without examining how elements of it are borrowed, rejected, enhanced, worked upon, transformed or canonized – that is, without understanding the local dynamics of craft, of classes, castes, and political and theocratic orders. The very concept of 'regimes of value' cannot be gauged without an understanding of the dominant and subaltern cosmologies, ideas and social structures. So, too, of how an instrument that travels can or may be elevated or 'improved' to function as an elite object of admiration, and get absorbed into defining currents of the 'traditional' or relegated to the margins of the lower classes, ethnicities and castes. This has occurred everywhere from Madagascar and China to Spain.

Furthermore, the liberation from Eurocentric narratives has spawned multiple and discrete accounts that rarely speak to each other: we have literatures on the Sanskrit or the Persian cosmopolis (Pollock, ed. 2003; Pollock 2006); significant 'mapping Asia' initiatives (Lachand Van Kley 1993); multiple Silk Road projects and literature (Liu 2011; Peterson 2002; Staniforth 1996; Whitfield 2004; F. Wood 2002); Indian Ocean studies (Beaujard 2007, 2011; Malekandathil 2010); work on the 'interlacustrine kingdoms' of the Great Lakes Region of Africa initiated by Archie Mafeje (1991); the admirable work of Jan Vansina on how MesoAfrican polities were born (Vansina 1990, 2003) – all dealing with bigger chunks of material and cultural exchange that traverse political boundaries. The closer we look at these systems and their boundaries, the more we become aware that there is a plethora of 'intermediaries' involving the servicing of regional mobilities of people, material and symbolic goods.

For example, Indian Ocean connections between large parts of Asia and Africa, stretching across several centuries, have been researched. The monsoon, with its seasonal reversal of winds and long periods between travel in one direction and the other, meant long expanses of time spent by maritime travellers in ports of destination. The monsoon also created varied environments in areas that it covered, with great potential for exchange of resources and commodities. With the Mediterranean to the far west and China to the Far East, land and maritime routes overlapped, aided by the arteries of the Red Sea and the Persian Gulf. It is undisputed that despite all the changes following the European intervention in the Indian Ocean, and the incorporation of large parts of it into the capitalist world economy, it still retains a number of its *longue durée* social and cultural characteristics, and music, myth and ritual are important ways of uncovering the connections.

This is true for the areas of northern Gujarat and Rajasthan whose pathways reach far, and for the Swahili and their oceanic dhow cultures that the eminent Zanzibari historian Abdul Sheriff has sketched out with commitment and detail (Sheriff 2010). Such cultures wove the Zanzibar–Kilwa–Madagascar–Mozambican archipelago of islands together with India, the Persian Gulf and the Red Sea. And interlaced with that was a system of slave traders, slave capturers and human chattel distributors and markets. And though we may be perplexed by the variety and intensity of the interactions, and by how even wretched giraffes sailed the seas at the relevant monsoonal times, we have to account also for the elephant in the room: China.

We are aware that AfroAsia is richly adorned with theoretical claims and their empirical consequences. By now the Eurocentric claims about backwardness have faded away, even though some of them survive in the sociological categories of development and modernization studies. Sociology was a fertile field for the growth and cultivation of such insights and for a definition of what 'other' societies lacked, always in relation to a European meta-narrative of modernity. Max Weber's contribution to such a view was enormous, although what he wrote about music (Weber 1969) remained rather marginal in appreciation of him as a canonical figure in the discipline. It was his work on the economic ethics of world religions (Ertman 2017) that came to define both the great difference between the east and the west and, explicated in his terms, their great divergence – how it was, for example, Hinduism's 'enchanted garden' and especially its caste system that helped block the development of a rational type of capitalism there, and so on.

Unlike most of sociology for a while, it was world systems theory that provided for some the capacity to speak about both European hegemony and prior world systems. The work of Immanuel Wallerstein (1974, 2000), Samir Amin (1971), Janet Abu-Lughod (1991), Christopher Chase-Dunn (1991) and Ho-fung Hung (2008) was key to both directions of thinking. Although the latter two continued to talk of world systems theory, Wallerstein insisted later that his was a world systems *analysis*, with theorization still a work in progress. Further historical work (social and economic) was to shatter a range of Eurocentric assumptions. Andre Gunder Frank's *ReOrient* (1998) bent the stick the other way, away from Europe towards China and a Sinocentrism.

Following discussions on the 'Great Divergence' between the east and the west in economic history, Frank's iconoclastic book asserted that 'Europe did not pull itself up through its own economic bootstraps, and certainly not thanks to any European "exceptionalism" of rationality, institutions, entrepreneurship, technology, geniality, in a word of race' (ibid.: 4). What occurred instead was that 'Europe used its American money (silver) to muscle in on and benefit from Asian production, markets and trade – in a word, to profit from the predominant position of Asia in the world economy. Europe climbed up on the back of Asia, then stood on Asian shoulders – temporarily' (ibid.: 5).

His summation, coming from the main intellectual of the older 'development of underdevelopment school', is stark:

> In view of my past work, of special interest to me and perhaps to many of my readers are the notions of 'development', 'modernization', 'capitalism', and even 'dependence', or call it what you will. All are procrustean and empty categories; because the original sin of Marx, Weber and their followers was to look for the 'origin', 'cause', 'nature', 'mechanism', indeed the 'essence' of it all essentially in European exceptionalism instead of in the real world economy/system. . . . They were all derived only from European/Western ethnocentrism, which was propagated around the world – West and East, North and South – as part and parcel of Western colonialism and cultural imperialism. (Ibid.: 338)

Frank's main point is not only that Asia, and in particular China and India, were the dominant socio-economies until the nineteenth century, but that their decline and Europe's rise were relational. Out of the pages of this, his final book, China emerges as a wounded and misunderstood giant whose decline was explicable but most probably temporary. Its re-emergence as a major power, therefore, has been obvious.

We concur with the view that Frank bends the stick the other way, and he has been taken to task for it (Abu-Lughod 2000; Chase-Dunn 2000), but his arguments were an important corrective. His idea that there was a significant world economy and a world system before European hegemony is well supported by reams of evidence. Such scholarship challenges in significant ways: (a) the very materialist conception of history in the Marxian tradition; (b) the notion of a transition to modernity in all its senses; and (c) the view that the world of the fifteenth to seventeenth centuries was undergoing an epochal change ushering in European hegemony. But whatever the lens we may be using, what pre-existed that period and what endured thereafter have to be seen in a new way. The robust debates on the transition from feudalism to capitalism appear so parochial, and confined to such a small area of the earth's surface, that continuing to talk about it without widening the frame will tell us very little.

Rather, a more complex dialectic of emergence is mandatory – it is no longer possible to speak of Europe's 'virgin birth', as Gurminder Bhambra (2014) argued in her attempt to create a global sociology. Instead we need to focus on an unfolding and entangled modernity – a task we tried to take on in our book, *Gauging and Engaging Deviance, 1600–2000* (Sitas *et al.* 2014). It was precisely the aim of this project to push further back and attempt to map the interconnections between citadels and political formations in earlier times. What was entangled then? Where could one start the story? Our first move involved crafting new narratives about regional, national and local forms of agency or genius.

In a Marxian sense, work is an important centrepiece for deliberation in such an undertaking. Work was and is a nature-imposed necessity, and its drudgery and pleasure took great twists and turns in the years of our study. As Marx argued, 'labour then, as the creator of use-values, as useful labour, is a condition of human existence which is independent of all forms of society; it is an eternal natural necessity which mediates the metabolism between [people] and nature and therefore human life itself' (Marx 1976: 133). The varieties of labour's expenditure as labour power differed vastly between and within regions. This is evident in the challenging work by a Sinologist like Timothy Brook, who brought the Ming world of the fifteenth century alive through his *Confusions of Pleasure* (1998), and in the narratives about Cairo, Baghdad, or Mapungubwe and Great Zimbabwe. But traces of far-flung places emerge everywhere in the narratives, in the work around harbours and transportation, in the manufacturing of goods and the location of trading networks. And as the 'backward' and 'traditional' disappear, urban forms reappear, different kinds of cosmopolitanism and indeed different takes on 'modernity'.

Othello and Energy Points

Perchance Othello and Mariam III met up in Cairo. We have alluded to that possibility anyway in our previous pages. Othello could have been tired of the Mamluk life, even though by then they were in control of Egypt and very much ran the affairs of and in Cairo. The slave-warrior life he had led would be over, now under the Abbasids, now under the Turks, now under all and sundry who could afford and feed such regiments. He was, as Shakespeare had him say, fed up with 'battle, sieges and tortures'. The first thoughts of becoming an 'extravagant and wheeling stranger' must have crossed his mind.

We can imagine him telling Mariam his stories of slavery and serfdom in the 'deserts, the quarries, the rocks and hills whose heads touch the heavens'. As stories go, these could have been real or made up, a habit that has not made storytellers in our domain less charming. He would have also shared his intention to change sides, as it were, and join the Franks – to be more precise, the Venetians. They were consorting with Mamluk leaders over opening the place where Moses split the seas to navigation, now that their access to the east had been nullified by the fall of Constantinople.

Mariam too would have related her travails, her abduction and ordeals at the hands of slaving men who were running out of their old ports to sell dark women. Now she was facing a difficult choice: could she find a way home following the Nile upstream? Egypt was a welcome place for her kind and she could even ask for help from the Bishop and Patriarch of Alexandria, who could send her with his envoys to Ethiopia. Or she could have listened with rapt attention to the stories of Jewish merchants there, the very same ones whose archives Amitav Ghosh consulted in crafting his novel, *In an Antique Land* (1992), about the thriving communities of the Habeshi in and around Calicut.

There must have been a reason for Othello to be hostile to the Turks and their regiments of horsemen and bombardier cannons, a reason that neither Venetian chroniclers nor Shakespeare could provide. Between them they had him fighting them on land and sea for the rest of his wretched life. But crossing over, let us say, to Cyprus controlled by the Luisignans until 1488, the closest Christian outpost to the Holy Lands, would have been dangerous for dark men like him, as their aristocracy, commanded by the fair queen Caterina Cornaro (whose sorrow Donizetti was to mythologize in Venice later), had large sugar estates and mills in need of slaves who by then were mostly black. The fact that the Luisignans were a vassal state to Egypt might have been a rather complicated matter; would that have enhanced his chances of a welcome, or would he have been a symbolic focus of their resentment? What he did not want was to end up back in chains.

Perhaps for a moment Othello could have hesitated and thought, 'let me follow this enchanting lady'. We as authors share such hesitation; we have no actual record of what kind of 'black' our 'lascivious Moor' was. So-called Moors avoided or tried to avoid enslaving people who were of their own ethnicity or shared their faith. In these wild years he could have been enslaved from anywhere – Ghana, Nigeria, Mali, Chad, Nubia, Abyssinia, even Zanj, Al-Hind, Sindh and Malabar. Here we are treading on dangerous ground, because even post-colonial Shakespeare scholars like Ania Loomba (1987) would have him from North Africa. The hesitation is obvious, because if he was from Malabar or Ethiopia, he could have told Mariam, 'I will follow you home', unless there was a very serious reason to avoid that home. On the other hand, it would fall foul of two other narratives, one real and one fictional: the real history needs to get him to Venice somehow and show his rise as a heroic warrior who would end up leading the resistance to the foraging Turks off Anatolia, and constructing his eponymous castle in Famagusta, Cyprus, in 1507. The fictional narrative would have its literary canon damaged if we chose otherwise: Shakespeare's racial classic needs his heroic rise, his love for Desdemona, his jealous rage, his duping by Iago, their tragic end in Cyprus. We decided to stop Othello from going south or east.

But we could have Mariam go north and west, that is, follow him to Venice, to the nerve-centre of another Christendom. This would not have been strange at all, because Ethiopian envoys and representatives from the Solomonic line, monks and traders made a few journeys there, as well as to Rome, Florence and further afield to Avignon. This would have afforded her a way back home so that she could not stand in the way of Desdemona, or we could have had her experience the fresh winds of a Renaissance: read Dante, admire the Florentines and pose for Da Vinci for a fresco or two, become part of the musical cultures that Jordi Savall (2018) has reconstructed in millenarian Venice. We had to deny her that experience too, because we were less concerned with the pathways to Donizetti or Vivaldi.

All things considered, she was destined to accompany her mistress to Al-Hind, where she was to marry a Habeshi commander of Mamluks. He would have been ensconced by now in the Delhi sultanate, enjoying some time of peace. Ibn Majid's ships could take her there, or at least to the coastline of the Indus, and from there she could find a safe passage to Gujarat or Punjab. Perhaps her mistress was there, free and married after a handsome ransom had been paid to the piratical scoundrels. We would rather have her board a ship commandeered by the very Ibn Majid himself and have her get to Calicut.

Had we been scripting a novel, we could have also shown how Garai III could end up in Delhi at a very good time for the creative arts. Or we could have pushed him up from the coastline of twenty-first-century Kerala to Vijayanagara; there was good money to be made there by foreign musicians. We could have had him in the highlands of Ethiopia.

What would have made dramatic sense would have been an encounter at the point of embarkation and disembarkation in Calicut. Would Garai have recognized Mariam, or would she have recognized him? Whom should we favour in this? Again, our research interferes: had she been on the ship to Calicut and if she wanted her dignity protected, she would have had to wear a veil. So the onus would have been on her to recognize him. But assuming that Bollywood-meets-Hollywood moment arrived, would we stop him from embarking to spend a life with her there, or would we insist that he or both of them sail away towards Africa? We could have them shipwrecked or disembarked in Madagascar, just to demonstrate the immense musicality there and its far-flung connections to Borneo and the coastline of Africa. Perhaps it would have been best to return him alone and leave it to future creative cohorts to make sense of all this.

Whomever we chose as characters on this journey and wherever we sent them, conjuring multiple destinations and emphasizing their agency and creativity, we would have to assert at the same time that their choices were prescribed by the dynamics on a polycentric map with its own pushes and pulls, magnetic fields of attraction and repulsion that were quite independent of our actors' wills.

That there was a polycentric world before European hegemony is correct, as much as it is a platitude. And even given this polycentricity, there were asymmetries and inequalities of power and wealth across the world system. Each centre exerted a different magnetic force, mediated on its margins by others. Our characters would have to jump over peculiar tectonic fissures. Such powerful ruling elites/classes/castes change the life conditions of all those they colonize, and of course smash through other emergent forms of development in the process; but even then, what the new rulers attempt to do is to create conditions for the eternal repetition of the same: their rule. They are concerned with accumulating more tribute and more wealth, more temples, mosques and churches, but their driving desire is to conserve a permanent present.

It is clear that the dynamics of change, as Marx argued way back, had to involve novel forms of production, circulation and exchange of the products of alienated labour. We know much more these days than he knew in his time, but the necessary redrafting of his ideas would show how sedentary agriculture in itself was not the long-term 'game changer'. Of course, it displaced pastoral and nomadic peoples and pushed hunter-gatherers off their prized lands and into the fallow margins, the deserts and the remote forests, as it slashed and burned forests or uncultivated lands into prosperity. It also had 'slower' (than now) serious environmental consequences in assaulting flora and fauna, and introduced narrow but fruitful monocultures. But as Sherratt (1981) tried to argue, it was the secondary products revolution, its novel forms of manufacturing and processing, the results of the exploitation of nature's bounty and the technologies to do so, that both maximized the surplus extraction and revolutionized forms of consumption, trade and work on the way to moving X widgets to Y. Unlike the exalted classes that demand eternal repetition, it was the working people who ushered in new forms of concentration in proto-urban, 'rurban' and urban assemblages.

The exalted classes would still be involved in their lavish theocratic and military displays and insisting on tighter and tighter controls of their 'umlands' and 'hinterlands', but by then, as Sherratt argued, manufacturers' and traders' inter-urban dynamism, synergistic forms of growth, their even and unequal development, and their calyx-like expansions were creating new centres and peripheries. All the exalted classes were bent on doing was to exercise some control of these energies to their benefit and, often, loss.[4]

For the purposes of this project, though, we had to dig deeper into the smaller scales of this expanding world system, and look at all these urban formations as synchronic and simultaneous forms of existence on the AfroAsian map. Each formation, from Calicut to Mapungubwe to Sofala and Vijayanagara, had its 'umlands' that provided it with sustenance; and within each urban cluster, we had to identify both centripetal and centrifugal forces, sucking material and symbolic goods in and exhaling them out. We had to explore how these energies felt within a 100-kilometre radius of each centre on this map in all directions, and beyond that, into their hinterlands which were often other formations' hinterlands too. It was obvious that much of the energy involved in these formations was about inland energies, away from coastal dynamics of trade that needed serious attention.

Surprisingly, every 500 kilometres or so on the map that hugs the AfroAsian seas, there was to be found an urban formation of note: Great Zimbabwe, Sofala, Kilwa/Zanzibar, Mogadishu, Aksum/Lalibela, Calicut, Vijayanagara, Khambat, Delhi, all the way to Baghdad, Damascus and so on. There were long-distance dynamics facilitated by Silk Roads, spice routes and what the dhow cultures of the ocean permitted and the seas allowed. And here, within these broader dynamics, there were clearly four energy points that animated each urban formation in turn: the Ethiopian, which did not control but animated the northern coastlines; Great Zimbabwe, which animated the trade in gold, ivory and later slavery; Vijayanagara, which animated the Hindu and Dravidian south and had Calicut as its 'hinterland' and vice versa; and the northern Umma, animated by the Delhi sultanate and indirectly touching Istanbul and Fez. These, in turn, were animated by broader Far Eastern, European and western African interconnections. In short, as Ctesiphon and Zoroastrian Persia succumbed to Islamic conquest, the new energy points superimposed themselves on the prior terrain that linked Japan and China to all possible destinations. Baghdad had a wondrous urban emergence and dragged all the energy points towards it, but this was a temporary phase that was quickly superseded.

Take Vijayanagara for example: it became, as the fifteenth century unfolded, a major energy point (Mahalingam 1951). Although most of the population was to be found in thousands of villages, they were interlinked with at least twenty-seven major towns, which in turn were interlinked to Vijayanagara city with its population of more than 500,000. Of course, strong class and caste divides structured its social interactions, and as a city that started as a pilgrimage point of temples and of enormous fairs, it emerged as a major manufacturing hub. Travellers described highly populated streets with throngs of elephants and haulage of goods and trading. It was estimated that there was a waged army of 24,000 horsemen on call and 12,000 policemen under the local bailiff.

Nobles ran the place for the royal house, assisted by thousands of officers and clerks. Supported by royal patronage and urban levies, astronomers, astrologers and medicine men made up the scientific community, and large numbers of architects, sculptors, musicians and dancers were involved in a major refinement of traditions. It is claimed that much of the Carnatic canon, even if it was not started there, was consolidated in Vijayanagara. The royal house itself was an embarrassment of riches, with a 4,000-strong harem from which 2,000 wives accompanied the king wherever he went, and as many eunuchs. And yes, all of this was on the back of the rural serfs and peasants, and urban slaves. There was a large market for black slaves in Bidar that fed into the Vijayanagara and plantation economies of the realm. It is unclear how work was organized and who performed it, but the proliferation of crafters, weavers, oil pressers, bakers and so on employed both free and unfree labour. At the heart of city politics was a 900-strong merchants' guild. This inland concentration did not diminish Calicut's own energies.

Similarly, one can start from the Great Zimbabwe formation and its transition and takeover from MweneMutapa, fan outwards from there to the north into the Zambia–Katanga region of copper mining and trade, and move across to Congo proper, up into the Great Lakes Region and the Ugandan–Burundian–Rwandan spaces, and southwards to the bifurcation between the Sotho/Tswana and Nguni, each space with urban formations and their umlands and hinterlands, and the intermediary formations inbetween. What can be deciphered through this in the lands of the 'Zanj' is that the dynamic was not about exporting raw materials and, later, slaves in return for manufactured goods. There was internal manufacturing and contiguous trade, exchange, movement of people, of livestock and, most importantly, cross-clan interaction (as most settlements sought exogamous relationships) despite political boundaries.

In this system of even and unequal growth, there were ruptures that accelerated reconfigurations. We have hinted at the environmental ones, the Little Ice Age, the famines and plagues, all elements for future research and measurement. The major ruptures, as is quite obvious, were firstly, the disappearance of Baghdad as an energy point, which immediately bifurcated the magnetic fields, creating a strong pull towards China on the eastern side of the map and an enforced distance of the Renaissance epicentres of Europe from the east. Furthermore, the Reconquista pulled Islamic energies towards Morocco and beyond, towards western and central Africa. Finally, the sacking of Constantinople tore apart European access to the east. Venetian capital had to find a way of convincing ships to move westward in order to find the east. Portuguese adventurers complied.

The Anti-Canon

In short, to return to our main preoccupation: the travels of musicality. Through them, we seek to argue the following:

1. Understanding the emergence and transformation of musical traditions, or more generally, art traditions, necessarily has to be about a critique of canons, of the 'ethno' of ethnomusicology and of various centrisms, whether Euro-, Indo-, or Islamo-centrisms. Further, it is necessary to understand cultural formations as having historical roots, rhizomes and influences that go far beyond what are commonly talked of as links between people and their cultures. Thus, the cultural influences in the Iberian Peninsula or 'Islamic' northern Africa or the Indian subcontinent can be seen, through music, to be constituted by connections that are

more extensive and involve more categories of people than what is known and acknowledged in historical or musicological work. This is important not only for dealing with arguments about cultural essentialism, but also to make sense of actually observed forms, to get to the root of what constitutes and changes them over time.

2. Over and above the critique, it is necessary to provide a different mapping of how music moved and how each setting mimicked, transformed, enhanced and nudged it all through long-distance movement of goods, symbolic or material, and people. It is the mapping of such aesthetic movements that, we believe, provides interesting ways of understanding cultural transformations.
3. The carriers of the music across all locations were to a large extent slaves, people in servitude, nomads and various other 'subaltern' people, large numbers of them being women, although the histories of the creation of musical traditions usually attribute their development to male rulers, conquerors and male-centred traditions, especially for the medieval period.

   Furthermore, the debates around Iberian or Andalusian music have been trapped within the Abrahamic traditions of Christianity, Islam and Judaism; what is known as 'modern' and 'rational' European music attributes its qualities to refined tastes of white bourgeois societies, and debates around Indian music are mostly about Hindu or Islamic influences, without an ability to break out of such straitjackets. However, careful listening as well as an unbiased uncovering of historical detail brings out clearly the role that the slaves, the wanderers, the street performers and nomads played not only in carrying musical forms but also in contributing to the development of musical canons, philosophies and perspectives.
4. Thus, what is seen as Hindustani or Carnatic is perhaps a profound sedentary elaboration of such travelling soundscapes; what came to be known as the European classical tradition perhaps needs to acknowledge influences from numerous 'others' and a decisive repression of many of them in liturgical and religious medieval music; what occurred in Ethiopia between the seventh and tenth centuries and in China during the Tang dynasty might be fascinating mutations of the very same; and so on. Therefore, we need a non-essentialist understanding of music as always on the move, *borrowed, elaborated, transformed, revolutionized and passed on within and across boundaries*. We also need to understand musicians

and composers as bearers of an *aesthetic acuity* which is open to the world of formed and transformed sound. Of course, in certain historical periods a canon becomes fixed, deviation is abhorred and masterful repetition of it becomes the marker of good music. Such constructions have unique local qualities, but we try to avoid claiming that they are a manifestation of an ethnic or religious essence.

There is a pressing need to bracket ethnomusicology away if this journey is to achieve its intended goal – to fathom how music moved and moves. This is a philosophical and socio-historical imperative and not an attempt to demean the work of the ethnomusicologists as such. Without them, all this would be hardly discernible. Bruno Nettl's wonderful introduction to the field, *The Study of Ethnomusicology: 31 Issues and Concepts*, is both convincing and hearty, and the credo that it is 'the study of music in culture' (Nettl 2005: 16) and a 'study of the world's music from a comparative and a relativistic perspective' (ibid.: 17), which is respectful and egalitarian, is noteworthy. And as a field it has spent the last two decades reflecting seriously about its own limitations and the ideas it has projected about musical 'others', and has expanded its scope to include trans-ethno movements and influences. There would be very few who would deny that the ethnomusicologists' gathering of tones and semitones from the 'out there' has enriched our lives, and that the cultural contextualization has helped in making difference and variety a fact (ibid.: 18). Yet, the bits seen in isolation from each other make the comprehension of the arc difficult and stifle any attempt to comprehend movement and change: we are left with Lorca's hermetic flowers – a wondrous but insufficient gift.

A bracketing of ethnomusicology, as argued above, has to go hand in hand with the rejection of the west-centric idea of music and its relation to modernity. This is drenched in highbrow and elitist conceptions of the music of the western imperium; it has been sharply articulated in Max Weber's *The Rational Foundations of Western Music* (1969: 19) and was perversely supported by scholars like Theodor Wisengrund Adorno (2001). For Weber, the 'beautiful', the 'profound' and even the 'ugly-as-sublime' were to be found in the west's compositional culture, that is, in the tension between the rationality and organization of its harmonic structures and the intensified, lyrical expressivity it permitted and controlled at the same time. To quote: 'without this [enharmonic] quality modern music would have been neither technically nor meaningfully possible. Its meaning rests on the fact that tone successions are not treated as an indifferent series of semitones' (Weber 1969: 20). Weber's contrasting 'other' was demeaning. It was the 'unorganized conglomeration of nonrational tone successions' (ibid.: 21). Each word carries with it a little devastation: 'unorganized' as opposed to 'organized', 'conglomeration' as opposed to 'composition', 'nonrational' as opposed to 'rational', 'tone succession' as opposed to 'harmony'; and he argues further that 'only the elevation of many-voiced music under notational art created the composer proper and guaranteed the polyphonic creations of the Western world in contrast to those of all other people, permanence, after-effect and continuing development' (ibid.: 39). All this needed a make-over, as it is no longer enough to ascribe achievement and rationality to the west and define the rest of the world's contribution as what Weber calls the 'nonrational tone successions'.

Yes, something distinctive did occur in Europe that enhanced compositional and organizational processes during the rise of bourgeois society. The road from the violin and the piano to Beethoven has been more than impressive. And Theodor Adorno has a point in his *Aesthetic Theory* when he states that 'Beethoven's music is as much a part of the revolutionary emancipation of the bourgeoisie as it [also] anticipates the latter's apologia' (Adorno 2001: 22). The achievement of a complex polyphony in Beethoven's work was at the same time an uneasy acceptance of a declining status quo. Yet even this achievement was not a virgin birth, unrelated to the world around it. The greatness in compositional form in Europe from the seventeenth century onwards until the late nineteenth century is not only based on a Bakhtinian appropriation of forms from the lower classes, as it has become fashionable to say, but also on appropriations from many peculiar 'others'.

More pressing, though, in this deliberation is the need to get rid of the perverse idea that ethnic, national or civilizational adjectives are a scientific correlate of musicality. Yes, as a construct of social power and sometimes as an empowering declaration, or even a statement of received notions based on territorial histories and cultural confinements, it is possible to place the adjective African, Greek or Persian, Tamil or Indian or Andalusian, next to music, but if we are serious about examining the craft itself, such a political act obfuscates more than it reveals.

To arrive at an understanding of emergences and transformations, there has to be a critique of the canon, of ethnic epithets, of Eurocentrism, of Indo- or Islamo- or other such essentialisms, and of the constant mild bickering within the Abrahamic traditions over, say, the music of al-Andalus. To give another example, it is not correct to say that 'X musicality is linked to ritual'; rather, it is more accurate to say that X power elites used musicality to define rituals of submission, defiance and social reproduction. That the relationship between music and ritual becomes canonical and indeed ingenious thereafter is another story. So it was with the elaborate organization of *rāgas* in Hindustani and Carnatic music – a remarkable achievement, but never a virgin birth nor a direct spiritual transmission from the pages of the Vedas.

Understanding how 'musicality' moved overland or by boat thus requires us to note that there were fascinating connections forged between far-flung places through music and musicians, connections that are not adequately acknowledged in historical or musicological work. It further points us to the fact that this period, from the eighth to the fifteenth century CE, also happens to be the period (as indicated by our mention of Al-Farabi) when philosophies and theories of music performance practice were beginning to be written, reflecting and articulating many of the pathways. While this is the beginning, also, of canon formation and exclusive identification as 'Islamic' or 'Indian' music or various other musical 'types', based on apparently distinct and unrelated essences and rules, the texts themselves are beginning to reflect the varied influences on the musical forms and, importantly, the kinds of people who created and carried the music.

We started with an evocative journey, and outlined a series of claims made up of fragments researched here and there to make a claim that another world was possible. But how do we account for its dynamics?

Theory

Ibn Khaldun's claims about musicality are rather idiosyncratic. To quote generously from his celebrated historical work:

> [The Arabs] did not know anything except [poetry], because at that time, they practised no science and knew no craft. The desert attitude was their dominant trait. . . . When such humming was applied to poetry, it was called singing. When it was applied to the praise of God or some kind of recitation [of the Qur'an], it was called *taghbir*. Abu Ishaqaz-Zajjaj explained this word as [derived from *al-ghdbir*, that is, melodies] reminding one of *al ghabir* 'that which remains', that is, the affairs of the other world. The Arabs continued this way during their desert and pre-Islamic period. Then, Islam made its appearance. [The Arabs] took possession of [all] the realms of the world. They deprived the non-Arabs of

> their rule and took it over. They had their well-known desert attitude and low standard of living. In addition, they possessed the thriving religion [of Islam] and that [Muslim] religious severity which is directed against all activities of leisure and all the things that are of no utility in one's religion or livelihood. Therefore, [music] was avoided to some degree. In their opinion, only the cadenced recitation of the Qur'an and the humming of poetry which had always been their way and custom, were pleasurable things . . . (Ibn Khaldun 2004: 101–02)

The fact that they took all artfulness and musicality from the Persians was also the sign of their eventual decay:

> Then, luxury and prosperity came to them, because they obtained the spoils of the nations. They came to lead splendid and refined lives and to appreciate leisure. The singers [now] left the Persians and Byzantines. They descended upon the Hijaz and became clients of the Arabs. They all sang accompanied by lutes, pandores, lyres, and flutes. The Arabs heard their melodious use of sound, and they set their poems to music accordingly. In Medina, Nashit al-Farlsi Tuways, and Sa'ib Khathir, a client of 'Abdallah b. Jafar (b. Abt Talib), made their appearance. They heard the poems of the Arabs and set them to music. They did it well, and they became famous. Ma'bad and his class of singers, as well as Ibn Surayj and his ilk, learned from them. Continual and gradual progress was made in the craft of singing. Eventually, in the days of the 'Abbasids, [the craft of singing] reached its perfection with Ibrahim b. al-Mahdi, Ibrahim al-Mawsili, [Ibrahim's] son Ishaq, and [Ishaq's] son Hammid. [The music] and the [musical] sessions of Baghdad during the ['Abbasid] dynasty have remained a topic of conversation down to the present time. (Ibid.: 102)

Ibn Khaldun's historical evidence is richer than his actual attempts to theorize music out of the sensation of 'glad-ness' (see Shehadi 1995). But he touches on what was also a significant emergence on the farthest point to the left of the *umma*'s map: the genius of Ziryab, the manumitted slave who was to define the Andalusian schools of music:

> The Mawsilis had a young [apprentice] servant, by name Ziryab, who had learned from them how to sing. He learned so well that they became jealous of him and sent him away to the West. He joined al-Hakam b. Hisham b. 'Abd-ar-Rahman I, the amir of Spain. He [al-Hakam] honoured him greatly. He rode out to welcome him. He showered him with gifts, fiefs, and allowances. He gave him a place in his dynasty as one of his boon companions. The musical

> heritage Ziryab left in Spain was transmitted down to the time of the *Reyes de taifas*. In Sevilla, [the craft of singing] was highly developed. After [Sevilla] had lost its affluence, [the craft of singing] was transplanted from there to the coast of Ifriqiyah and the Maghrib. It spread over the cities there. A sprinkling of it is still left there, despite retrogression in the civilization of the region and the decreasing power of its dynasties. (Ibid.: 137)

Ziryab, as we have already stated, was the son of a manumitted black slave from Baghdad. Indeed, was he from the lands of the *ngoma* (discussed in chapter four) and the frivolity of dance and rhythm? Or was he from the Habeshi lines of Martha's people or the Nubians further north?

Ibn Khaldun's *Maqaddimah*, however jaundiced it was about sub-Saharan Africans and however narrow its understanding of music's subservience to mathematics (ibid.: 372 – it claims that 'it is the knowledge of the properties of sounds and modes and their numerical measurements. Its fruit is the knowledge of musical melody'), his idea of refinement was deeply sociological (ibid.: 138–39). It was about the

> transition of dynasties from desert life to sedentary culture. . . . It enslaved people of the former dynasties and employed them in their occupations and their household needs. From any of them, they selected skilled masters of the various crafts . . . developing a culture of luxury and refinement in food, drink, clothing, buildings, weapons, carpets, household goods . . . [and] music. (Ibid.: 139)

There are many arguments to be had with the ideas of that remarkable historical sociologist. His account of pre-Islamic creativity among Arab people is rather poor. The compilation of such poetry, for example the odes contained in the pre-Islamic Arabic collection of *Mu'allaqat*, are as fine a set of compositions as any. As Michael A. Sells states in his introduction to his translations of six of these odes, through their imagery of 'spring rains, flowing streams, flowering meadows, desert animals birthing and nursing . . . in idyllic tranquillity', a recalled wholeness is re-membered and re-collected in sorrow, as lost beloved gardens, as laments (Sells 1989: 5); and in the lyrics of unrequited love we find the basic landscape of the very lyrics we have been searching for. One of the seven legendary poets who produced these poems was Antara, an Ethiopian manumitted slave, a poet and a military hero whose lyrics about blackness would get Ziryab into trouble three hundred years later in northern Africa on his journey to al-Andalus. Suffice it to say that we are running ahead of our narrative. There was creativity and poise in what was to be the Arabic core of the Islamic world, enhanced and transformed in and through Persian creativity.

Unfortunately, too, Ibn Khaldun's engagement with the actual theorization of music and the actual philosophers of Baghdad, whose writings became both defining and canonical, seems superficial: Al-Farabi and Ibn Sina are not in his range. Al-Farabi's *Great Book of Music*, especially, is an unparalleled contribution, and he must also have been making a remarkable political point: the detractors of Baghdadi musicality were plentiful in the power elites of the day, so the act of making music a part of the general philosophy of mathematics, and of the philosophy and science of sound, gave it a political sanction. Furthermore, his deductive-inductive approach to musical complexity, combining on the one hand Neo-Platonic ideas that had journeyed from Alexandria and Antioch alongside Syriac and Nestorian Christians to Ctesiphon under the Persian Sassanids (at a time of Christian 'fundamentalism'), and on the other a focus on the actual performance aesthetics of the Al-Mawsili family (who migrated from the very same Persia to Baghdad), provides a key, too, to how Ziryab must have worked in and through the Umayyad courts in al-Andalus. Al-Farabi's work describes and canonizes a significant aesthetic constellation.

We shall return to Baghdad later, after we have cleared the pathways, the routes and movements of material and symbolic goods, people, ideas and information, to make sense of a world before European foraging, settlement and colonialism. Perhaps from Ibn Khaldun, we can keep a sense of an internal and external logic of the rise and decline of polities, and of a multilayered evolution that always synthesizes and syncretizes from defeated remnants of the past.

The concept of a 'constellation' was borrowed from Theodor Adorno's work; it is about a diverse universe of concepts and elements that are held together with difficulty by an organizing principle – they include ideological narratives, insights, inferences and the like, in our desperate philosophical attempt to bring the non-conceptual into the conceptual and discursive order. So, it is about the formal and unformed elements and yarns that constitute an artist's universe of creativity and allow her to navigate her art or craft. An artist may be located in the confluence of many such constellations. Or, as in the case of Mariam in Basra, be forced into one which makes sense to the elite cultures of Baghdad and far-off al-Andalus.

We would also like to comprehend such an idea in its broadest sense in all contexts, avoiding distinctions of taste, of high or low, elite or popular, devotional, social or political or purely commercial. Yes, there are aesthetic dominants, processes of inclusion and exclusion, canonized individuals (Al-Mawsili, Ziryab), canonical works, aesthetic gatekeepers, classifiers and power investments and cruel dynamics. Sometimes aesthetic constellations of some kind become dominant, canonized – and often, not.

It has not changed much: perhaps an ensemble of us might be sitting in Johannesburg listening with total attention to a piece by Cecil Taylor, and then one of us, for example, plays the church organ in the afternoon and finds herself or himself down at the drinking hole where some of their buddies gather with guitars and sing. Late at night she/he might be settling down to earn her/his real bread by being some politician's speechwriter. She/he might be going through an intense period of compositional creativity which might bring together all the diversities of sound she/he has encountered, or none of them at all.

Here is where we need to bring in another concept: aesthetic acuity. The distinctions made between 'high' and 'low' – that is, the distinction between those who do and do not possess the ability to distinguish the 'pure' and the 'vulgar', 'authentic' and 'inauthentic', 'good art' and 'aesthetic excellence', and so on, are about the hierarchical structuring of society and not about 'aesthetic acuity'. Put differently, the construction of 'aesthetic dominants' and the 'canonization' of some works and not others is less about aesthetics as such than about the monopolization of value by aesthetic status groups.

'Aesthetic acuity' is the range of trained and socialized aesthetic, visceral and practical sensibilities that accrue in a person by virtue of her occupying one or more particular aesthetic constellations, each of which is constituted by specific symbols and signifiers, grammar and history, and which influence her perception, creativity and responses. For example, an Indian composer listening to Toumani Diabaté's kora in Delhi is at the same time imagining the felt connections to local Bengali river music, to the major notes a variety of instruments produce, and perhaps to voices of poetry she once heard. If you are serious about your craft, you are quite open to the different, the 'vulgar' as a poet or a musician. There is no innovation without it – so instead of cultivating class, caste and race bigotry at the gates of the profound, you listen, like, dislike, copy, enhance.

In the previous chapter, we followed our fictional Garai and Mariam through three incarnations in order to provide some human weave for our yarn. We made them musical. Garai's musicality was a mix of talent and training. He would have had his talent groomed in the age-sets of his cultural formation. There he would have been identified as talented, and perhaps sent to learn how to make or play bows, flutes and the ancestor of the mbira. He would also experience further forms of engagement with sound and harmony, call and response, and tonal variation in the esoteric sects of metal workers and in the sects of healing and ancestral ritual. His aesthetic acuity, his openness to other sounds, would have been inculcated there. His judgement of good or bad music would very much depend on his existence within a cultural formation and his exposure to others.

We need to also distinguish between creative ecosystems and spaces of performance – although common to all societies, they differ in their social constitution. The former is a cultural formation that involves a relation to the sources of instrumentation and their manufacture; it could be a clan or a caste, a social assemblage, that makes the creativity possible. The latter are the permissible performance spaces in a society where creative teams are mixed up with audiences, participants and forms of patronage. Musicality occurs in many spaces, formal and informal, in palaces or fields, on boats and in carceral encampments. We attempted to show through Garai and Mariam the existence of creative ecosystems and performance assemblages of many kinds, from al-Andalus to Mapungubwe.

No matter what forms of travel and interaction we might be concerned with, aesthetic interaction is about aesthetic constellations, acuities on the move in and through them, and the tension between creative ecosystems and performance spaces. What might be this history of interaction and travel, then, and why is it important? How would this be related to the manner in which such an aesthetic constellation emerged? There is a realization that this arc of music and the words that accompany its songs show remarkable commonality, despite significant variations, from Kashmir or Kerala to Mali, for example, and that interrogating how this might have come about could lead to new directions in understanding music, societal change and emotional landscapes. We therefore intend to reconstruct the actors and cultural formations of the *longue durée* that made all this possible and to bring them into sharp relief, as far as the available archives and scholarship permit – to reconstruct their lives, their social servitude, their creativity, their work, the words they composed and sang, and where possible, their music.

Since most of them were women enslaved or in servitude of many cultures and faiths from all imaginable slave routes, and importantly coming in large numbers from Africa, it will be vital to deepen the already exciting insights. For instance, Suzanne Meyers Sawa has brought to light in her work the importance and centrality of women (S.M. Sawa 2002), and more and more writings confirm our sense that women from everywhere were at the epicentre of creativity in poetry, performance and music.[5] Of late, the *qiyan* form the centre-point of fascinating accounts (Gordon and Hain, eds 2017). What needs deeper exploration is precisely their centrality in the development of the craft.

As we are more specifically interested in the soundscapes of the lament, mostly in its minor note tonalities and Phrygian forms, so that an aesthetic arc of sorrow can be reconstructed, we need to search creatively for the broader musical landscape that made this possible. The broader music we are aware of, after all, 'talks' about migration, separation, refugeedom, persecution and intense nostalgia, and expresses itself in varied ways through combinations which in the Indian tradition are classified under the Bhairavi family of scales. They would be closest to the natural minor scale in western classical music, the songs of lamentation in Africa's *ngoma* styles, the Phrygian scale in ancient Greek music, and related to the Hijaz *maqām* in Turkish, Persian or Egyptian classical music systems.

Further, across these vast distances, the soundscape of the lament also underpins contemporary musical expression around these themes, indicating a historical trajectory across space and time that has left deep imprints through emotion and the power of the forms that might have travelled. So, from the *heer* on the Indian subcontinent to the *amanes* or *rembetika* or *mirologia* in Greece, Cyprus or Turkey, to the *nuba*, *melhun* or *muwashshah* in Egypt, Tunisia or Morocco, to the *soleares*, *seguriyas* or *bulerias* flamenco songs in southern Spain, similar echoes are heard. The effort here is located, as it should be, at the intersection of creative work and aesthetics, poetics, musicology and historical materialism.

We encountered, for example, the world of the *qiyan* and the world of the ordinary *jawari* – both would have shared a sense of loss and longing for the homes they had been removed from. But in the elite spaces of Baghdadi musicality and the music of the haunts or the streets, their feelings would have operated through different filters: the successful *qiyan* looking on their lowly pasts with a mixture of disdain and longing; the *jawari* murmuring about their present and sharing the longing for their pasts. But for a moment try and imagine what happened to the *qiyan* when music was silenced and they were rendered homeless and craft-less by a *fatwa*. Imagine thousands of them losing voice, status and livelihood, and finding a home either in travelling troupes or in new forms of slavery. Where did they travel?

Historical Conjecture

To make sense of this complex period and its landscapes, we divided our account into two periods: the seventh to the eleventh century and the eleventh to the fifteenth century CE. We called the first period the era of theocratic proxy states, that is, where the powers that ruled did so through an explicit divine mandate whereby each, for lack of a better word, ethnospace justified its ruthless exploitation in and through the 'theocratic', until there was a shift to a later stage in which more secular concerns of power and possession underpinned such justifications. The elites of these states, each aware of the 'other' 'over there', were nonetheless quite self-absorbed in their earthly missions and the extraction of surplus from their immediate countryside. This was common to the Maya and the Han, as much as to the epicentres of Mapungubwe and Mouziris/Kochi. There was a remarkable co-emergence of urban formations that ushered each other into prominence at this time, and if size mattered at all, we see that most of the fourteen such formations with more than a hundred thousand people were to be found in the east, with only Cordoba in Europe, and Cairo and Constantinople in the eastern Mediterranean.

The eleventh century was a vital turning point, a kind of pivot in world history. From the eleventh to the fifteenth century the dynamism of the world of interactions is still to be located in the east, with Beijing featuring as the largest city; Genoa, Venice and Paris appear on the scene, but everywhere there seems to be a synergistic growth. In southern Africa, it seems that Zimbabwe takes over the mantle from Mapungubwe, and we know from the hard work of archaeologists the implications of the changes from Central Cattle Pattern societies to the sedentary agrarian and mining and metal-working societies of the Zimbabwe Pattern. For reasons that will be discussed later, by the end of the fifteenth century, southern Africa's hinterland had disengaged from this dynamic and, as Shadreck Chirikure (2015) here insists, we have to look at agency because the 'hinterland' was not just the *tabula rasa* of world trade.

Our task is to work hard to understand the rise and fall of polities, and the articulation between the world and Africa beyond but including its coastlines. In all this bustle and criss-crossing, slavery had a significant role to play – indeed servitude in AfroAsia was different from its transatlantic counterpart, but it was a serious endeavour.

Slavery has been seen as a mode of production in its own right, but more often than not it forms part of the assemblage of activities that constitute a polity or a social formation. The only difference between it and other forms of servitude is that the owner/master has control over the person that includes his or her productive and reproductive powers. The period under consideration involved more than that. Other forms of servitude involved voluntary total or partial bondage, debt bondage, and a variety of entrapments that defied imagination in their cruelty. Although the right to take the life of a slave was proscribed in the Sassanid, Abbasid and Sinic domains, this did not mean that extreme forms of violence and even death were not the fate of slaves.

We can twist slavery and turn it because it does not fit the image of a shiny past; and we can rely on the unreliable figures as an alibi to minimize its impact and its extent (E. Harris 1992). But it was there, clearly, as all qualitative accounts of every urban household and institution mention slaves. There was a forced movement of people through the coastal towns of eastern Africa and their distribution in the Gulf, the Abbasid lands and northern and southern Al-Hind, and then of people from India and the Malay archipelago trafficked to other destinations. Parts of this trade in slaves have been researched, but rarely synthesized. Women were more prized than men, and they were carted off into domestic, entertainment and sex-work servitude; by contrast, it seems the men were shipped off to plantations and armies. These transactions reached China, where remarkable and racially discomforting accounts are beginning to be researched about dispositions and racial prejudices around the Qunlun expressed in literature and travel narratives. In Muslim lands, slave conversion to Islam presented a problem which escalated pressures towards manumission and attempts to exempt converted slaves from 'freedom'. In 1505, a judicial *fatwa* in what is now Iran/Iraq decreed that converts who were slaves need not be freed.

We are aware that not all clusters fit exactly the chronology we have imposed: southern Africa's first phase extends to the late thirteenth century, Cairo's is disrupted in the ninth and thirteenth centuries, Baghdad is ravaged in the early thirteenth century, whereas Ethiopian citadels fit the chronology better but their change of command is radical and discontinuous. What is evident though, at the broadest level, is that urbanity is on the 'up' with Baghdad providing a serious energy point by the eleventh century, and the volume of urban formations comprising more than a hundred thousand people shifting decisively towards China by the 1500s with Beijing gaining both size and prestige as it grows to house more than a million people (Brook 1998).

Here, Sinologists may object too – isn't 1368 a local and a global pivot?

Isn't the prior period one of Yuan (or Mongol) rule, and the latter one of the flourishing of the Ming? We are convinced by Timothy Brook's *The Troubled Empire* (2010). He argues for a compromise that the Ming consolidated what Khubilai had started when he imposed his rule as 'Heaven's Deputee', establishing a theocratic state. But as Heaven remained aloof from the crises and troubles that befell his domain – the Little Ice Age, droughts, floods, famine, locusts and epidemics – he learned to expect little from that quarter, and started establishing instead a sturdy bureaucracy, a well-organized military command and a centralized administration to control both need and greed (Brook 2010: 79). The Ming flourished on the back of this.

There were different 'rhythmics' in the time under investigation, too. Although the notion of entanglement hints at synchronicity, the dynamics could not be synchronous. The asynchrony is still governed by the natural cycles of the monsoon, the planting and harvesting seasons, the limits of physical endurance in overland trade, the manufacturing cycles, the patterns induced by festivals and pilgrimages. There are also the very patterned movements of pastoral people and the ones deduced from astrological observations. As absolutist states consolidate, the annual tax is paid in kind or cash. So, the postmodern abandonment of the imperial and national calendrical time leads us straight to very precise cycles. It is unavoidable to distinguish between night and day, and to conform to annual seasonal cycles (however much they differ between the Aztecs and the Hindus). What creates variety is the space between the two. So, as Clare Oxby notes (1998), Berbers in Kabyia operated between three calendars: Gregorian for their administrative dues, Muslim for their religious rituals and Roman for their agricultural cycles. Their 'rhythmic' was never arbitrary.

Hence, with a few narrative adjustments here and there, we thought our periodization would allow us to talk more easily about the world of slavery, bondage, spice, gold, iron, art and music, looking also at energy points and clusters in their flourishing and decline. Timothy Brook makes a further vital point: the Ming were in turn actively engaged in 'weaving the commercial webs that were tying them to the rest of the world and by so doing creating the conditions for the rise of capitalist enterprise in Europe' (Brook 2010: 217). Usually, the dramatic cessation of the Zheng He maritime project is seen as a decisive and inexplicable withdrawal. That it was. But our assessment of it needs to be modified: 'in consolidating the trade networks of [the] South China Sea made up of Chinese merchants from the North and Arab traders from the South, a relatively autonomous trading system was established' (ibid.: 227). Frank (1998) was right – the west needed the Potosi silver and some cannons to buy into all that.

We take from Ibn Khaldun the sense of the rise and fall of earthly powers, a sense of non-teleological history, but have some problems with his assessment of both Arabic and Baghdadi prowess and decline; we take from Marx the idea of contradictory emergence of polities and the relationship between surplus extraction and dynamism; we take from Sherratt a world of interconnections and the power of urban forms and hegemonic regimes of value; we try to find a midway between regimes of production and accumulation and trade, and try to locate, through the movement of slaves and people in servitude, the emergence of constellations and acuities that let our project make sense. We shall return to the key energy points of this world system of interactions in the fourth chapter. Before doing so, we need to address some key methodological problems that are implied in our effort to collect musical and performative material for our journey.

There is a formidable scholarship on many of the spaces we will be visiting. Persia is unthinkable without the introductory work of Ella Zonis (1973), and that of Hormoz Farhat (1990) and Bruno Nettl (1992). Our Baghdad station would have been lost without Henry George Farmer's work on Arabian music (1925a, 1925b, 1929), and works by Don Michael Randel (1976), Owen Wright (1978), and Jean Jenkins and Poul Rovsing Olsen (1976). Above all, as will be seen below, we have relied on G.D. Sawa's (1989) canonical *Music Performance Practice in the Early 'Abbasid Era 132–320 AH/750–932*. So al-Andalusal has a growing cast of eminent scholars: see Anwar J. Chejne (1974), Amnon Shiloah (1991), Owen Wright (1992), Jareer Abu-Haidar (1993) and Nadir Marouf (1995). They all provide enough portraiture and analysis to make the nuances of the emerging cultural formations sensible.

Notes

1 One of the present authors, Ari Sitas, had the pleasure of meeting Andrew and Susan Sherratt at a mini-conference on world systems and urbanity that the late Professor Hermann Schwengel organized in Freiburg in 2005; see Schwengel (2006). On a long historical view, Norman Yoffe (2012) was also useful.

2 For a quick journalistic summary, see https://theconversation.com/archaeology-shows-how-ancient-african-societies-managed-pandemics-138217, accessed 23 April 2020.

3 For a discussion of Chinese debates and accounts of this idea, see also Brook (1989).

4 See also Chandler (1987).

5 See Richardson (2009) and Gordon (2004).

CHAPTER THREE

Methods in the Madness

We are writing at a time when the past is being sought and reconstructed by musicians and musicologists with an urgency that is quite uncanny. For example, the 'early music' master, composer and performer Jordi Savall's work is conscious of the medieval roots of the pentagram (or the set of five lines with four spaces between them which is used as the basis for staff or stave notation in western music), but to it he is juxtaposing other soundscapes.[1] He is facing east and south and his music, in reconstructing the music of Jerusalem, Granada, Venice and the slave routes (Savall 2008, 2009, 2016, 2017) from a vast collection of works of medieval music reconstruction, is an act of profound craft and humanism. But he alerts his publics to how difficult the task is of reconstructing such music from the archives given the scarcity of description and notation, which he overcomes with craft-based imagination. It is the craft of the 'must have sounded like that', knowing deeply the range of instruments, their limits and their possibilities. The fascination with ancient routes is increasing exponentially, exemplified by YoYo Ma's portrayal of Silk Road music with deep roots in the past in Morgan Neville's 2015 film, *The Music of Strangers*, Tan Dun's *Buddha Passion* (he had toyed with Marco Polo before[2]) and new work on the antiquity of the kora in northern Africa which places us in good company.[3]

The revival, reconstruction and performance of 'early' or 'medieval' or 'ancient' music is not new, and has, at least over the past half-century, been driven by several imperatives: academic, political and creative. The debates that are easily available are many and encompass how, why and for whom such endeavours of 'going into the musical past' are relevant. Of course, there are differences in the kinds of such material that are available, particularly material that is written about, skewed heavily in favour of the revivals in the European tradition. The initiatives are several in the non-European tradition as well, but perhaps not as much written about, relying on oral and aural transmission.[4]

Bagby (2002a, 2002b), in addressing questions about such retrievals in the west, or what he refers to as 'performance informed by historical imagination', asks how various forms of documentation like 'musical notation, descriptions of performance situations, treatises, methods, visual representations of music-making, playable instruments, etc.' can indicate how the music of the past might be performed in the present.

Such documentation, even if available and detailed,

> is still missing the one crucial element of musical performance, which we would most need and desire to possess: the actual sound, the presence of a living master. Barring the discovery of time-travel, we shall never meet our master (and of course, there is always the terrifying sub-scenario of this time-machine fantasy: what would happen if we had access to the original sound and to the master's living art, but we simply did not like what we heard?). Deprived of this essential face-to-face musical experience, we are forever doomed to confront our own past musical cultures through a veil of conjecture and intuition, with our contemporary tastes and preferences silently informing our musical choices (Bagby 2002a: 340).

This is a valid note of caution, no doubt, and those engaged in this exercise of approximating performance of past music in the present day from well-documented sources would do so keeping in mind this possibility of inauthenticity.

> [E]very performance of medieval music . . . is by its nature a reconstruction. For that matter, every performance of a music which is not 'our own' is a reconstruction. The sad truth is that the actual music of the Middle Ages no longer exists, since all the musicians who created it, performed it and lived through it are long dead. The surviving manuscripts, depictions of instruments and descriptions of performances are simply artefacts, not music. We live in a reconstructed musical universe, filled with sounds made by the living but based on documents . . . made by the dead. (Ibid.)

The concern with the 'artefact' or the document that is trustworthy as evidence in musical reconstruction misses out on an important dimension of musical performance particularly in the non-west, namely interpretation and improvisation, even of highly codified and 'written down' music. Also, the reconstruction might happen, not necessarily from sources in the past to performance in the present, but from the present in the direction of looking for documents, artefacts or other traces in the past. This would fall into the category of what Bagby calls 'historically informed imaginative performance' (Bagby 2002b: 343), which would need to acknowledge, however, the loss of 'authenticity' or, more importantly, exact verifiability. The argument is clearly a response to the claims to authenticity that are often made by musicians performing music of the past, and the caution being insisted upon is useful.

However, if we are interested in a two-way reconstruction – using performance in the contemporary period to provide us with traces of the past and working through a variety of artefacts and materials from the past to imagine what music of the past might have been like, and how that finds reflection in the music of the contemporary period – the usual desire for authenticity has to be necessarily discarded. Particularly in our case, we are trying not only to reconstruct music and, with it, the histories and social formations of the past, but also to focus on intertwined pasts of vast regions of the globe that were interconnected through several kinds of migration. At the same time, in sifting through the available material we recognize the deep embeddedness of the areas being considered in local histories and social and cultural formations. As we have noted in an earlier paper (Damodaran and Sitas 2016), our objective is, significantly, not to elevate our quest into a search for 'the exacting evidence', but to distil and point to elements that indicate connections beyond the usually acknowledged and researched ones.

A powerful reason for reconstructing the past in music can be found in a whole range of initiatives, including Savall's, to engage with 'old traditions' and musical reconstructions for a politics of the present. For example, Indian musicians have for more than three decades now been studying and performing repertoires that were excavated from the past, often from centuries before, as a response to divisive politics, inter-religious violence and the rise of right-wing nationalism. Musicians like Shubha Mudgal, Madan Gopal Singh, Dhruv Sangari, the musicians of the Kabir Project[5] from north India, and T.M. Krishna and others from the south have worked through various old repertoires with a critical view; and a vast corpus of such music, largely from Sufi and Bhakti traditions from the twelfth century onwards, has come to address and reconstellate questions of nation, identity and politics. These initiatives have challenged right-wing cultural assertions frontally, and also shaped popular music-listening cultures in the country by providing contemporary interpretations (Manuel 2008; Moss and Rahman 2013). A significant part of Savall's performative work, like that of several people involved in reviving Andalusian repertoires, has similarly worked with contemporary remnants of traditions claiming centuries-old roots to address politics in the present.

Savall also leaves us with a serious question: the juxtaposition of the liturgical west and the orient in, let us say, Granada, leaves us wondering why such proximity turns into a proto-pentagram in the west, devoid of any traces of the kind of microtones that we are trying to deal with, so evident in the Moorish lamentations that he has reconstructed. Elements of it remain, too, in the Byzantine liturgical traditions. How is it that the west's liturgical tradition became devoid of the very 'buccal undulations' that Lorca and a great Spanish composer like Falla were looking for (Orringer 2016)? Was there an act of repression? Were there prohibitions that created a canon? Or was canonization an attempt to make sense of varied influences and movements? The periods that Savall talks about were tetchy times of rising fanaticism, of the crusades, of the origins of the move towards the Reconquista. The key is there in his 'The Forgotten Kingdom' (Savall 2010), a threnody about the savage extermination of the heretical Cathars, sanctioned by official decree and executed with aplomb by crusaders within France. The laments reach east and south, the Cathar prayers are somewhere in between, the western liturgy is repressively enharmonic, about to swaddle all excess. But the music reconstructed across several albums by Savall is based on the strength of an oral tradition that has preserved the music of several parts of the pre-colonial world down the centuries.[6]

However, even Savall's extensive and detailed performative work perhaps limits itself to the Abrahamic traditions and is a demonstration of music from across ten centuries of the courtly and the liturgical, not really about the 'buccal undulations' that Lorca identified in the 'deep song' (Lorca 1922), coming either from the less privileged populations in the geographies of the Abrahamic traditions or from beyond those boundaries, far into the east or the south. Our enquiries require us to look in both directions, that is, first to extend our search beyond the boundaries of, say, the Abrahamic traditions, or the Chinese or Indian or Ethiopian traditions in themselves, to see how and when they extend towards each other; and second, to explore how these connecting traditions reflected the music-making of those from the margins of society in class, race, caste or religious terms.

What is particularly difficult is that the project of uncovering the 'note road' or 'melody road', in our case, would encompass not only the liturgical or court traditions, presumably with the greater certainty of finding records that describe how such music or performance might have occurred in the past, but also that we have set out to uncover the music of the people who wandered, were enslaved and so on. We are interested in carrying out an archaeology of melodies along the routes of these migrations which can lead us to a matrix of melodies along our metaphoric minor note road from 'below', dotted with the minor notes of the wanderers, the minstrels, the sheep-herders and the Roma.

What is important to note and study for our work? What, from the initiatives outlined above, are we choosing to draw upon as methodological points, and what are our sources?

Following the 'Sounds Like'

The starting point for the musical aspects of this project, consisting of variants of Lorca's deep song, or Phrygian tonalities, or the Bhairavi/Bhairav family, was western and north-western India and adjoining parts of Pakistan, with a ballad form called the *heer*. The presence of four minor notes in the Bhairavi melody (on which the canonical *heer*, detailed more in the next chapter, is based) or three in the Bhairav formed the basis for the 'sounds like', or 'listening for', to begin with. That these melodies, traced as they were found in contemporary renderings into western Asia and parts of the Mediterranean, were very often laments and songs about loss or separation, provided another basis for the 'listening for'. In other words, melodies that are minor-note-based, with recognizably similar cadences in modes of rendering and being part of lament traditions of one sort or the other, recognized primarily by the ear, began the exercise of the 'sounds like'. We have found such melodies proliferating through all the regions that we are focusing on. Further, be it a Bhairavi or a Phrygian tonality in Lorca's deep song, the music appears to have had an appeal that went far beyond specific histories or cultural markers. As the travels took place, the music seems to have absorbed as well as shaped emotional registers to the extent of making the connection between them seem universal. If not, why do a La Caita in Spain, a *rembetika* in Athens, a Parvin Alipour in Lorestan and a Sheila Bhatia in Punjab express love, separation and loss through similar combinations of notes and perhaps very similar melismatic cadences?

The 'sounds like', however, could be a limiting exercise, even a tautological one, if limited to a certain set of melodies, even if they are numerous and found to be proliferating across the geographies being considered. Again, the *heer*, with its melodic variations (said to be more than 50 in number) provides a useful template to locate variety. For example, a certain variant that is sung in the part of Punjab bordering the desert sounds very similar to some melodies that are part of the Mande tradition in Mali and Senegal. What is being emphasized here is that even as we call attention to minor-note-based melodies in the Phrygian range to talk about a lament voicing or melodic pattern that is common, this is not being done in a limiting sense at all. We are mindful of the largely pentatonic musical traditions that permeate many parts of Africa and also China, whereas the Indo-Arabo-Andalusian world has an abundance of heptatonic melodies and scales. Our attempt has been to identify various melodic pathways and musical traditions that could be the result of travels and interactions.

For this book, we began the Garai travelogue in southern Africa, and moved across land and sea towards India. Based on the oral record, we can construct several travelogues over and above the Garai ones we have traced. For example, we can follow the passing on of the Shirin story; we can follow the migrations of northern African people into southern Spain, and follow the Roma and other travelling bands of people. We had to ask a broader question: how far could we go to uncover actual connections, beyond the fact that aesthetic acuity allows for imaginative reconstructions of the 'sounds like'? Our listening carefully to all those in AfroAsia who claim antiquity made us believe that the connections were obvious. But could we move from the subjective and the intuitive to something more substantive and demonstrable? This is especially important because most of the work that does look at such connections, which we have ploughed through extensively, tends to limit itself to specific parts of the world or to particular traditions. Be it work in comparative musicology or ethnomusicology, the research is thus clustered geographically, for obvious reasons like availability of historical sources and the difficulty of disentangling the long distances and local effects. Our work has extended itself beyond the distances that most research traverses.

We have hypothesized that the travels – of people, of myths, of religious influences – have left remarkable traces in the form of melodies. Could we be metaphoric archaeologists and find the bone that could allow for the reconstruction of the skeleton? Or attribute greater connections than are usually acknowledged through the 'sounds like'?

Theorizing the 'Trace'

Mapping on the basis of the 'sounds like' can open up a large vista of possibilities, which can make it possible to explicate proximities to and distances from it. It can allow for the testing of what is being said by purveyors of a variety of traditions and clarify whether indeed there is a resemblance or not. On the other hand, the hundreds of musicians and ensembles that claim deep historical connections can be brought into the comparison and differentiation. There will always be the distinction between what they say and what they play – oral historians have often made the point that there have to be traces of pasts in what is being retold – but with careful attention the inventions can always be carefully sifted out, however understandable they may be in terms of the contemporary politics of authenticity. Here, the work of Carolyn Hamilton (2002), a South African historian concerned with the pre-colonial past, has made the eloquent methodological point that to reach beyond the colonial archive that inscribed an ahistorical tribalism on African people and others, we have to insist and imagine that there are 'traces' in both the way the past is narrated and the way, in our terms, it is played. Narratives, textual and performative, are productive, and it matters little whether they are exactly about the real or the mythical. Stories related in performative traditions or traces found in actual performance that shape the narrative are important sources for this project.

Picken and Nickson, in analysing the remnants of evidence for music of the Tang courts in China, argue that large parts of Asia show the persistence of musical construction over more than 1,200 years, making the search for traces even more important (Picken and Nickson, eds 2006). In the sources that we list below, we have looked for traces of various sorts.

Manuscripts and Other Textual Material

The musicological treatises that originated in Baghdad provided us with an interesting entry point for comparative analysis. G.D. Sawa's pathbreaking reconstruction of music in the early Abbasid period (eighth to tenth centuries), combining the insights and information provided in books by Al-Isfahani and Al-Farabi, showed the continuities between pre-Islamic Persian music and Islamic Persian and Arabic musical systems (Sawa 1989). Picken and Nickson provided the template for the comparison of manuscripts from India, China, Japan and Indonesia (Picken and Nickson, eds 2006). In Ethiopia, the text by Saint Yared written 1,500 years ago that forms the basis for liturgical and non-liturgical music to this day (Zemedu and Assabie 2014), was another example. Placing these textual sources side by side and then zooming out to cover geographies that went beyond each of their briefs provided important insights about possible connections and, more importantly, the imperatives for codification in these different contexts. It also provided a comparative picture of the relationship between social status, servitude and musicianship that indicated cross-cutting influences.

Computational Analysis

Musicological work has moved further ahead with computational analysis or music content recognition techniques that conduct a technical analysis of musical forms and identify patterns that indicate similarities or departures. Broadly coming under the heading of computational musicology, such analyses, which tend to be more accurate than the human ear, have been done for specific musical traditions that we are considering (Serra 2014, 2017). They consist of processes referred to as physical or low-level content description from audio signals of recordings (without what are called high-level musical and contextual knowledge), content-based generalizations about the data (such as knowledge about genres, instrumentation and melody) and analysis of the information that is generated, resulting in painstaking transcription that attempts to capture as much detail as possible. For example, Kroher *et al.* (2018) use the 'audio approach' that is appreciative of the lack of scores or specific ornamentation and microtonality to compare a piece called *martinete* from flamenco and an Arab-Andalusian form called *inshad*, and analyse their similarities and differences in terms of ornamentation, vibrato, melodic line and scale. Caro Repetto *et al.* (2015) conduct similar analysis for recognizing the *nawbat* of the Arab-Andalusian tradition.

Such analysis, even if only in a nascent stage for non-western musics, as Kroher *et al.* (2018) acknowledge, addresses an important dimension of understanding music historically: it allows us to make connections between living traditions in the contemporary period, the same or similar traditions recorded, say, in the first 50 years of the past century (when ethnomusicological recordings, largely made under colonial regimes, were collected and preserved in various archives), and documents and artefacts from the distant past. Mark Aranha (2021) and Neo Muyanga (2020) have worked with transcription techniques and computational analysis for some of the material collected on this project. This approach could be used on a wider scale from Al-Hind to al-Andalus, and from Africa to the south Indian or north-west Indian coast.

One could take the entirety of the International Library of African Music and scan it across a large landscape of sounds to create theories about similarity and variation.[7]

Archaelogical Traces

Archaeological findings, inscriptions and epigraphic evidence can be employed as sources to comment on musical cultures in the distant past, and comparisons between different sets of evidence or for different regions allow influences to be traced. Notations found on rock faces or on objects found in archaeological digs, inscriptions or epigraphical evidence found similarly, and iconography, revealing instruments, musicians or performances, are used by music scholars in combination with other historical and sociological information to put together 'musical universes' of areas being studied. For example, in constructing the musical universe of ancient Israel/Palestine in pre-Biblical times, Braun and Braun (2002) underline their method of finding the pre-semantic and pre-iconographic meanings of instruments named in the oldest texts available (like the Bible, in this case), and combining this with the semantic meanings of the names using anthropological, archaeological, semiotic and organological methods or models for understanding the significance of instruments across the ages. They note that what is available through later texts might reflect what was in use at the time of their writing; but still, being the only texts available, they would be the most proximate sources of evidence.

When names or images of instruments or of musicians and performances, or physical evidence of instruments are found, the first step, then, is to identify them using multiple sources. Historical organology, for example, arrives at categories of instruments and their classification based on the physical and technical qualities of the instruments, which in turn are also historically located in terms of their period of use. When an instrument that is found in a region is seen to be different from those found there in general, it is located using organological models, but also in terms of its specific use where it is found, in combination with or separately from other instruments in that region. Its topos, the mythological, historical and theological context of its use, then becomes important to identify in order to uncover the meaning of the instrument. When families or categories of instruments are found along routes of travel and migration, comparative organology thus becomes an exercise in combining technical characteristics of instruments with the knowledges about those histories.

Linguistic and Semiotic Evidence

Linguists have traced for us evidence of similarities between and migration of population groups from one region to another on the basis of similarities in language, syntax and the meanings of words. The travels of the Roma from central and western India through large parts of AfroAsia and Europe over centuries, for example, have been traced through linguistic evidence, among several other kinds of sources. The symbolic meanings of words and what they signify is another way of tracing connections that appear between places and communities, even if there is no objectively accepted link between them. One set of traditions that has allowed us to trace connections much beyond typically available scholarship, utilizing linguistic and semiotic evidence, is spirit, trance and healing traditions. An example is the complex of drumming, performance, healing and spirit practices, referred to as *ngoma* in central and southern Africa. However, hardly any found source from the deep past is available for *ngoma* as it travelled.[8] What is available is evidence of the linguistic and semiotic elements that go into musical meaning in cultures that are African, or have African origins or links through AfroAsian connections in, say, parts of India, Pakistan, Iran, Oman and other parts of the Persian Gulf where African populations were distributed across the centuries. A trance, drumming and performative Sufi tradition of the Sidi community in India, which has African origins, is called *Sidi goma*, and has been linked to the African *ngoma* traditions (Basu 2008; Caitlin-Jairazbhoy 2012). Most unexpectedly, however, one of the well-established spirit propitiation and worship traditions from within the Hindu religious tradition in the province of Karnataka in south India yielded a backward link in the form of epigraphical evidence from the medieval period. Here, as with *Sidi goma*, a living spirit worship tradition that has strong musical and performative elements encompasses the worship of a spirit, Bobbare, who has been linked to African traditions. Techniques of visual art history employed by Shobha Talengala (2017) in her work in our project combine examination of the visual dimensions of contemporary performance with a study of the implications of epigraphic inscriptions beginning in the eleventh century, and point us towards the significance of deified characters of African origin, such as Bobbare, who were nested within a large pantheon of spirit characters belonging within the Hindu tradition, and were absorbed into a larger process of Brahmanical hegemonic religious practice.

Our research has pointed to more such spiritual and religious traditions in India and elsewhere, in combination with the work of other scholars. The claims to antiquity may evaporate, but unconscious lineages can be traced. In contemporary times, what is said might be interesting for its mythological power despite the archive: for example, there are stories of Kappiri, the beheaded black slave in south India who is a cult figure of certain communities belonging to the lower castes in central Kerala, and has produced rituals and music in the district of Kochi. According to fieldwork done among people from these communities (Jeyachandran 2014), he appears, as an African man smoking a cigar at various locations where there are tiny shrines dedicated to him, to this day, whether real or not! Similarly, eleventh-century stories in Zanzibar about a hundred Shirazi castaways in southern Zanzibar who mixed with the locals, preserved a solar calendar, and evolved a syncretic ritual that involves the sacrifice (symbolic now) of a virgin, the burning of the craft she is on and the sinking of the craft through its stoning by women, mythical or not, bring forth complex interconnections. The songs sung now claim antiquity, and the story talks of people way back in the mists of time.

Spirit worship traditions thus provided us with an important entry point into tracing links between communities, both where histories of long-term migration were known and also where no such obvious connections could be established historically for the communities themselves, but could be understood given the histories of the regions. In Talengala's work, for example, the history of the communities that worship Bobbare in the present would not attest to AfroAsian lineage, but Mangalore and its surrounds have historically been important in Indian Ocean trade.

This is but one example of connections discovered between parts of the world based, to begin with, on linguistic and semiotic evidence, and then supplemented with fieldwork and other evidence like performance. Such examples abound in the work done on this project.

Poetry and Song Lyrics

The words of songs and the poetic traditions that have endured across centuries, through manuscripts as well as through oral transmission, provide important traces of distant pasts and entanglements. To give but a few examples: the metaphor of the 'blackbird' used in present-day flamenco songs of the Gitanos of Spain, that possibly refers to Ziryab, the musician who was chased out of Baghdad first and then out of what is present-day Tunisia, and who was called the 'blackbird' (Gatlif 1993);[9] the trope of the *atlal* or ruins (Cooper 2018) that recurs across the centuries in Arabic poetry from the pre-Islamic period and the early days of Islam (referred to as *wuquf 'ala al-atlal*, or 'stopping by the ruins'), and has found new life in the work of a generation of artists reacting to the losses due to war and state violence across the Middle East; the many versions of the words *zanj* (*zindj*, *zang*, *zangi*) or Berber (Bobbare, Baburiya). Even if not fully immersing ourselves in language and metaphor as philologists and linguists do, we have, through words and expressions found in poetry and songs, arrived at several connections that are typically not pointed out.

As Cooper (2018) writes about the trope of the ruins,

> the motif of the *atlal* ('ruins') originates in the pre-Islamic period, among the so-called Jahili ('agnostic' or Pre-Islamic) poets. It's thought that its originator was the 6th Century poet-king Imru' al-Qais. Al-Qais was the last king of the kingdom of Kindah, and is often hailed as the father of Arabic poetry. He spent much of his life banished from his kingdom, ostensibly due to his excessive love of poetry, and during his exile he wandered the lands of Arabia and wrote poetry. Legend has it that one of his poems was later written in gold and included in the *Mu'allaqat* (the Hanging Poems), seven pieces of poetry supposedly suspended from the Kaaba at Mecca, Islam's holiest shrine. In his contribution to the *Mu'allaqat*, al-Qais describes a character stopping for a time at the ruins of a campsite and remembering his beloved in the ruins. . . . The word *wuquf* that gives the trope its name holds the double meaning of 'standing' and 'stopping', so this portion of the poem usually forms a moment of stillness and meditation, outside of time. The landscape comes to represent loss and longing, a container for memory . . . the *atlal* trope endured through the ages, and today in the Middle East, a new generation of artists is returning to this ancient trope and using it to make sense of the loss and destruction experienced in countries with recent experience of war: most prominently in Iraq and Palestine.

Our uncovering of traces involves similar exercises for musical and poetic traditions in different parts of AfroAsia that we are covering. We are, however, also making a distinction between the forms that endured through formally acknowledged sources such as manuscripts, and those repeated in orally or aurally handed-down traditions.

Thus we have both the lyrics and poems of Baghdad, and, with Ziryab's alleged words, the Sephardic and courtly poetry of the Umayyads, and the Persian and Indian subcontinent's lore from Nizami to Amir Khusrow, Waris Shah, Shah Abdul Latif Bhitai and Kabir, to mention just a few. We have also found collections of women's songs of Africa that range from the twelfth century (very few) to the nineteenth century (the majority).[10] The latter claim antiquity, and there are continuities in themes about suffering, womanhood, rites of passage, marriage, death and love. There are laments scattered in this archive too. However stretched the time is, patterns of call and response and collective singing endure, and so does the dancing that so irked Ibn Khaldun and alerted slavers, as we have seen, to an inherent talent. Is there a code that is enduring? Is there a prototype?

We cannot state clearly whether an enduring code or prototype exists across centuries, but there are certainly patterns with words that come deeply entrenched from different traditions and yet point towards each other.[11]

To summarize this discussion on the sources and methods that we have used to arrive at musical connections in AfroAsia in the colonial period, the multiplicity of traces we have identified can be seen to come together in what poet and philosopher A.K. Ramanujan calls 'symbol pools' that are context-dependent and yet influenced by time, movement and crossings (Ramanujan 1999). Thus words, musical phrases, names of people and places, textual and archaeological evidence observed across short and long distances in the AfroAsian landscape have provided us with material to uncover connections that we discuss in this book.

Notes

[1] The pentagram is known to have been preceded by notation based on neumes, which first made their appearance in musical notation in the ninth century CE as symbols placed above the text to indicate the melodic gesture for that syllable (Strayer 2013) and the general melodic contour, but not the intervallic distance between them. They were used together with oral instruction and memory to aid performers in actual performance. This kind of neume started becoming diastemic or graphical representation (as against phonetic notation in the Greek, Chinese, Arabic or Indian systems) with the introduction of lines to depict pitches by the tenth century, and eventually, through the medieval period, developed into staff notation which allowed for playing of music by musicians without having heard it previously. The separation of musical performance from memory, because of the vast transformations in notation from the neume to the pentagram (which is seen to be precise and complete in itself), is also considered superior and as contributing to the rationality of western classical music.

[2] A performance of Buddha Passion by the Shanghai Symphony Orchestra in July 2020 (Tan Dun 2020) is available at https://youtu.be/KuAZOvEhQ0M. 'Tan Dun's Buddha Passion – the first of its kind among a history of Christian Passions – weaves stories that have lived in the hearts and minds of the eastern world for thousands of years. Inspired by the ancient city of Dunhuang and its awe-inspiring Mogao caves, the music powerfully illustrates the lessons of Buddha . . . [the work is inspired] by the powerful history of spiritual and cultural exchange of the Mogao Caves, as well as the

groundbreaking musical history discovered in the Dunhuang murals from the fourth to fourteenth century' (Dun, n.d.).

3 In the Sahel region of West Africa, the kora and balafon musical instruments are used by griots or storytellers to recite and perform stories from epics and narratives of the past – for example, Toumani Diabaté's *The Mande Variations* (Diabaté 2008).

4 The concern with exact evidence about the past in order to reconstruct its music is greater in the European tradition precisely because of the availability of notations that are considered 'precise' in the modern period, where oral transmission or memory are seen to play a smaller role. Performing music that is orally transmitted, even if helped along through notation where it is available, is a characteristic of many non-western musical systems, and reconstruction of old music in such contexts does not necessarily ask such questions of performers, as improvisation and interpretation are not considered to diminish the seriousness of the music. Some of the questions raised in the European tradition can be found in Bagby (2002a) and McGee (1998).

5 See http//kabirproject.org.

6 In *The Forgotten Kingdom*, Savall explores the classical period of the troubadour school from around the turn of the thirteenth century and also provides a comprehensive historical and artistic background, with the extermination of the Cathars being a disturbing and violent component that changed the history of the Languedoc region of southern France, considered part of Occitania. The troubadour tradition, which originated in Occitania and in turn was strongly influenced by the Andalusian music tradition, subsequently spread to Italy, Spain and Greece. In *Venezia Millenaria*, Savall brings out music from over a thousand years in Venice, from the Byzantine empire to the Napoleonic Wars, that interacted closely with music from the east and shaped western music substantially (Savall 2018). In *Granada*, he presents music from the foundation of Granada in the Zirid period to the time of Castilian rule when Muslims were forced to convert to Catholicism.

7 The International Library of African Music (ILAM), housed at Rhodes University, Grahamstown, South Africa, was founded by Hugh Tracey in 1954. See https://www.ru.ac.za.ilam.

8 Janzen (1992) and Janzen (2017) are studies of the various practices of *ngoma* as healing and spirit practices, and their music based in Africa.

9 The film *Latcho Drom* by Tony Gatlif, which traces the music of various Roma communities along the routes that they travelled over centuries, features a song by La Caita, the famed Roma Spanish singer, referring to the blackbird. More will be said about this song in the next chapter.

10 Our sources for these African songs include Daymond *et al.*, eds (2003); Finnegan (1976); Joris and Tengour, eds (2012); Kalu, ed. (2007); Lihamba *et al.*, eds (2007); Opland, ed. (1992); Opland (1998); Sadiqi *et al.* eds (2009) and Sutherland-Addy and Diaw, eds (2005).

11 There is perhaps a difference in the poetic codes between the songs of those who composed and sang for the elites and those sung for the lower-middle and working classes – although both favoured and unfavoured slave women had to get a few things right, specifically the balance between the devotional and the 'hadith' in which allusions to the Prophet and holiness would have been plentiful, and songs about wine, humour, repartee and satire, epics and panegyrics, and what at their most important could have been called elegiac (Kilpatrick 2003).

CHAPTER FOUR

AfroAsian Musics

Interconnections and Imprints

Dil-e-daar jogi de hatth jode
Mainu apna karo fakir saayee
Tere daras didaar de vekhne hoon
Aaya des pardes main cheer sayee

(I fold my hands to you, O mendicant of love
Make me yours, O fakir
To catch a glimpse of you
I have pierced through lands, near and distant)

Thus runs a verse in the sung version of the classic ballad of *Heer–Ranjha*, the popular *heer* form that is heard in the Punjab provinces of both present-day India and Pakistan. The *heer* form is used to relate the love story of Heer–Ranjha, as well as to depict love and joy, or to lament separation and dislocations associated with migration, social conflict and other issues that cause ruptures in society.

Waris Shah, the Punjabi Sufi poet, is said to have written the modern-day version of the Heer–Ranjha story, commonly referred to as *Heer Waris Shah*, in the eighteenth century, and said to be the creator of the canonical sung *heer* form based on the north Indian rāga Bhairavi or the Phrygian scale/mode. While the canonical *heer* is Bhairavi-based, those who have documented it and/or sing its different versions talk about more than 50 versions of the *heer* that can be found.[1]

The canonical *heer*, like the one from the Heer–Ranjha story described above, is elaborate, with clearly demarcated sections to the melody and

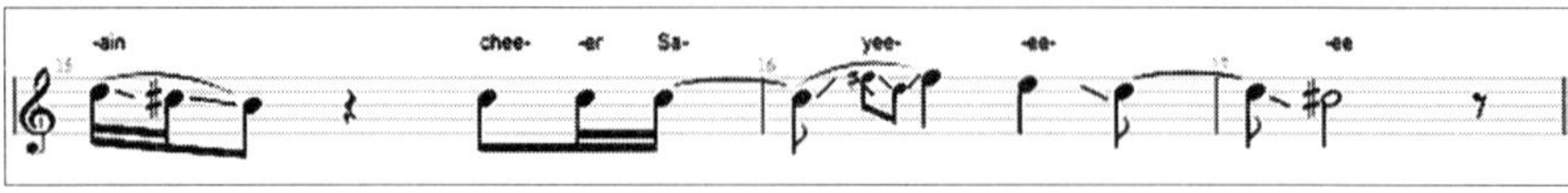

Figure 4.1 'Heer', Madan Gopal Singh. (Transcription by Mark Aranha.)

distinct musical form. In the first section of the melody, transcribed above, we can see the setting of the mood with a line containing notes that veer around the tonic *sa* (*do*), including notes that go into the octave below the *sa,* notably *komal ni* (flat seventh). The first line, when completed, then leads into a second and third line that go into a long tone with vibrato, or melismatic runs using the higher notes, finally coming back to the first line's melody again to close the section. This structure allows a build-up to more sections in the song that begin at higher levels in the melody, also going up to notes in the octave above the high *sa* of the octave, to *komal re* and *komal ga* (flat second and flat third). The melismatic runs are employed to elaborate the melody and also to effectively move up the scale or to come down the scale at the end of the sections. In addition, there is a signature descending phrase (which we will discuss in more detail later) that is employed at various places in the melody, and that becomes like a code. Expression in the song is elaborate, and enabled through the combination of the lyrics, the ambitus or range of the melody which extends often over three octaves, and the nuanced and carefully modulated melismatic runs.

The singing of the *heer* changes with the terrain and perhaps the social histories of the areas that it covers. Closer to the Afghanistan border of Punjab in both India and Pakistan, there is a version that is based on the Bhairavi, but much less elaborate than the canonical *heer.* It is sung at a high pitch in a loud, throaty and less modulated style, with the melody range limited to three or four notes of the scale in segments and with the other notes being sung in a different section, again with the section itself having a limited range of notes. In other words, there is hardly any melodic elaboration; it is sung at a faster tempo and the tunes of the segments get repeated as the singing continues for a long time, narrating the story.

Towards the desert side of the Punjab, bordering Rajasthan, the *heer* transforms into major mode, similar to the *maand* songs sung by desert nomads. This melody, expansive and elaborate, has an imploring quality, beginning at a high point in the scale and then looping and meandering through several high notes to come down gradually to the tonic *sa.* The way in which the looping is done with the voice (or *meend* as it is referred to in north Indian music) is similar to the continuous bowed playing of fretless string instruments like the sarangi, which is a common instrument in the desert region. The *maand* group of melodies is in a major scale, but often a *komal ni* or flat seventh note is used to bring in pathos or deeper emotion.

The story of Heer and Ranjha as well as the *heer* melodic family circulate across the regions with variations that could be attributed to time, geography and specific histories. The Bhairavi and its variants are associated with long common histories of the north-western frontiers of India and Pakistan, and extending into territories across Afghanistan, Iran and farther in West Asia. In India and Pakistan alone, variants such as the Sindhi Behravi or the Sindhu Bhairavi associate the melodies with the province of Sindh that traverses the borderlands between the two countries, marked by the Sindhu or Indus river. In south Indian music, the Bhairavi that we are referring to is called the Sindhu Bhairavi, an obvious reference to its association with the Sindhu/ Indus river.

The Bhairavi rāga or its variants (the range of rāgas Ahir Bhairav, Bhairav, Jogiya, Basant Mukhari in the north Indian tradition) appear in many locations along the route we are describing, namely India, Pakistan, Iran, several countries in West Asia, the Balkans, North Africa and Spain.[2] The Bhairavi is the Phrygian scale in the western musical system and close to the Hijaz *maqām* in the *maqāmat* classification system found in many parts of West Asia, Turkey and North Africa.

As we move across the map further west, a very similar melody, in the notes of the Ahir Bhairav rāga, is found in the singing of another love story, of Shirin–Khusrow, in Khorasan in Iran among Khorasani musicians belonging to the nomadic Bakhtiari community. This is an example of the way in which the story of Shirin and Khusrow II, the fascinating empress and emperor of the late Sassanid period (fifth century CE), has come down over the centuries. Khusrow was a Zoroastrian, Shirin was a Syriac Nestorian Christian. Their story is nested within the history of Nestorian Christianity and the persecution of those who practised it, ultimately resulting in their banishment towards Ethiopia in one direction and Kerala in southern India in another. From around the seventh century onwards, but particularly from the ninth century, the love story of Shirin and Khusrow came to be written about and idealized. In later versions that came from Islamic interpretations, there was a third person, Farhad, in the love triangle. Ferdowsi celebrates Shirin's valour and asserts, after her suicide, that 'her death was praised by all the world' (Ferdowsi 2007: 831). Later it was crafted as a symbol of nationhood and loss over several centuries across Persia, Turkey, Armenia, Azerbaijan, Byzantium, India and Afghanistan.

A contemporary rendering of the story of Shirin and Khusrow by Parvin Alipour has similar characteristics to the canonical *heer*, both in the way in which it is introduced by the flute at the beginning and how the voice comes in with the word 'Khusrow'.[3] The setting of the scene or mood with the interaction between the instrument and the voice is an important characteristic of Sufi singing in India and Pakistan, and appears so in the Alipour melody as well. An additional characteristic in Alipour's rendering similar to the *heer* is the descending melismatic or *legato* phrase from the fourth, through the minor third and the minor second to the first – a phrase that repeats like a code in the melody and appears to define its 'mood' as a lament.

A third example that we take up here is from the other end of our musical map in the west, in Spain: a 1922 recording of a 'deep song' by Federico García Lorca on the piano and the singer La Argentinita.[4] Drawing upon the echoes of laments from the east that are found in *bulerias*, *seguiriyas* and *soleares* from the flamenco repertoire (or, more specifically, from the forms that reflect the history of the Roma people in Spain) (Manuel 1989), the song that is performed is interesting for its 'typical' markers. While the song's overall ambience is also coloured by the piano and its western style, La Argentinita's voice sings the typical descending phrase that we identified in the Heer and Shirin melodies above as the minor note-based lament.

An interesting variant from the flamenco repertoire is a rendition of a song about a blackbird, '*Pajaro Negro*', by the Spanish Gitano (Roma) singer, La Caita.[5] While at first the song does not conform to the kind of lament that we have described above, careful listening reveals, through the interaction of the clapping (*palmas*), guitar-playing and La Caita's voice, the characteristic descending phrase of the lament in both the guitar and the voice. The guitar changes scales in the melody, and the voice enunciates the descending lament phrase with staccato movements between the notes and with a looping of the notes as the voice descends, but the phrase is recognizably there. The staccato movements and the raspy voicing, characteristic of many kinds of flamenco songs attributed to the Gitanos, give the song an expression of urgent anger. What is further interesting are the lyrics with historical references to the persecution of the Roma, which run as follows:

> You, you're a stork
> That has landed on earth

Figure 4.2 'El Pajaro Negro', La Caita. (Transcription by Mark Aranha.)

> Me, I'm a blackbird who has taken flight
> Why does your wicked mouth spit on me
> What is it to you
> That my skin is dark and my hair gypsy dark
> From Isabel the Catholic
> To Hitler and Franco
> We have been the victims of their wars.

The blackbird, while obviously referring to the dark-skinned Roma, perhaps also alludes to Ziryab, the slave musician of African origin who was banished from Baghdad in the ninth century and is said to be the progenitor of what came to be known as the Andalusian music tradition.

A fifth example is of a *rembetika* or *rebetiko* song from Greece, which, like other musical traditions characteristic of Greece, Turkey and Cyprus, employs the Phrygian scale and incorporates the features of a typical lament.[6] The *rembetika* musical corpus came into existence as underground music among migrants from Asia Minor in Greece from the 1920s, and typically came to represent sentiments of lamenting the past that they had left behind, being persecuted as immigrants and remaining poor, as well as love, celebration and social commentary. The *dromos* (literally 'road', but referring to the combination and progression of notes used) in *rembetika* are often based on *maqāms* in Turkish classical music, with the Hijaz being one of them.

A final example is a Sephardic Jewish Arabic Gitano song from Morocco, which is one of the centres of the Andalusian music tradition. This carries the

Figure 4.3 'Rembetika: Greek Music from the Underground, No. 8'.
(Transcription by Mark Aranha.)

Phrygian imprint as well as the descending lament phrase in much the same way as the canonical Bhairavi-based *heer*, the Bakhtiari Shirin and Lorca–La Argentinita's deep song.

What we are pointing out through these examples are the similarities between pieces of music performed in contemporary times, picked up initially through listening and then examined more carefully for the elements that suggest similarity. From the 'sounds like', we find in the above examples similar melodic contours (in the broad Phrygian range, with minor seconds, thirds, sixths and sevenths used with variations), phrases that are characteristically employed (like the descending segments in laments), intense and often sorrowful rendering, matched with poignant lyrics and also a certain kind of setting with arrangements of instruments and voice.

If a melody or a melodic phrase or a style of singing or musical performance is found to appear across long distances to sing of loss and separation, how can we make their contemporary renderings lead us to connections that we know existed many centuries ago? What kinds of traces would we focus on to reveal affinities between musical forms or to point out distinct differences?

Figure 4.4 'Grabacion', Federico Garcia Lorca and La Argentinita. (Transcription by Mark Aranha.)

In other words, if we want to get to the musical impulses around our energy points, what tropes would we employ?

This chapter attempts to lay out the different categories of music that appear to suggest long historical connections around some of the routes of the Silk Road, the Indian Ocean trade routes, and various other smaller, water-based or land-based routes that we have identified.

We began above with the examples of the Bhairavi-like melodies found along some segments of the mapped routes. If this subset may be part of the matrix of Lorca's deep song, signified by the minor note-based laments that we have described, our research has also pointed us to various other kinds of music from communities that inhabit the areas around our energy points and suggest the *longue durée* connections that we have mapped. We provide a historical and contemporary description of genres across these different kinds of music and analyse them in terms of two very broad categories: first, musics of the 'low', or of communities that have historically been at the margins of society and associated with 'lowly' social status, including music that comes from spirit possession and trance rituals that show uncannily similar forms across several segments of these routes; and second, musics that have been codified as 'classical' traditions across different cultures along the same routes.

The rest of this chapter is divided into two major sections based on these categories: diasporic musics of the 'low' (including performing spirits and possession) and the codification of the classical. What is being attempted here is to move away from standard received categories like 'folk' and 'classical', as the division into the two sections is not to make this kind of distinction between 'high' and 'low', but to tease out the class- and social identity-related structural distinctions that separated musics of different kinds from about the seventh century CE onwards.

Diasporic Musics of the 'Low'

We began the Garai narrative in chapter one with his first incarnation, beginning in southern Africa, and traced his travels through East Africa to Baghdad and then to India. In uncovering musical traditions, let us imagine Garai III after he arrives in India, on the western coast, through the port of Khambat (Cambay) in Gujarat. Or, perhaps, we can imagine that he arrived from the north-western frontiers, through Sindh, across the land routes along the Silk Road. He would possibly have been greeted in Gujarat by people who looked somewhat like himself, those who came to call themselves Sidis, or, if he wandered southward towards Bharuch, by livestock herders, the Maldhari Jatts, who were moving between Sindh and Khambat in their yearly nomadic sojourns. Both communities, albeit quite different in their social practices and economic activities, are Muslim and practise Sufism.

This covers two of the routes we have referred to above: the Gujarat–Rajasthan–Sindh route into West Asia and the East Africa–Gujarat route.

Historians as well as anthropologists have in more recent decades come to understand the Gujarat–Rajasthan–Sindh territories as 'frontier regions' or 'mobile regions' that are contiguous and connected by old histories of movement of people and goods, both material and symbolic.[7] The Thar Desert, Kothiyal argues for example, which has historically existed as a frontier connecting regions like Punjab, Multan, Sindh, Gujarat and Rajasthan with each other, can be defined as a region

> through the mobility of its inhabitants, who were warriors, pastoralists, traders, ascetics and bards, often in overlapping capacities, exchanging mobile wealth and equally mobile narratives. . . . The historical understanding of the Thar Desert, like that of other such spaces, is couched in familiar frames of barrenness and waste. Yet, a closer look at the Thar Desert reveals a rich history of movements of a large number of itinerant groups, of settlements and depopulations, as well as of a cultural milieu where memories of movements have been immortalized in the rich folkloric traditions of the region. The recurrent patterns of circulation of people, resources and lore united the Thar as a region encompassing several political states with shared histories of mobility. (Kothiyal 2016: 2)

With the region having been partitioned in the Indian subcontinent in 1947 into Sindh, Multan and parts of Punjab in Pakistan, and the remaining parts of Punjab, Gujarat and Rajasthan in India, these communities experienced major ruptures in their existing livelihoods as nomads and pastoralists, and also in their cultural practices.

Let us look, for example, at nomadic communities like the Maldhari Jatts. Who might have been the Maldhari Jatts? The anthropologist Farhana Ibrahim's work points us to the history of these people whose lives historically have been structured around migration in search of livelihood, across both land and sea. While studies have focused on the seafaring traditions of Kachchh that supported trade and migration (for example, Simpson 2007), she argues that there is almost no contemporary scholarship that refers to the overland migration which occurred across the Rann into Sindh, and thence to Central Asia and beyond:

> This movement for trade was often conducted by and under the auspices of the animal-rearing (maldhari) groups who dominated the Rann territory. Once upon a time the eastern arm of the river Indus flowed along western Kachchh, providing a waterway to the Arabian Sea, as well as north into the Rann. The entire area of the Rann itself was once the sea and Kachchh was an island surrounded by water. Seismic changes converted this from primarily a water body to a desert-like formation which is the former sea bed, a fact borne out by the periodic discovery of sea-fossils. Then, traders came and went across these now desolate marshes. An area that was once at the centre of trading routes that connected the subcontinent to Central Asia is now a landlocked border area with no through traffic except under the guise of illegality. The Muslim maldhari communities used to cross frequently, to sell the ghï (clarified butter) that formed the mainstay of their income. The Jatts are one of these itinerant maldhari groups who live in the areas surrounding the Great Rann. (Ibrahim 2004: 170)

Ibrahim thus argues that the pastoral nomadic populations of this region need to be situated within the larger landscape of trade and migration that has historically influenced the socio-economic profile of Kachchh, facilitated both by the proximity of the sea and by the lack of opportunities that a robust agrarian system would have otherwise provided. Based on the earliest records available for Kachchh, the main sources of income seem to have come from either trade or livestock. Kachchhis were known for their maritime prowess, and as seafarers, the sea contributed to their livelihoods and fortunes. Port towns like Lakhpat, Jakhau, Mandvi and Mundra retain even today, albeit to differing degrees, reminders of an earlier prosperity.

Further, in medieval Gujarat and Rajasthan, migration was synced between menial and pastoral networks, and the nomadic or itinerant way of life was shared by various other communities as well, like the Rabaris, Kolhus and Mirasis, apart from the Jatts. All these communities have remained poor and continue to belong to the lowest strata in the social hierarchy.

Music, we find, is a medium through which memories circulate as narratives in this region, and the music of the Maldhari Jatts is a good example of this. Musical traditions continue to be contiguous despite the partition, carried through the singing and performance of the epic narratives of the region, notably love stories like 'Umar-Marvi Jo Kisso', 'Sassui–Punnu', 'Dhola–Maru', 'Heer–Ranjha' and so on. The category of music called 'Sindhi Kalam' and the singing of compositions by the eighteenth-century Sufi mystic

Shah Abdul Latif Bhitai, whose poetic and musical genius brought to life the characters in the love stories in an incredibly refreshing way, are part of the musical corpus that we believe represents very old and long-distance links.

Researchers in our project collected some of the musical material by travelling to various towns in Gujarat and Rajasthan and recording the music of customary musicians among the Jatt, Mir, Hudkal and other communities.[8] The songs of Bhitai and the love stories interpreted by him in musical and poetic form are found commonly across the region. It is only very recently that there have been English-language translations and descriptions of the rich material set down as poetry and melodies in the *Risalo*, a fabulous text by Bhitai (Virmani and Rikhi 2019). In their detailed analysis of the musical and poetic content of the *Risalo*, which draws from its contemporary interpretation by musicians in Kachchh as well as from historical information about the life and experiences of the mystic himself, Virmani and Rikhi provide us with rich content for understanding the circulation of musical narratives.

There is deep yearning that finds expression in the songs of Bhitai, sung, for example, by the Jatt musicians. The songs are of two distinct styles found within the *Shah jo Raag* (compositions or Raags of Shah) – *kaafi* and *wayee.*[9] The *kaafi* and the *wayee,* in different ways, are forms about loneliness, about being alone. Contemporary recordings from our fieldwork and from other sources demonstrate the nuances of this music of loneliness.[10] The *kaafi* is sung to the accompaniment of the harmonium and the banjo, and the *wayee* to the five-string dumboor or damburo. Bhitai himself would have created his enormous poetic corpus on the basis of what he might have observed, which would have come down across the centuries in the region. The *wayee,* in some accounts, is attributed to Maulana Rumi and was popularized by Latif's ancestor, Shah Karim (ibid.: 54).

If the *Risalo* provides a rich textual (in the form of available manuscripts) and additionally created (as a living corpus, with additions over the centuries that do not find reference in the manuscripts) context for the circulation of moods and the various love stories that are about travel and yearning, less codified sung forms also proliferate – for example, in Rajasthan. And in both Gujarat and Rajasthan on the Indian side, and in Multan and Sindh in Pakistan, indigenous codification systems which musicians refer to as rāgas are found. In our fieldwork among musicians belonging to the Hudkal and Mir communities in Rajasthan and the Meghwal and Fakirani Jatts in Gujarat, we found fascinating variants of the Sassui–Punnu, Umar–Marvi and Dhola–Maru love stories in musical form. Many of the communities practise Sufism, which, in its local forms, in turn reflects multiple influences from far and wide. More will be said on this later.

Coming back to the communities that we met through our project work in Gujarat and Rajasthan, tropes of the desert, sea, camels and the crow proliferate in the music (Dash 2019). The musical imprint of travel and yearning is unmistakably there, as the following song by two musicians of the Hudkal community demonstrates: [11]

> I long for you, my love
> No one longs for me
> Because of this longing
> My being becomes my cage
> Oh lover of the one with teary eyes
> I long for you, my love
> Come soon from far away
> I long for you.

A word about the classification system before we move further west beyond Sindh on the north-western side, or across the ocean from Gujarat, or eastwards into China. Komal Kothari's famous ethnographic musicological studies in western Rajasthan (Neuman, Chaudhuri and Kothari 2006) point us to an understanding of rāgas as they obtain in 'folk' traditions that are relevant to the entire region. It is among the professional music communities, or the ones that function within customary obligation systems in the village hierarchy that the concept of a rāga is mostly found, according to them. The melodic concept of rāgas is related to their musical function as scale types with characteristic phrases, as in the Hindustani system, but rāgas differ from the latter in that they cannot be elaborated. According to Neuman, Chaudhuri and Kothari (ibid.: 95), 'one does not "develop" a rāga so much as utilize it as an attribute of a composition', a mood, an emotion. So, in the *Risalo*, what is written down as a *sur*, or a melody, is also interpreted as a rāga, and the Langa and Manganiyar musicians studied by Neuman and others refer to them as rāgas. Among the Langa musicians, Neuman, Chaudhuri and Kothari (2006) record specific rāgas such as Sindhi Sorath, Jangla, Kafi, Sameri Mand and Sindhi Bhairavi among others, which we believe could be indicative of longer-distance contiguities with the *maqām* tradition that is found all the way to North Africa. Ayesha Sheth, a researcher in the Recentring AfroAsia (RAA) project, has traced the etymological roots of a specific rāga, Jangula, to the term Zanj, used to denote populations of Ethiopian origin (or perhaps, more generally, African origin), arguing that Rāga Jangulā is believed to have developed from the similar-sounding Persian Zangūlā, with both the *maqām* and rāga having the same tonal material. These are also similar to the Arabic mode Zanjāran, and the Turkish Zengule (Sheth 2017). Chroniclers record another similar-sounding rāga, *Zangula*, distinguished from *Jangula* by one note, which could have similar origins as well, although according to Sheth (2017) they are recorded as different rāgas falling under a different classificatory category (called *that*). More will be said about this later, and also about the relationship between the 'folk' rāgas and the classical canon.

Our detailed interviews with Sufi musician and philosopher Madan Gopal Singh about how the story of Heer and Ranjha is rendered musically and interacts with the text created by Waris Shah in the eighteenth century allows us to extend the analysis, through the form of the *qissa*, beyond the north-western part of the Indian subcontinent into West Asia on the one hand, and southwards into south India on the other. The *qissa* (folktale or epic in Arabic) tradition of storytelling is said to have come into north India from the Arabic and Persian worlds in the Islamic period, and in turn imbibed pre-Islamic cultural influences in different places where it is found. The epic story of Heer Ranjha by Waris Shah is acknowledged as one of the most important *qissa*s in Punjabi literature. Interestingly, a form of music called *qissapaattu* (*qissa* song) is found in the *Mappilapattu* repertoire in the Malabar region of Kerala, also considered to have been influenced by Arabic and Persian migration and influences. This too will be dealt with later.

Two crucial eighteenth-century texts from the Gujarat–Rajasthan–Punjab–Sindh–Multan region (the *Risalo* and *Heer–Ranjha*) thus allow us to imagine how these two writers, positioned at that time, were making sense of overland and maritime mobilities, and writing of separation, loss and migration. Movement, a central driver of sociality and finding immediate reflection in art forms, influenced strongly by local developments, is thus a crucial trope in how we are tracing connections.

How would these musical forms manifest themselves beyond the Indian subcontinent, or in the contiguous 'mobile regions' of historiography and anthropology? But before we talk about the *qissa* and forms of poetry-storytelling-singing that reflected movement, and local interpretations and inflections across parts of the world that existing research does not take into account when exploring connections, let us follow the trail of the Jatts. Garai I, if he travelled along overland routes through Persia, might have been surprised at musician groups that were beginning to be reviled as 'lowly', even though they had been invited to bring music into parts of Persia some centuries before by the emperor himself.

In the tenth century CE, the Arab historian Hamza-I Isfahani of Isfahan wrote that in the reign of the Sassanian king Bahram Gour V (420–438 CE), 12,000 Luri musicians were sent by the Indian king Shangul to settle in various parts of Persia and to entertain people with their music. Isfahani's account referred to these people as Koulis, a term commonly understood in present-day Iran to refer to people who had migrated from Kabul (Amanolahi and Norbeck 1975). Within another fifty years, the Persian poet Ferdowsi, in his *Shahnameh* (The Book of Kings) written in 1011, mentioned the same legend (the number of Luri musicians was now 10,000) and that Bahram gave the Luri crops to sow as reward for their service: 'They ate the corn and asked for more. Consequently, the Shah sent the Luri out into the world on the back of their animals' (Badalkhan 2005: 24). Arab chroniclers refer to the descendants of these migrants as Zotts, a version of the Indian term Jatts, and Persian records refer to them as the Luris. In an allusion to the route that could have been taken by nomadic populations along a long migration corridor from western India, the legend of the Luris points to the centrality of music and musicians in the migration.

Amanolahi and Norbeck (1975) report that while studies done of the community of the Luris (said to be Iranian gypsies) earlier on in the twentieth century as well as their own informants maintained that the word Kouli was a corruption of Kabuli (from Kabul in present-day Afghanistan), an anonymous author of a tenth-century Persian geography text, *Hudd al-'alam* (published in 982 CE), located Koul somewhere in north-west India, south of Kandahar. Isfahani further associated the Koulis with the Zotts or the Zatts, who in turn were described thus by Mas'udi, a contemporary of Isfahani:

> The occurrence of famine in India forced the Zot (Zatt), to migrate in large numbers to several Persian provinces including Kerman, Fars, and Khuzistan . . . they became powerful, they harassed the trade routes in Khuzistan. . . . Consequently, the Caliph Al-Mu'tasim had to fight them in 835 AD. The Zot were defeated and moved to Syria. (Mas'udi, quoted in Amanolahi and Norbeck 1975: 20)

Khaqani, a poet, described the wandering Luris thus:

> My bewildered heart wanders like the wandering Lulis,
> Once again it searches for a new dwelling. (Badalkhan 2005: 23)

Figure 4.5 Jatt musicians Sumar Kado (left) and Mitho Khan (right) in Bagaadiya village, Banni, Gujarat. (Photo by Kathyayini Dash, 2019.)

Figure 4.6 Sumar Kado and Mitho Khan with their group. (Photo by Kathyayini Dash, 2019.)

Research into the identities and histories of the communities that these legends represent is mixed and often contradictory (ibid.). What is important for our purpose here is that a variety of names are found for the peripatetic people being referred to here in present-day Pakistan and Iran, such as Luri, Luti, Motreb and more, and that they might bear ancestry from Indian populations designated Jatts, Rabaris, Kalbelias and so on. Anthropological research into the community of Jatts in Gujarat (Ibrahim 2004), as well as musicological research (Dash 2019), has found them referring to their origins in Greece and Syria, and also found their music and sociality to be associated with the province of Sindh and with Sufism. For several communities like the Jatts in India, the connections in one way or the other with Sindh seem apparent, as we described earlier, also connecting them to the desert corridor stretching from western India into West Asia and possibly beyond.

The Luris, in turn, are also associated with Roma migration from north-western parts of India, said to have taken place from the fifth century CE or so as they moved into West and Central Asia and made their way into the Balkans and Europe, to arrive in Cordoba by about the eleventh century. A whole lot of population groups with close contact to India lived – and still live – in today's eastern Turkey, Iraq, Iran, Afghanistan and so on. Like some of today's and probably most of the earlier Roma, they all tend to adopt itinerant professions in metal-processing and entertainment, and have historically suffered social ostracism. They are excluded from the majority population and their contact with the latter is typically restricted to economic relations only. The tracing of routes that the Roma might have taken as they moved out of parts of central and then north-western India has taken place largely due to linguists identifying connections in languages spoken by these communities. Some of these groups speak Indo-Aryan languages: the Dom, Karači or Kurbati of what is now referred to as the Middle East (Syria, Palestine, Jordan; in the past also Iraq, Iran, Azerbaijan) speak Domari; the Parya in Tajikistan use a variety of Rajasthani; the Inku and Jat in Afghanistan use a central Indo-Aryan language, just like the Doma from the Hunza Valley in northern Pakistan. Other population groups from the Caucasus to Sudan know secret languages whose lexicon is completely or partially of Indo-Aryan origin; among them are the Karači and Luti in Iran, the Nawar in Egypt, the Bahlawan in Sudan, and the Boša or Lom in Armenia whose language is called Lomavren. In India itself, there are groups of nomads in various regions who specialize in services, such as blacksmiths, basket weavers, musicians and dancers. Within the caste system, these nomads are called Dom (Kenrick 2004; Moorjani *et al.* 2013).

Linguists today assume that apart from the length of stay, it is mainly the means of contact between different population groups that determines their linguistic relationship. Similarly, musicologists could perhaps glean from the musical expressions of Roma populations how their relationships with local communities might have evolved, but also how these relationships could point to travel. Parvulescu and Boatcă (2020), in looking at contemporary music among Romani musicians from Romania, have argued that 'aesthetic labour' is an overlooked dimension of diasporic mobility. The clues provided by linguists, as well as work like that done by Parvalescu and Boatca, are helpful for the better-known routes taken by the Roma, but the story from the Indian side is often seen only as a beginning, the point of origin of the Roma. The connections between the diasporic distribution of the Roma and other nomadic communities like the Luris, Doms or Jatts, also allowing for reverse movements into parts of India or their interaction with the nomads of the 'frontier' regions that Kothiyal (2016) and Ibrahim (2004) talk about, are not interrogated. It is music that can offer us a lens into these crisscrossing movements, and hence the recurring traces in musical traditions.

Coming back to the diaspora that the Jatts might be a part of, as we head north-west of India and Pakistan towards present-day Iran, fieldwork by Amanolahi and Norbeck (1975) among Luti, Tushmal, Luri and Bakhtiari people in Luristan and Bakhtiari, Iran, demonstrates that the Luti traditionally gained a livelihood by 'serving as entertainers, playing musical instruments, singing, and dancing, by producing handicrafts such as wooden plows, bowls, spoons and other simple tools and utensils, by performing circumcisions, a defiling activity, and by begging' (Amanolahi and Norbeck 1975: 25). According to them, the Luti occupy the lowest rank in Iranian society and they are regarded by the dominant Iranian population as polluted and innately inferior.

The chain of migrations and the connections established hitherto are demonstrated interestingly by Badalkhan (2005). The Luri musicians of Baluchistan, acknowledged to have migrated mostly from north-western India and said to be designated as minstrels (*pahlawans*) customarily performing for ethnic Balochis, play drums of different kinds, flutes (nal) and the sorud fiddle, carved out of a single piece of wood and shaped strangely like a skull. It has a shimmering, spooky sound, with resonant sympathetic strings. Other local instruments include the damburag (a long-necked lute, like the dumboor of the Jatts), donali (also called the double ney) and the benjo (the keyed zither or banjo of the Jatts). In the mountains of central Iran, the raucous sorna (or shawm) is played amongst the Bakhtiari and also in Lorestan, which is also famous for its folk kamancheh (bowed-string instrument) players, much like the kamaicha players in western Rajasthan.

The diffusion of musical instruments like lutes, harps, oboes and fiddles along the Silk Road, stretching from China in the east through India and into the west as far as Europe and down into North Africa, has been documented, and the direction of diffusion has been pointed to (Lawergren 2010; Levin 2002). Through the influence of Buddhism, Hinduism and Islam, and of nomadic and sedentary musical traditions, the instruments thus firmly carry the imprint of travels through the centuries. The Central Asian and Persian short-necked lute called barbat, Levin (2002) notes, is the ancestor of the Middle Eastern oud and the European lute, as well as of the Japanese biwa and Chinese pipa. It moved from the region of its origin, possibly among nomadic people, to China in the east to become the pipa, and through West Asia to be called the oud, travelling then towards southern Europe and North Africa. Chinese documents record the pipa as belonging to the 'northern barbarians' or nomads (ibid.), and in combination with the legends of Ziryab, the manumitted slave of African origin who is said to have carried the oud to North Africa and eventually to Cordoba, and of Shirin and Khusrow whose court is said to have included the legendary musician Barbat, the travels of the lute can be traced. Similarly,

> Turkic and Mongolian horsemen from Inner Asia were not only lutenists, but also were probably the world's earliest fiddlers. Upright fiddles strung with horsehair strings, played with horsehair bows, and often featuring a carved horse's head at the end of the neck . . . may have inspired the round-bodied spike fiddles played in West Asia (kamanche, ghijak) and Indonesia (rebab) and the carved fiddles of the Indian subcontinent (sorud, sarinda, sarangi). Loud oboes called surnai in Central Asia became the shahnai in India, suona in China, and zurna in Anatolia. (Ibid.)

As for harps, with one kind (the arched variety) originating in India and another (the angular variety) in Persia and further west, they were seen to be part of music traditions in China between the fifth and the fourteenth century CE, as evidenced through illustrations in the Magao grottoes near Donhuang and in the Kizil grottoes near Kucha, reflecting diffusion from the western side. The arched harps from India travelled to Gandhara and Bactria in modern-day Afghanistan and Sogdia in Uzbekistan (Lawergren 2010).

It was not only westward movement from north-western India that would prove important in understanding musical interaction or influences on important routes in AfroAsia, but also the melding of cultures that was happening towards the east, in China and beyond, that was to define musical traditions. Our research points us to two important dimensions that we emphasize again and again: one, that the musical traditions that still exist, for example in parts of China, bear imprints of Silk Road movements and have been absorbed both into the Chinese classical canon and into 'folk' traditions; two, that the interactions between musics that are designated as lowly and 'savage' bring out traces of old connections in AfroAsia, with social distinctions often surviving up to the present. As for the musics from different parts of AfroAsia that we are analysing in this chapter, the latter are explored through existing research on contemporary traditions, whereas the first – that is, the emergence of the 'high' or more elite and classicized traditions – is researched based on historical work, which forms part of the next section.

Sheng (2000), in a fascinating account of his own travels into various Silk Road towns from Xi'an to Kashgar in north-western China, in a bid to seek out remnants and traces of the music, discusses the *hua'er* musical form of Qinghai. The town was not initially part of the Silk Road, but when warlords, marauders and robbers made the usual passage through the narrow Gansu Corridor impossible to travel, trading caravans took an alternative route to northern Gansu, a prominent Silk Road town, via the Qilian mountains in eastern Qinghai, one of the places where *hua'er* is found.

Hua'er, which means flowers, is a form of love song sung in the fields and mountains, and has 'zestful, often erotic content' (Sheng 2000: 2); it is performed at festivals dedicated exclusively to the form. Having been part of extensive collection and documentation exercises in this region of China over the twentieth century, and also banned for ten years after the Cultural Revolution and then revived again, *hua'er* is said to have come into existence during the Ming dynasty (1368–1644), and developed as a result of migrations into the region spanning rural areas of southern Ningxia, central and southern Gansu, and eastern Qinghai (Mu 1994). It is sung with variations reflecting linguistic and ethnic differences, yet showing similarities, by all communities in the region (ibid). An important aspect of *hua'er* music is that its erotic content and associated sexual customs during festivals denote the form as 'savage' and as required to be sung outside the boundaries of the village, in the fields and the mountains. Mu (1994) notes:

> Historically hua'er activities have never been accorded legal status. However

> according to some studies local laws specifically concerning hua'er singing activities have been enforced in certain areas which explicitly prohibited such activities from taking place inside or near villages. These laws do not, however, forbid hua'er singing far away from residential areas; they thus virtually acquiesce to singing out in the fields. (Ibid.: 104)

Describing his experience of *hua'er* music among the Tu people, who are from a branch of Mongols that moved to Tibetan-ruled Qinghai after the fourteenth century and speak a language with Tibetan and Mongolian elements, Sheng says:

> This year the festival took place in aspen woods along the banks of a dried river in Danma, a small town surrounded by mountains in Huzhu County. During the three-day festival, all young men and women, dressed up in their finest clothes, sang and wooed each other with love songs. One afternoon, when the day was at its hottest, the festival was also at its zenith. Standing in the middle of the riverbed, I had the overwhelming experience of being in a 'hua'er ocean', as Qinghai is nicknamed. When all of the small groups sang different hua'er tunes in the same key by chance, the sound of one melody falling as the other was rising, enhanced by echoes from the valley, formed a truly remarkable polyphonic composition. Later, the sounds of many groups singing in different keys from different parts of the valley swelled in Charles-Ivesian cacophony – but enlarged a thousandfold – and transformed music and nature into a masterpiece no composer could have written. (Sheng 2000: 2)

Sheng also talks about Yulin singing and Xiliang music, two kinds of music that reflect Silk Road influences and would be considered 'folk' varieties, and the Uygur *maqām* and elements of the Qin opera that are part of the classical traditions of China. The latter are taken up in the next section.

During the Silk Road period the route to Donhuang along the Gansu Corridor, home to the famous Donhuang caves with their terracotta warriors, was the principal passageway for caravan traders travelling west to reach the Taklamakan Desert in Xinjiang, seeing its peak during the Tang dynasty. Towns in the region were of mixed ethnicities; and Xiliang music, a form blending the music and dance styles of Central Asia and north-western China, came into existence and remained popular for five centuries (Sheng, n.d.).

Let us go back to the legend of the Zotts about whom Sykes reports:

> At the beginning of the eighth century of our era, a large number of Jatt, termed Zott by the Arabs, had been transported with their buffaloes from the Lower

> Indus to the marches of the Tigris. As soon as they were settled, they began to rob and kill . . . compell[ing] successive Caliphs to send armies to subdue them . . . the Zott surrendered and after being exhibited in boats to the delighted citizens of Baghdad wearing their national garb and playing their instruments, were exiled to Kanikin on the Turkish frontier . . . and to the frontiers of Syria. (Sykes 1921: 11)

If Baghdad, as we know, became the meeting point for cultures from various parts of AfroAsia, the Zotts or the Jatts could perhaps have been in the midst of or even in contact with the musicians of the Abbasid kingdom. If the nomadic frontiers were to extend through the Roma into Europe by the eleventh to thirteenth centuries, surely there would have been interaction along the nomadic routes to and of al-Andalus. Can we say, then, that the Sahara and its territories, and the areas that they were in interaction with, could be brought into musical conversation with the nomadic corridors stretching from western and north-western India?

Haul, Qaul, Maqām

An interesting musical route or resemblance that is not discussed much by historians or musicologists is that between the modal systems of the *haul*, which applies to poetic and musical forms in five countries in North Africa, and the *qaul* or its derivative, the *qawwali*, in the Indian subcontinent. Even though the *haul* has been more prevalent in present-day Mauritania, the system spread through Hassanya-speaking communities across countries in North Africa, and can also be said to relate historically and musically to the *noubat* in Andalusi music (performed in Algeria, Morocco, Tunisia and Libya), the *maqāmat* in Egypt, Turkey or Iraq that were Ottoman-influenced, the Persian *maqāmat*, the Greek modes and forms deriving from the spread of the *qaul* eastwards, like the *qawwali* form, and the Hindustani rāga system.

In this sense, the long and complex array of travel routes from al-Andalus to Al-Hind have one very distinct connection through the modal systems of the *haul*, *qaul* and *maqāmat*. Admittedly, Islam provided a key vehicle for the dissemination and transmission of important elements of the modal systems, but two points are important to remember here: one, that what this led to in musical systems are variations reflecting local and regional histories, yet retaining key ingredients that allow us to trace the influences; and two, that while these modal systems developed into 'schools' of music and underwent classicization processes over time, their dissemination through non-elite classes of people can also be traced through both performative aspects as well as historical knowledge of who travelled.

Here, as with the frontier region of the Thar in India and Pakistan, we have to read between the lines of historiographical and anthropological/ethnomusicological methods to look, for example, at North Africa. There are two ways of looking at North Africa: to see there a multiplicity of ethnic formations, some sedentary and some nomadic, paying or refusing to pay tribute to primarily Islamic aristocracies, and envision further the Umayyad holdings in the Iberian peninsula with al-Andalus and Cordoba as fascinating entrepôts; or, to see the entire terrain as one of movement – of people, of animals, of goods, of symbolic forms and influences. A terrain covered by thousands of camels and their loads in formation, trudging across desert sands and mountains to shift gold and slaves, and later spices and precious stones, in all directions. These caravans and the caravanserais dotted in between urban formations would replicate themselves all the way to China along the manifold Silk Roads of the time. Finally, there would have been the thousands and thousands of believers trudging their way to Mecca and back.

The musical traces to be examined lie between the music of the Berbers, whose ancestors were some of the earliest inhabitants of Mediterranean North Africa (with the largest Berber populations in Morocco and Algeria), the Gnawa (brotherhoods of former slaves and descendants of indigenous and migrant Sahrawis, forming a large segment of the population in Mauritania and the Saharan segments of other countries), and the descendants of the Arab migrants from the Arabian Gulf. Of the three sets of communities, the Berbers are said to have been relatively isolated culturally and influenced by Islam only from the 1800s, but to have been responsible for bringing Mediterranean arts and technology southwards because they controlled the trans-Saharan trade routes (Reimer 2020).

Of course, the linkages between what is now Morocco and West Africa, and the traces of those linkages that still exist in western Morocco, Mauritania and Ghana/Shongay, are more than evident, whether one looks at wandering musicians, at their strings and poetic forms (performed by professional, hereditary poet-musicians, the *griots*), at the healing rhythms and chants of the Gnawa, at the forms that shifted towards the mountains after Arabic invasions, or at the Berber-controlled caravan traders trudging along major routes. Of course, Morocco is also defined by the more elite *nuba* traditions that migrated from al-Andalus down to the flamenco-like performances of the rebab, the oud and castanets.

Among musical forms that are common to many parts of the Sahrawi region and much of North Africa, we can find Sufi forms that accompany Zikr or Dhikr ceremonies (in remembrance of Allah) which combine music with healing rituals. These encompass Berber Tuareg communities as well as Gnawa brotherhoods, with the latter drawing more from African customs but in fact venerating Sufi saints like Sidi Marzuk in Tunisia or Sidi Mohammad-el-Merheni in Morocco. We will be saying more about healing and possession practices later, but for now, this might be a hint towards the origins of the Sidi community in India.

In Mauritania, Mali, Niger and southern Algeria, the *griots* perform the *haul*, which is considered 'classical' in that it is based on a familiarity with Arabic, Moorish poetry and musical styles and music theory (Stone, ed. 2017: 43). According to Amoros (2016: 45), 'performative aspects of interaction' can be seen between the *haul* and the other modal systems mentioned earlier 'in relation to the vocal nuances such as the melismatic ways of elongating the notes; the relationship between music and poetry, lute-instrument techniques from various instruments in the vast studied regions such as the *ataque* in the sarod, oud, ngoni and tidinit; and certain song-structures'.

Norris (1962) discusses the migration of Yemeni communities of Ibn Halal and Ibn Hassan during the fourteenth and fifteenth centuries to Trabel Bidan, a pre-colonial territory related to the linguistic area where Hassanya, the main national language in Mauritania and Western Sahara, is spoken.

After the Yemenite communities settled in Trabel Bidan, the interconnectedness between Africa (Saharan and sub-Saharan) and the Arabian Gulf was via two commercial routes: a desert route (from Western Sahara towards Sudan and the Arabian Gulf) and a coastal route (from Mauritania through Spain and North Africa). The pilgrimage to Mecca was one of the main foundations for the continuous interaction of the Hassani people with the Arabian Peninsula. Yemenites migrating to Western Sahara or pilgrims on their way to Mecca from Western Sahara would have provided the regular encounters between Yemen and Trabel Bidan, and between Yemen and north-western as well as south India. In the Sahara, Hassanya identity was established on the basis of the interaction of Yemenite and Berber cultures. The Berber Sanhaya, who were the predominant Berber community in Western Sahara, were mostly Christians or Jewish (Rodriguez 2011: 16), and had lived in what later became Trabel Bidan from the third century CE; by the seventh century, the Berber empire had expanded from Spain to Ghana through different Berber communities. With the arrival of the Yemenite Arabs during the fourteenth and fifteenth centuries, recognition of the territory designated Trabel Bidan took place and Islam became well-established.

According to Amoros (2012), musicians called *igagwen* and poets called *chorfa* or *zuaia* in Trabel Bidan, and musicians-cum-poets called *jelis* or *griots*, were the carriers of stories and epics in musical form in the Mande empire (mostly in Mali, Senegal, Burkina Faso, Guinea and Gambia), with local traditions interacting with Islamic influences from the Arabian peninsula. Duran (2015) notes that *jelis*, keepers of history and epic stories, 'entertained the nobility with their epic songs and stories about the major events in Mande history'. The *igagwen* in Trabel Bidan were musicians, whereas the responsibility of preserving oral history through music rested with the *chorfa* or *zuaia*, poets dedicated to the study of the Qur'an and Hassanya history. A relationship thus existed between the poet and the musician which has been carried down to the present in Mauritania and Western Sahara. In any case, the *haul* came into existence as a musical form across the region reflecting these various influences.

The Qur'an's recitational forms provided one basis for the development of *haul*, along with the use of local instruments from Saharan and sub-Saharan Africa. According to Amoros (2018: 7),

> Charry (1996: 3) notes that many instruments from Trabel Bidan and the Mande region (Senegal, Gambia, Guinea, Mali, Niger and Burkina Faso) remain similar such as *ardin* and *kora, t'bal* and *djembe* or *tidinit* and *ngoni*. According to Charry (ibid.), except for the *tidinit*, a lute brought by the Shanaja Almoravids from Egypt in the 7th century, none of the instruments comes from Arabic-speaking countries.

The instruments used in the *haul* modal system in Mauritania are the ardin (a twelve-string harp), the tidinit (a four-string lute) and the tbel (a frame drum). The ardin is made out of a calabash for resonance, a goatskin and twelve nylon strings. It is a drone instrument used for accompaniment and only played by women. In Mali, Niger and southern Algeria, where the tradition is performed by Tuaregs, the tahardent is used in place of the tidinit, and is very similar to it. According to the Garland Encyclopaedia (Stone, ed. 2017: 44), melodies across the region vary from less ornamented, repetitive styles to highly ornamented and melismatic styles, with local traditions being reflected in rhythms. Pentatonicism is common, and melodic use of an augmented fourth above a tonic is common. Microtonicism is present in

Berber and Arab styles, while the songs of the Gnawa make use of seconds and thirds, rarely heard in Berber or Arab music.

Like the circulation of poetic and musical narratives in the Thar Desert in interaction with oceanic movements, the Sahara and its musics can thus be considered contiguous and influenced by long migrations through nomadic corridors, making it a 'frontier region'.

The *haul*, spirit possession rituals (discussed below) and the music of al-Andalus from Africa therefore need to be seen as reflecting, and in turn extending across very long distances and showing connections with, musical traditions which are acknowledged, if at all, very briefly in understandings of musical influences. In typical accounts, Africa figures mostly as being at the receiving end of imperial and religious expansion, or as being the source of human chattel that would retain some features of cultural forms of the places they came from. What we are trying to point out is that the modalities of class formation and power operated in multiple ways in the pre-colonial world, and this was true across the different geographies that are under consideration here. Cultural formations and forms came into existence in interaction with each other, and retained traces of long-distance movements. While we have tried to identify the traces that lead us to these long-distance likenesses, we also acknowledge that these similarities can only be understood if we see the musics in interaction with local dynamics of provision of the means of subsistence and the creation of wealth, the emergence of polities or state formation, and, in most cases along our routes, the history of colonialism.

We now turn to spirit possession forms and healing rituals as one important dimension of the movement of cultural forms.

Performing Spirits and Possession

There is another set of tropes around rituals and ceremonies of spirit worship, propitiation, trance and healing, that lend themselves to comparison and suggestion of AfroAsian connections through music and performance. Ethnographers, historians and ethnomusicologists have provided for us carefully argued case studies of various forms of spirit worship and propitiation at various energy points in the Indian Ocean world – Makran, Gujarat, Oman, Somalia, Zanzibar and Ethiopia. Towards the Persian Gulf, encompassing Oman, the southern part of Iran and Pakistan, extending across Baluchistan, and along the western coast of India lining Gujarat, there are communities that are seen to have descended from African migrants, such as the Sidis of Gujarat and Karnataka, the Sheedis of Karachi in Pakistan, and various people designated as Afro-Omanis or Afro-Iranians. From the research done in the RAA project (Koela 2019; Talengala 2017), we can add to this both sites (such as the Mangalore–Malabar coast in south-western India and Gujarat in western India) and methods by which spirit possession and healing rituals can be studied as performative traditions, to point us to connections between communities in the AfroAsian world that we are looking at. Music in such traditions – singing, instrumentation and drumming – allows us to understand these links.

Along the west coast of India, covering the states of Gujarat, Karnataka, Maharashtra and today's Telangana, Sindh and Baluchistan provinces of Pakistan and Baluchistan in Iran, and down into Sri Lanka, descendants of Africans who settled in their host societies came to be known as Sidi. Basu (2008: 161) notes:

> From the times when sailing ships were the only means of transport, the appellation 'Sidi' was given indiscriminately to African slaves and sailors working on ships and in Indian Ocean ports. The sea journey from Africa to distant lands in South Asia thus transformed displaced people from the hinterland of the Swahili coast into 'Sidi'.

African-derived forms of music referred to as *goma* are an important example of 'dhow cultures' or cultures transmitted historically through seafaring, trade and slavery. While scholars like Basu (2008) attribute the transmission of music and ritual performance traditions of the Sidis to connections with Zanzibar through the seventeenth to late nineteenth centuries, we might hypothesize that the transmission could have occurred through multiple routes, including overland. Further, *goma* among the Sidis are likely to have drawn not only from influences on the Swahili coast or other littoral influences, but also from the hinterland of Africa. As we discussed in the previous section on the Sufi traditions in North Africa, the term 'Sidi' is used for venerating saints in Tunisia and Morocco, which is possibly a hint of population movements involving North Africans into the South Asian and Persian Gulf littoral regions.

If Garai III came in contact with people from the Sidi community in Gujarat as he entered through Cambay, or through the landlocked Rann of Kachchh, they would possibly have been engaged in the agate trade for which the area is famous. If he travelled via the Gulf, along sea routes or overland, he would perhaps have found them engaged in pearl-diving. The Sidis are acknowledged as one of the most prominent communities of African origin in India, with musical traditions that clearly point to their origins.

Ibn Battuta, for example, noted in the mid-fourteenth century, the legendary bravery of Habshi soldiers and sailors. He travelled on a ship with fifty Abyssinians on board to protect them against pirate attacks; he called them 'the guarantors of safety on the Indian Ocean' (O. Ali 2011). While boarding a Chinese junk ship at Calicut in south India, he observed Abyssinians carrying javelins and swords, and others with drums and bugles, indicating the use of Africans on ships travelling to the Far East.

The sharing of an African ancestry and the denomination 'Sidi', however, have not resulted in a unified Sidi identity in India, Pakistan, Iran and Oman. Each of these Sidi communities is deeply embedded in its respective host region and looks back to different histories. Moreover, local Sidi communities are not homogeneous but include people speaking different languages, living in rural and urban environments, and adhering to different religions (there are, for example, Hindu, Christian and Muslim Sidis in Karnataka). What the Sidi people do have in common, though, are constraints of poverty stemming from lower-class and lower-caste status across the region.

In the Indian Ocean maritime world, music provided a mode of communication for people working together on ships or in ports, loading and unloading boats. Seamen and labourers in ports came from different places and a range of cultural backgrounds, and they often did not understand each other's language. But they made music together; the Sidis were known to sing, drum and dance on dhows and in ports. The term used for this kind of music is *goma*, which has etymological kinship with the Bantu word *ngoma*. This, we would argue, goes back to movements of people from various parts of Africa into Asia, and the other way around, over several centuries in the pre-colonial period.

Ibn Khaldun, for example, recorded African proclivities to dance, even if he did not appreciate them – in his magnum opus, he makes quite a few derogatory remarks about Black Africa, and just one sardonic sentence where he says that given any melody, Africans dance in abandon. That people in sub-Saharan Africa do so in most social formations is not in dispute: music, rhythm, dance, song, storytelling and poetry have intermingled since time immemorial to constitute a widespread tradition that bears the name '*ngoma*'. The same word refers to drums and drumming traditions from Uganda and northern Kenya to the southernmost tip of the continent. However, even though the word is the same in Bugandan, Swahili and, let us say, isiZulu, *ngoma* music displays fascinating variations – from complex drumming ensembles (Uganda) to polyvocal versions (in the KwaZulu–Natal Midlands). The bulk of our understanding of it comes from oral traditions and work emphasizing the vitality of the *ngoma* traditions in ritual performance. The Venda of southern Africa, who claim the closest allegiance to Mapungubwe and Great Zimbabwe, situate the *ngoma* as a complex inheritance which combines storytelling, spiritual ecstasy, ritual and song with a range of drumming rhythms. There is reverence among them towards an enormous drum which belongs to royal ensembles, and in performance their drums differ from many others.

Basu notes that,

> in South, Central and East Africa, *ngoma* is a complex term that contains several related meanings: first, *ngoma* is a type of a drum; secondly, *ngoma* means drumming, singing and dancing performed in a call-response pattern; thirdly, *ngoma* refers to performers organized in associations or *ngoma* cells; and finally in a more encompassing sense, *ngoma* is the umbrella term for cults of affliction associated with spirit possession and the healing of consequent mental or physical disorder. As anthropologists working in Africa have shown, however, *ngoma* does not refer to a fixed tradition but to continually shifting practices. (Basu 2008: 164)

Even on the African mainland, *ngoma* travelled with inland migrants, was modified in the process, and helped people to adapt to different urban contexts. For example, there has been a return of some forms of this musical tradition by people from the Indonesian archipelago brought to southern Africa as slaves by the Dutch East India Company, in the form of *goema* in the southern Cape in South Africa (Bruinders and Layne 2006; Layne 2019).

In Gujarat, the basic elements of *goma* performances consist of men and women dancing in circles, specific rhythmical styles, a collection of instruments some of which clearly display an African origin (such as the footed drum), and singing in a call-response pattern. Moreover, the word *goma* refers to as many embedded meanings of music as *ngoma*. It is related to a specific cosmology and to healing of possession illness in cults of affliction.

Basu (2008) refers to a specific dimension of *ngoma* that takes place in both Zanzibar and Gujarat, involving the veneration of Habshi or Ethiopian spirits. *Ngoma ya habshia* in Zanzibar denotes a cult of affliction related specifically to a class of Ethiopian spirits (*masheitani yahabshia*), whereas in Gujarat Sidis honour an assembly of African-Sufi patron saints also figuring in cults of affliction, of whom one is named 'Bava Habash'. Like *habshia* spirits, Bava Habash is ascribed an Ethiopian origin, is believed to have followed Sidi seafarers to Gujarat, was transformed into a Muslim Ethiopian saint, and embodies himself in possession rituals accompanied by *goma* music. Bava Habash, in turn, is the elder brother of Bava Gor, the most revered Sufi among people of African descent in South Asia. Bava Gor, originally named Sidi Mubarak Nob, is said to have travelled from eastern Africa during the fourteenth century and made Ratanpur, in Gujarat, his home. The African became the patron saint of the agate bead industry, having been credited with augmenting the trade in the quartz stone between eastern Africa, the Persian Gulf and India. Before arriving in India, Bava Gor spent time in Mecca and the area of Basra in lower Iraq, where he studied with Sufis of the Rifa'i order who gave him the honorific title Baba Ghaur, meaning 'master of deep meditation' in Arabic. According to oral tradition, Bava Gor's sister Mai Misra also travelled to India and developed her own Sufi following. She came to India, it is believed, to vanquish a demoness from Hindu mythology. Mai Misra, whose name is derived from *misr* (Arabic for 'north-east Africa'), is particularly venerated for her powers of fertility. Respect for her may be seen in the coconut rattles used by the Sidis that bear her name. In Gujarat as well as in other parts of India, Sidis play the malunga, a single-string braced musical bow found in many eastern African communities (and as far away as Brazil, where it is called berimbau). The hand that holds the malunga also holds the *mai misra* rattle below it, which is attached to a gourd resonator to amplify the instrument.

If Sidi musical and performance practices in present-day India bear resemblance to African *ngoma* traditions, these are also found among the Sheedis in Pakistan and similar communities in Iran, all along the Makran coast. The Arabs had entered Makran in 644 CE, 70 years before the conquest of Sindh; subsequently, three different expeditions were targeted towards this part of Asia for the spread of the Islamic faith under Hajjaj, the commander of Caliph Walid I of Iraq. One was directed towards Kabul, a second towards Samarkand and a third to India through Makran, which became an important gateway into India for at least three centuries (Badalkhan 2002). During the twelfth century, the Baloch ethnic group became important in consolidating the Sultanate of Makran. Makran emerged as an important seaport for trade from Arabia to China and into the Far East and South-East Asia. Afzal-e-Kirmani, the sixth century CE historian, reported that apart from Makran, another city, Tiz, was also a major centre for trade, where 'the inhabitants of

Figure 4.7 Sidi bow master Sultan in Vijapur, Gujarat.
(Photo by Nkosenathi Ernie Koela, 2017.)

Hind, Sindh, Abyssinia and Zanzibar trade were [found]. . . . Every kind of ambergis, logwood . . . and slaves of Hind, Abyssinia and Zanzibar . . . find their market here' (ibid.: 244–45).

Sabir Badalkhan, a respected ethnomusicologist of the region, notes that while about 30 per cent of the population of about one million in the region are descendants of slaves from Africa, they neither call themselves Afro-

Baloch nor claim African descent, having been completely absorbed into ethnic Balochi identity (Badalkhan 2002). That being said, the Shidis and Gulams, two communities of African descent, belong to the third and lowest stratum in a three-tiered classification of Balochi society, often distinguished by physical traits. Badalkhan also mentions several proverbs among Balochis that refer to Zangis, people of African descent.

Musical traditions bear the distinct imprints of African pasts or interactions between populations, particularly through the dhow experiences, both at sea and in the ports. Two music–dance forms, the *amba* and the *leywa*, also identified clearly by their drumming patterns, according to Badalkhan (2002), appear to have distinct African roots. The former are work songs and songs dedicated to the Prophet, whereas the latter is a festive singing and dancing style with often sexually charged lyrics. While Balochis believe that the forms moved from their coast to eastern Africa, Badalkhan believes the origin of these forms to be African. Andersen Bakewell, a reputed ethnomusicologist, argues that these forms are found in the entire Indian Ocean region in his collections (ibid.). Badalkhan traces the etymology of the name *amba* to the Swahili term *wimbo*, which means 'song in general and . . . song of 12 syllables in the line' (ibid.: 271). *Amba*, interestingly, is also found among fishermen along the Kerala and Tamil Nadu coasts, and also on the Lakshadweep Islands in the Arabian Sea. *Leywa* is found in Makran and Oman, with the difference that it often leads to a trance in Makran. *Malid*, *gwat* and *damal* are also spirit possession and trance rituals found in Baluchistan, with *damal* showing continuities with Sidi traditions, and the *gwat* and *malid* being found also in the Gulf. Further, the Somali *zar* is found on the coast of Baluchistan, in Iranian south Khuzistan and in Cairo.

So much for the various forms of spirit possession and healing rituals, and their associated music and dance traditions along the western and north-western India–West Asia route that draw heavily from African traditions. If we move southwards within India, down the Mangalore–Malabar coast, spirit and healing traditions can be seen that have been less formally acknowledged in the literature. Research by Talengala (2017) and published work by Jeyachandran (2014) point us to two important 'spirits' that have African links, and whose presence in traditions is seen through impersonation of spirits and their propitiation in regular performative rituals. One such spirit is Bobbare, venerated over five centuries by a wide spectrum of communities along the west coast of India, in the states of Karnataka and Kerala. The other is Kappiri, the cigar-smoking spirit who is said to have been the custodian of the wealth of Portuguese colonizers in Kochi, Kerala.

Bobbare, a *bhuta* or spirit, is highly venerated and worshipped in the *Bhutaradhane* tradition, which includes a variety of worship practices but popularly indicates the possession ceremonies performed for spirit propitiation in the coastal belt of south Karnataka, also known as Tulunadu. *Bhuta* in Tulu, the language used widely across the region, refers to spirits, and the *bhuta* pantheon includes categories such as totemic animals, ancestral spirits and spirits of heroic figures from history. A performative living tradition enacted primarily through complex rituals encompassing epic ballads, musical accompaniments and oracular spirit impersonation, the narrative of each spirit presents itself through its own specific story called *paaddana.* This is a richly descriptive oral text which relates the individual history of a *bhuta,* its origin, its powers and the manner of its transformation into a spirit deserving to be worshipped. The *paaddana* is sung by the family members of the spirit impersonator, and can differ widely in its details depending on the patron, the impersonator and the space of performance, even when the spirit remains the same. According to Talengala (2018), a particularly remarkable myth created a vivid visual picture in its portrayal of the Bobbare *bhuta* as a spirit who straddled 'the Arabian Sea with one foot on the Western Ghats and the other

Figure 4.8 Performance of 'Bobbare Bhuta', Kasargod, Kerala. Photos by Shobha Talengala, 2019.

across the ocean on the Barbary Coast' (Prabhu 1996: 237). The myth of spirit worship was heard in the fishing villages around the city of Mangalore, an important port city for the present-day district of South Karnataka and the larger surrounding area known as South Canara or Dakshina Kannada.

In the fourteenth century, Ibn Battuta described Mangalore as a bustling trade hub frequented by Persians and Yemenis (Dunn 1986). Mangalore has in fact been on trade routes since the medieval period and is possibly famous since the Roman period, going back in history as far as Ptolemy's chronicles. Described vividly in an account from the twelfth century (in Dunn 1986), the town of Mangalore appeared as an important node in Indian Ocean trade and was uncovered by Amitav Ghosh within the scattered papers of the Cairo Geniza. In his book *In an Antique Land* (1992), Ghosh recounts the lives of an Indian slave in the medieval period, Bomma, and his master/owner, Abraham Ben Yiju, a Tunisian Jewish trader. Abraham Ben Yiju emerged within the written record in the form of a letter sent to him in 1148 CE by his friend Khalaf ibn Ishaq, a merchant in Aden, found in the Geniza records.

Talengala argues that

> it is possible that the name Bomma was revealed to be more than a number in a forgotten archive and was in fact evidence of the importance of spirits and their worship as early as the twelfth century. Bobbare similiarly might have contained within its linguistic usage a kernel of an earlier history; it might be a record of forgotten visitors to these shores. . . . Bobbare, as a Muslim *bhuta*, assumes significance as it exemplifies the deification of a member of a historically marginalized community. The word itself, according to Prabhu (1996: 237), was not only a derivative of the word Berber, but had probably arisen due to the association between the west coast of India and Somalia. While the original references might have blurred in the intervening period, the influences and memories of it in the region must have been so significant that they surfaced within its longest surviving tradition. (Talengala 2017: 6)

Talengala's research has found that the position of Bobbare in the spirit pantheon is unique, as it mobilizes multiple elements; it is not just one of the few spirits to have been mentioned in epigraphic form in the sixteenth century, and memorialized in stone, wood, brass and silver in shore-based shrines and Hindu temples as a guardian spirit from the seventeenth century onwards. It also had its narrative ballads recorded in colonial records in the nineteenth century, and continues to resonate in the region in the twenty-first century. She also points out a fascinating facet of this spirit of the sea which emerged in the work of Jayasuriya and Angenot (2008), wherein a closer investigation into the term Baburu as used in Maldives reveals that it refers to an African of Berber origin. The possible associations between Bobbare and Baburu/Barbari present a new area hitherto unexplored that might yield evidence of further historic links between Africa and Asia in the pre-colonial period.

Like Bobbare, who is hardly acknowledged as belonging to an AfroAsian tradition, Kappiri represents the spirits of Africans who suffered violent deaths and who have become represented as a suppressed soul who wanders the landscape of Kochi. With the deification of the spirits of murdered Africans and their integration into local worship culture, the collective souls of the Africans (Kappirikal) are often talked about as a singular spirit who endured suffering and bore the sufferings of the rest. Kappiri shrines exist in Fort Kochi and Mattancherry in Kochi; they are devoid of any religious figures and are noticeable because of their blazing candles and the strong scent of burning incense, and also because of the unusual offerings left at the shrines such as alcohol and cigars. Jeyachandran (2014) reports oral accounts of people who claim sightings of the cigar-smoking spirit through shadows cast on walls near the shrines. There are also ceremonies that propitiate Kappiri with music and dance.

Figure 4.9 Kappiri shrine in Mattancherry, Kochi, Kerala.

Contemporary musical and ritual traditions among various communities along our routes who have historically suffered marginalization and/or persecution, considered 'low', 'savage' or 'outcast', thus allow us to 'trace' the past in interesting ways and produce 'maps' that are driven by their music and other performative traditions.

What, then, of 'classical' musics that were part of performative traditions of ruling establishments and patronage systems, and which are said to have come down across centuries, codified and distilled into 'high' musical systems? What was the relationship between these systems of music, their forms of patronage and those who performed them? Would we be able to trace AfroAsian links in how various classical music systems evolved along our routes?

The Emergence of the Classical Canons

If we consider China, India, Persia and Baghdad between the seventh and twelfth centuries CE, we see the coming into existence of cultures of 'cosmopolitanism', notably driven by musical cultures. In China during the Tang era, India from the seventh century onwards, and Persia and Baghdad under the Abbasids from the ninth century, we see specific dimensions of this culture, marked by two tendencies: one, to systematize, classify and institutionalize extant musical traditions; and two, the undergirding of these processes with systematic control and subjugation of musical performers, even as their craft was celebrated and elevated. Carefully institutionalized systems of social stratification emerged, with musicians and other performers being members of enslaved or subjugated groups in the population, dominated and patronized by political institutions of various kinds.

The centrality of music in social life and in entertainment in courts generated vigorous debates on what constituted music, who a musician was, what it meant to be a musician and how to codify music. In the Islamic world, it also involved debates on the legal position or permissibility of music in Islam (Nielson 2012).

It was also in this period that theories and philosophies of music, and the distinctions between 'high' and 'low' musics and performers began to be spelled out and in fact written down. What is remarkable to note is that quite generalizably, the intermingling of cultures through deliberate exchange of people and through migrations unrelated to processes of deliberate exchange was reflected in the kinds of musical systems that came into existence. Whether it was Chinese or Persian or Arabic classical music, all were responding to the influences of various 'other' kinds of music and musicians, in addition to reflecting local dynamics.

If we use the two tendencies noted above as distinguishing features of the emergence of musical systems reflecting varied influences, the Chinese, Persian, Arabic and Indian systems can be examined for the period from the seventh to the fifteenth centuries CE.

China from the Tang Period

In China, the systematic codification of music started occurring with the Tang dynasty from the seventh century CE. Even before this, Chinese musical practice had incorporated various elements drawn from the country's western borders, and the acculturation and assimilation that resulted during this period have been studied by many scholars (Picken and Nickson, eds 1997; Xiaodun and Xiaohui 2004; Zhang 2015). Tang music continued a system of codification that had started during the early Sui dynasty (581–618 CE), when a court repertory called the *qibu-yue* (music of seven parts) was performed and recorded systematically. The *qibu-yue* consisted of the *guo-ji* (a mixture of music of the Chinese Han nationality and China's western bordering regions), *qingshang-ji* (music of the Chinese Han nationality), *gaoli-ji* (music of Korea), *tianzhu-ji* (music of ancient India), *anguo-ji* (music of ancient middle Asia, present-day Uzbekistan), *qiuci-ji* (music of *qiuci*, present-day Kushe in Xingjiang) and *wenkang-ji* (a dance in which people wear masks). From the sixth century onwards, a complex bureaucratic system, *yuebu*, had also developed that governed the transmission of music through the systematic migration of musicians and their training within a relatively 'closed' system that maintained the family unit (Xiaodun and Xiaohui 2004). It is said that these systems and institutions of classification represented a new historical phenomenon at the time when Chinese court music entered the '*yanyue* (banquet music) period' and when the music of the 'western regions' was becoming prominent (ibid.). In other words, the codification during the Tang period reflected the multiple influences from outside China's borders seen in the seven-part court music, as well as the setting up of a bureaucratic system for administering music and musicians.

Yueling, or laws governing music, would be sanctioned by the court, and the *yuebu* would represent the musical organization set up in accordance with court-sanctioned regulatory requirements for state ritualistic purposes. Different types of bureaucratic organizations existed for governing music that came through foreign relationships and that which came out of national and regional interactions. The transmission of court music depended mainly on two types of music-makers: performers who played the role of practitioners of the tradition, and musician scholars who were the theoreticians and regulators of the tradition. The number of players and instruments, as well as the ranks of the users of the instruments, constituted essential aspects of the musical organization.

The classification and institutionalization that occurred under the Tang period was also a response, among other factors, to large-scale internal migrations of people, among them musicians. During the time-span of four hundred years between the Han and the Tang dynasties, frequent military confrontations between China and neighbouring nations had resulted in large-scale population migrations. The *yanyue* or banquet music came into existence as a result of the amalgamation and convergence of migratory routes and their music cultures in the cities of Luoyang and Changan before the Tang dynasty. Given the migrations and the assertion of regional cultures, there had to be a regulation of the transmission and pedagogy of music. The traditional method of music transmission had been through the family unit since the time of the Han, and within this mode of transmission (*jiaxue*), musicians and theorists of different regions and cultures emerged as advocates for the music cultures of their respective regions.

The bureaucratic basis of *yuebu* was a systematically organized unit made up of instruments, performers and costumes. Through the systematization of the *yuebu*, what was transmitted was not merely the music itself (that is, its theory, repertoires, styles, performance practices and so on), but a whole system that included regulation of the role of musicians, their methods of training and so forth (Xiaodun and Xiaohui 2004).

The Tang court's musical influence was widespread, affecting Far Eastern music in Korea, Vietnam, Mongolia and other parts of this region as well (Van Khê 1985). Within the Tang dynasty's banquet music, there developed music for entertainment, with dances and instrumental ensembles from other Asian countries including a Korean ensemble, the *gaoliji*. Chinese music of the Tang dynasty was learnt by musicians of the Japanese court; this tradition has remained in existence until the present and is referred to as *tōgaku*, meaning music of the Tang dynasty or music originating in China. *Tangak*, meaning music of the Tang dynasty, also exists presently in Korea, and refers to either music originating in China or music performed on instruments originating in China, such as the tang-pip'a (a pear-shaped lute of the Tang dynasty) or the tang-jok (a transverse flute of the Tang dynasty). In the thirteenth century, after conquering China, the Mongols founded the Yuan dynasty (1280–1367), a relatively short-lived dynasty during which several ritual musical instruments such as gong and stone chimes were introduced into Mongolia (ibid.).

Musicianship was marked by servitude and bondage, together stemming from the low social status of musicians. Along with the codification of various styles and the bureaucratic control system for the performance and transmission of music through the family unit, the systematic devaluation of musicians' social status was maintained. In China, according to Zhang (2015), a registration system of musician households that started from the northern Wei period (534–50 CE) defined, institutionalized and perpetuated the existing social status of musician households for more than a millennium. Interestingly, musicianship was also associated with criminality, or the latter was merged with musicianship through punishment. A considerable number of musician households belonged to relatives and their descendants of criminals, and family members of bandits were registered to musician households. This, in turn, was considered to be one of the most severe punishments possible, indicating the low social status of those musician households.

Individuals belonging to such musician households were controlled by the government differently from the rest of the registered population and, when it became necessary, could be given out as gifts (Zhang 2015). An important Tang musical institution, the Jiaofang or Court Entertainment Bureau, was established, an event symbolizing the institutional separation of popular music from 'sacrificial' music, and almost all Jiaofang musicians during the Tang and later Song periods came from registered musician households that belonged to the *jianmin* (people of lowly social status) category.

Following the practice of having 'music erudites' teach music in the Sui period (581–618 CE), the Tang government regarded music teaching highly from the very beginning. The Tang music erudites belonged to the Court of Imperial Sacrifices, and the position of 'instructorial erudite' could be held by skilful registered musicians after strict and extensive training (ibid.). Once advanced to this position, the musicians could escape their *jianmin* identity and ascend to a higher social rank. A category of musicians referred to as *taichang*, who belonged to the highest echelon within the *jianmin* class, could have more freedom in marriage, property allowances and other privileges than regular registered musicians or craftsmen. For example, they could be registered in local prefects or districts, receive land from the government as commoners, marry with commoners, as well as enjoy other benefits as did the commoners. A *taichang* musician was distinguished from a commoner by his long-term duty to provide music service to the government. In comparison, musicians from categories where craftwork and musicianship were considered equivalent could not be registered in local prefects or districts; they could only 'marry with those in the same musical professions' and were forbidden to marry with commoners or officials (ibid.: 207).

The rigour of the classical system was indicated by the long time it took to acquire mastery of the required number of melodies. It was said that it generally took about one thousand five hundred days to learn to play forty or fifty difficult melodies, and from four to twenty-four years to train a qualified musician.

Tight control of musical and entertainment activities took place where both the identity and the profession were degraded. The government-owned *jianmin* were despised by people of higher status, and, as a result, the general public was deterred from professional involvement in music or drama as performers or as audience.

Coming specifically to female entertainers, there were registered female entertainers working in the drinking houses who were trained not only to entertain the court members, officials, soldiers and the public at government-sponsored festivals, but also to make money for both the government and military bureaus by performing on the stages set up and managed by the government and the army. Zhang (2015) argues that the latter were cheap labourers monopolized by both the government and the military for the purpose of profit, and were handily exploited by the government either as prostitutes or as servants, being placed in government-run programmes to serve clients in order to fulfil their duty as registered musicians.

The presence of attractive female entertainers was important for government-owned drinking houses as a means to increase wine sales in the 'pleasure precincts'. Wine departments organized wine rituals during celebrations and parades that featured female entertainers, who would be arranged by rank according to their beauty or how they dressed along with other theatrical and acrobatic performers, in order to attract customers, also divided by rank and class, to the drinking houses.

Some categories of female performers could pay for an exemption from serving the military, and some registered musician households could buy their way out of the labour of performance if they so desired and had enough money. There was also the *hegu* phenomenon of governmental employment of 'indentured' entertainers, who were musicians hired with money from the registered musician households that paid for their absence.

Bright Sheng's work on music of the Silk Road alerts us to the history of the Qin opera as reflecting the influences of its routes. Qin opera, whose history can be traced back to as early as the Qin dynasty (in the second century BCE), originated in Xi'an and is sung in its dialect. Like all Chinese classical operas, it combines music, dance and drama. Lute-like (that is, plucked) instruments were the first musical instruments brought into China via the Silk Road, and the pipa and sanxian, two early descendants of the lute family closely related to the oud, were the original lead instruments in Qin opera. Bowed instruments were introduced into China from Central Asia, and the xiqin, a bowed sanxian, emerged during the Sung Dynasty (960–1279) and became the chief accompanying instrument for the opera, to be replaced by the banhu, a louder and more flexible bowed fiddle. Sheng notes that in the instrumental interludes, fragments of musical traditions apparently from lands west of the old China can be heard in contemporary performance:

> The dramatically charged singing music is divided into two categories: happy and sorrowful tunes. The happy tunes, commonly believed to derive from folksongs of Shaanxi and Gansu, are based on pentatonic scales (i.e. five notes in each octave), like most mainstream Chinese music. What fascinates me the most are the unusual sorrowful tunes, which, I suspect older, appear to have a closer relationship with the music cultures from Central Asia, and share many of their traits. These tunes are based on the scale of eight pitches in an octave, a phenomenon peculiar for Chinese music. Highlighting the exoticism, sorrowful melodies emphasize the dissonant intervals of the scale – tritones and major and minor sevenths and ninths. In addition, Qin opera possesses other Central Asian characteristics, such as microtonal pitch bending, and the fiercely heartfelt singing style which sometimes resembles shouting more than singing. (Sheng 2000, n.d.)

Another significant musical form that is important to include as part of Silk Road music is the twelve-*mukam* tradition of the Uygur community of Xinjiang in China's north-western corner (Millward, n.d.). The *maqām* (or *makam*, *mugham*) as a mode of classification of melodies that came to characterize classical traditions in Egypt, Persia, Baghdad and al-Andalus is known to have been a principal carrier of Persian–Arabic traditions between Al-Hind and al-Andalus. There is much less acknowledgement in English-language sources of the Chinese variant of the *maqām*, the twelve-*mukam*, which is a thriving tradition in China and, more importantly, is associated with the kinds of routes that we are discussing here. During the Silk Road era, Xinjiang is said to have contained people from most of the kingdoms in Central and West Asia, which included present-day Iran, Iraq, Pakistan, Afghanistan, Tashkent, Kazakhstan, Kyrgyzstan, Tajikistan and Uzbekistan. It did not become a Chinese province until 1884, during the Qing dynasty, though Chinese suzerainties had it briefly under their dominion during the Han and Tang dynasties. Eventually the Uygurs of Turkic origin, and initially resident in the Altai mountains between the sixth and ninth centuries, migrated after their defeat by the Kyrgyz: some travelled south-west across the Tian mountains to settle in the oases surrounding the Taklamakan desert, while others moved east and founded kingdoms in northern Gansu.

There have been several debates and assumptions about the origins of the Uygur *mukam* tradition, with attempts to either deny its Arabic or Islamic roots by attributing its beginnings to before the fifth century CE, or to consider it an easy derivative of the Arabic or Turkish *maqām* traditions (Harris 2008). According to Sheng (2000, n.d.), many features in Uygur *mukam* music bear a close relation to old Chinese classical music:

> The structure of Uygur *mukam* resembles that of Tang Daqu, a large-scale musical form popular during the Tang Dynasty. In many ways, this model – essentially, a large suite divided into three sections (slow moderate fast) – also shaped the form of long arias in Qin opera. Like Xiliang music, Uygur *mukam* incorporates singing, instrument playing, and dancing all in one. The first *adagio* singing section, sometimes meterless, is followed by a lengthy *andante* instrumental section, and the suite concludes with fast dance music. Often, a long suite consists of many alternating sections of *adagio* and *andante*, but the fast dance music is always at the end. Each *mukam* can last from a few minutes to a few hours, depending on the occasion and the space in which the music is performed. The expressive mode ranges from sentimental to savage. Customarily, the ensemble size also varies from a few people to a small orchestra of a dozen. This flexibility makes *mukam* popular and fitting for any social occasion.

While similarities of structure, tuning systems and instruments bespeak Uygur *mukam*'s origins in the region over a thousand years ago, according to Sheng, making it a unique kind of music, it will also be useful to consider its lineage within the corpus of traditions like the *qaul*, *maqāmat* and *haul* across the region from al-Andalus to Al-Hind.

Arabic Classical Music

Arabic musical practice, like that of the Chinese, also saw the emergence of substantive systematization and codification between the ninth and eleventh centuries. The *Kitab-al-Aghani* (Book of Songs) by Abu-l-Faraj al-Isfahani is considered to be one of the most important sources for the history of poetry, culture and music, along with the *Kitab-al-Musiqi al-Kabir* (Great Book of Music) by Al-Farabi, both together demonstrating the presence of a vibrant musical culture in the Arab world from the third century CE or so.[12] The *Kitab-al-Musiqi*, commissioned by a patron in Harun-al-Rashid's time, is important for the study of Middle Eastern civilization from pre-Islamic times to the tenth century.

Running to twenty-three volumes, the *Kitab-al-Aghani* is an important source for the actual songs that existed in the tenth century in Baghdad. Its way of describing songs reveals information about the melodic and rhythmic modes employed, along with the lines and metres of the poetry, the names of the poets and composers, philological notes on the lines and the sources of their musical settings. The schematic used to list songs contains these headings, and usually only some were actually listed, but often one or more of the musical variables would be listed, indicating that they were songs that were sung, not merely named in the list and not only poetry. Kilpatrick (2003) observes that given this schematic, three types of songs are found: first, those that were being performed in Al-Isfahani's time and where the sources were known; second, those whose melody had been lost but whose musical indications were still present in the sources; and third, those that were part of the repertoire but their indications did not exist in the sources. Songs were handed down through a combination of oral and written methods. A major source of the musical material was collections of songs compiled in the ninth century (ibid.: 35). Kilpatrick notes that this method was a 'unique feat in combining material' (ibid.: 38). G.D. Sawa comments that the compilation technique is important to note; it is based on a tradition of Muslim historiography and the use of the *isnad*, the listing of the chain of authorities on whose reports the details of an event are based (G.D. Sawa 1989: 26).

The *Kitab-al-Musiqi* by Al-Farabi, written in the tenth century, was significant because it systematized theories that reflected actual musical practice. Apart from these two monumental works, numerous other writings on music from the ninth century have been critical in laying the foundations of Arabic musical practice. Examples of these are the *Kitab-al-Muwashah* (The Book of Brocade) by the grammarian Abu Tayib ibn Muhammad ibn Ishaq ibn al-Washsha, the *Risala-al-Qiyan* (Epistle on the Singing Girls) by the satirist Abu Uthman 'Amr ibn Bahr al-Jahiz, and the *Dhamm al-Malahi* (Censure of Instruments of Diversion) by Abu Bakr Abdullah ibn Muhammad.[13] Nielson (2012) notes that music literature from this period falls broadly into three categories: *ghina*, *sama* and *musiqa*. All three categories of music fall under the overarching category of *adab* (literature, *belles-lettres*), but *ghina* and *sama* include poetry, chronicles, histories and treatises as well as performance practices, stories about musicians, and so on, whereas *musiqa* includes exclusively music, theory, practical musicianship, philosophy and aesthetics.

Music performance, according to Al-Farabi, was prior to theory, and his work contained a description of *iqa*s, 'movement[s] of musical notes separated by equal time values in consecutive and equal time periods' (G.D. Sawa 1989: 39), and their practice based on the common practices of performers. He discussed the art of musical instruments, the way in which notes would be extracted from them and the timbres available on the instruments on the basis of the performances of specific practitioners, but distinguished his terminology from popular terminology based on grammar (ibid.: 16). Al-Farabi was also an accomplished performer. Melodies, according to Al-Isfahani, could be divided into sad, comic and soft ones which could lull people to sleep, and it was said that Al-Farabi himself could perform in a way that made people laugh, cry and sleep at the same time. G.D. Sawa, commenting on this, notes the impossibility of such an event, but ascribes such a story to the important place that Al-Farabi occupied in the world of music. He and other scholars of the music of the region consider him to have been the most important Middle Eastern music theorist (Farmer 1925a, 1925b; G.D. Sawa 1989; Shiloah 2000).

The basic unit around which music theory emerged, based on Ishaq-al-Mawsili's work and reflected in both the *Kitab-al-Aghani* and the *Kitab-al-Musiqi*, was the *iqa* (G.D. Sawa 1989: 39). The way in which the notes moved within an *iqa* was through *naqrah* (attacks), like the plucking of an instrument or the beating of a drum. The fundamental forms of the *iqa*s were general formulas or metres from which specific rhythmic modes or rhythms could be obtained through *tashbiqat* (fillings), *taziynat* (ornaments), and *madulat* and *taghyirat* (modifications and changes) (ibid.: 46). Al-Farabi described sixteen different types of ornamental techniques that could be used to embellish the *iqa*s and produce specific rhythmic modes.

In 715 CE, the Umayyad musician Ibn Misjah had systematized musical modes. Al-Farabi also wrote extensively about melodic modes in the *Kitab-al-Musiqi*, drawing on Ishaq-al-Mawsili who had tried to re-establish Ibn Misjah's musical modes, and who defined modes in terms of the tonic and the lute frets of the middle and ring finger. In his work with Ibn Misjah's melodic modes (*nagham*), one of Al-Mawsili's objectives was to counter the introduction of 'foreign' notes into the tone system. Al-Farabi based his work on that of Al-Mawsili, even if he was critical of it. In writing about the history, Al-Farabi stated that Persian notes were added to the system by the singers Alluyah and Mukhariq (*circa* 850 CE) and the lutenist Zalzal (842 CE), introducing what came to be known as the Zalzalian seconds and thirds.

Even if Al-Mawsili denied it in his work, the tone system that developed had its roots in pre-Islamic Arabia according to Al-Farabi, who described it through the fretting of the tanbur (pandore) in pre-Islamic times, subsequently seen in the Baghdad tunbur.[14]

Whether a system of melodic modes existed or not in these works has been a matter of debate, with Owen Wright (cited in G.D. Sawa 1989: 49) stating that it might be misleading to assume that all the different ways of interpreting the melodic modes lead to 'an orderly series of equally important notes anchored to a stable tonic', which a mode would need to be. G.D. Sawa, however, states that a consistent concept of mode as defined by Wright did emerge in Al-Farabi's work, as well as in that of Al-Mawsili and Ibn Munajjim (ibid.: 78). A detailed elaboration of the tone system, leading to melodic modes, was also accompanied by an elaborate system of melodic ornamentation, with four basic techniques: *al-takthir* (multiplying), *al-tafkhim* (making more abundant and richer), *al-tazyin* (embellishment) and *al-tabdil* (replacement).

In writing about the second technique, *al-tafkhim*, Al-Farabi details the role of *muqaribat* or approximating notes, that are distinguished clearly from *mujawirat* or neighbouring notes (also referred to by him as transposition notes), in that the former are notes played 'in between the frets' (ibid.: 95) and hence make the mode 'more abundant'. Further, the transposition takes place at higher or lower octaves as well, and can also add a harmonic element. Importantly, the transposition possibility allows for the intricacy of the melody to unfold through the *muqaribat* as well as for two or more singers to sing in unison at different octaves using the same notes, or for them to use harmonic fourth or fifth notes (*al-tabdil*) to embellish the melody. G.D.

Sawa notes that despite the presence of these harmonic notes, singers never sang in parallel fourths or fifths, that is, the melody would not be paralleled harmonically. Instead, '[a] note or more can be replaced by its lower or higher octave, lower or higher fifth, lower or higher octave+fifth, lower or higher fourth, lower or higher octave+fourth' (ibid.: 97).

In Al-Farabi's world, instrumental music was subordinate to vocal music, and consisted of preludes, intervals and postludes to songs; instruments also accompanied the voice, imitating it closely in unison or octave. Melodic ornaments, according to G.D. Sawa, consisted of tremolos and replacements and additions of notes also outside the range of the formal melody. The combination of melodic and rhythmic ornaments provided a heterophonic texture to music in his time, with unaccompanied vocal singing as well as vocal music accompanied by instruments.

Al-Farabi also provided great detail about the practice of performance centred around the *majlis* (a place where people sat together to converse), an institution that endured from pre-Islamic right up to Sassanid times (ibid.: 112). In the Abbasid period, the *majlis* could be called at any time, depending on the whim of the patron, mostly the caliph, and all musicians – male or female slave singers, and free singers whether Arabs, non-Arabs or of mixed descent – were expected to be on call, irrespective of the time of day or night.

Another important institutional mechanism relating to the *majlis* was the *nawbah*, a specific musician's or poet's designated day of performance in the week, a practice that G.D. Sawa traces to at least Harun-al-Rashid in the early part of the ninth century CE. Even if contradictory in principle, both practices – of summoning musicians or poets at any time and of designating days in the week for their performance – would be used simultaneously in the formal *majlis*.

Informal *majalis* (the plural of *majlis*) also existed as important venues for performance; they lacked the patron–musician relationship and could be convened by any hosts, musicians or their friends. An informal *majlis* could be convened without an invitation, and in that sense, happen spontaneously; the musician or poet was a host, in contrast to the formal *majlis* where the musician was a guest (ibid.: 118). In the twentieth century, many of these techniques and practices were still to be found according to G.D. Sawa, pointing to continuity in practice over many centuries.

Gender played an important role in performance practice in the Persian and Arabic music world, and much has been written about the role of women musicians, a large number of them being slaves (Nielson 2012). There was a long tradition of patronage of singing girls, *qiyan*, of *mukhannathun* or cross-gender male singers, and of specialists in mourning and elegists, who could be of either gender; their performances were shaped by traditional expectations of gendered musical performance. There was a distinction between singing girls and concubines, with the singing girl being the most visible form of musical entertainment in pre-Islamic Arabia. From pre-Islamic times, 'singing girl' could refer to any woman musician, including slaves and women of free birth, but eventually it came to signify a special class of courtesans. References to singing girls in pre-Islamic poetry and Islamic histories depict them as professional singers and instrumentalists who were owned by the wealthy, as well as being available for hire and for private amusement. Singing girls were also available for sex, and were always associated with wine, either literally in their capacity as servants who served wine or metaphorically because of their ability to inebriate the senses. From the Islamic period, several references in the *hadith*s demonstrate that singing girls were employed to entertain in a variety of different ways, and that the type of entertainment they provided carried certain social implications for the patron. Ownership and patronage of singing girls became a status symbol for courtiers and those seeking upward mobility. With the growth of a middle class, increased wealth and stability in the Abbasid seat of power, and the establishment of laws relating to marriage and adultery, a courtesan–patron dynamic began to develop which was to find its way as a developed system into parts of the world where the music travelled, like India and the region of al-Andalus.

Singing girls were acquired through trade or conquest, carefully trained, and extremely expensive to own and maintain. Prospective singing girls were selected based on physical beauty, country of origin, aptitude and market preferences. Their training included music, poetry, Qur'anic recitation and, since they were frequently foreign, the Arabic language. They were given descriptive names, such as Jamila (beautiful) or Bas-Bas (caress). Singing girls were also expected to memorize thousands of songs and poems, and were viewed by many as living archives. Their preferred instrument remained the lute, though they also played different types of plucked stringed and hand percussion instruments. The performance expectations of singing girls differed from those of male musicians, because singing girls were also expected to perform as courtesans. As slaves, singing girls could not be veiled and frequently performed in mixed company; therefore, they had many opportunities to solicit patronage through a carefully crafted display of intimacy and availability.

Slavery in the early Islamic era could be a temporary state and was not an impediment to social advancement. Singing girls and other female slaves had the opportunity to earn their freedom through the birth of a child, to be freed for marriage or to buy their freedom outright. It was often stated that since an ambitious singing girl could potentially earn the affection of the caliph or enough money to purchase her own singing girls, there was politicking and examples of intrigues, including assassination attempts, torture and such.

Until the eighth century, it was women who were court musicians, and the first celebrated musicians were foreign men or men of foreign extraction, the *musiqar* or *mughanni*. Whether it was the 'foreign' slave women or the men from abroad who introduced them, the new techniques that they brought with them were incorporated into existing traditions.

An important category of musicians from pre-Islamic times were the *mukhannathun*, the 'effeminates' or catamites, whose beauty and voices were coveted in the early period but whose musical role declined by the ninth century. They continued to remain at court, though their performances now focused on theatrics or buffoonery with less emphasis on music. Court preferences for sexual companions shifted from adult or young men to young slave boys who, like singing girls (and all slave women) were considered sexually available. The texts of the period have lively debates on the relative merits of young women versus young men as sexual partners (Caswell 2011; Nielsen 2012). At one point, this gender play extended to dressing singing girls as boys and serving boys as singing girls, then having them sing and recite poetry associated with their adopted gender.

Though there are many sources from the ninth and tenth centuries that reference singing girls, the ninth-century writers Al-Jahiz and Ibn al-Washsha were among the first to use them symbolically as representatives of a larger social problem (Gordon 2009).

Al-Jahiz, in his *Risala al-Qiyan* (Epistle on the Singing Girls), refers to them as *qiyan*; he is one of the few to distinguish them specifically from *jawari* (female slaves, musical concubines) (ibid.). One of the significant differences in the position taken by Al-Jahiz in relation to that of Ibn al-Washsha is that while Al-Jahiz attributes the moral turpitude of singing girls to greed, he acknowledges that they are still capable of emotion and regret. Ibn al-Washsha, however, expresses the belief that the bad intentions of singing girls are not a product of circumstance or human failure, but somehow ingrained in their souls. The immorality of the singing girls was the subject of other writings in later periods as well. Variations on Ibn al-Washsha's position regarding the inherent immoral qualities of singing girls can be found in descriptions by later authors such as Ibn Abi'l Dunya (Nielsen 2012).

Several studies thus provide detailed analysis of the Arab classical music system that was codified from the ninth century onwards (Farmer 1929; Myrne 2010; G.D. Sawa 1985, 1989). Nielsen (2012) notes that we also get glimpses of music practices outside the mainstream art performance in what was an ethnically diverse and heterogeneous cultural world, even if they are less detailed. She asks:

> Are we to assume that such musical genres of non-Arab and possibly pre-Islamic origin as, for instance, Persian and Khurasan instrumental compositions, *taraiq* and *dawashln*, as well as music-making on instruments like the Soghdian shahrud and Khurasan tunbur, described by al-Farabi, were governed by the same rhythmic principles as art singing (*ghina*) and other genres of performance practised in cultural centres, like Damascus and Baghdad, and codified by music theorists from their intellectual milieux? Or could it be that some forms of temporal organization of music remained unexamined, as they lay outside the realm of art music and were not identified with the concept of *iqa*? (Nielsen 2012: 22)

How can we make sense of the traces that can be seen through such 'glimpses'? How would the various impulses being carried through people who did not necessarily enter the world of classical music, even to be there by virtue of their inferior status, be related to larger histories of migrations across the vast geographies that we are studying?

The Classical Music of al-Andalus

The Arabic musical system had spread, by the ninth century, into al-Andalus. The identification of Andalusian music as 'traditional' or 'classical' is based on the persistence of musical forms that 'voice' the Arab-Islamic presence in southern Spain for several centuries until the thirteenth century, and that possess the characteristics of the interactions with Spanish music which then travelled to North Africa in the thirteenth century. Andalusian music is largely of two types: that which came from Granada, found in Morocco, and that from Cordoba, found in Syria. The music is found in different styles across the Maghreb and the Levant, or Tunisia, Algeria, Morocco, Syria and Libya, presently. This tradition in turn is said to have influenced the music in the Arab world, in Sephardic Jewish communities, and also of the Occitanian and Catalan troubadours of later periods (Farmer 1925a; Ferreira 2000;

Reynolds 2009; Shannon 2007).

Three musical genres, the *nubah*, *muwashshah* and *zajal*, are considered to be the hallmarks of the Andalusian music tradition. Ziryab, the multi-talented genius who moved from the Abbasid court in Baghdad to the Umayyad court in Cordoba having traversed parts of North Africa, is credited with developing the concept of the *nubah*, a suite form containing pieces composed in a single mode and grouped according to rhythmic structure. The twenty-four *nubat* established by Ziryab are considered to be the basic structural elements upon which early Andalusian music was founded. While until the 1960s, it was Ziryab's contribution that was said to have been the most important one, the discovery of a fragmentary text by Al-Tifashi from the twelfth/thirteenth century in the 1960s has brought out the role of Ibn Bajja (Avempace) in developing the tradition. Al-Tifashi's text contributed substantially to the reimagination of the Andalusian tradition, and also documented the musical instruments as well as the differences in the singing styles of Ifriqiyah (modern-day Tunisia), Morocco and al-Andalus (Reynolds 2009). A further contribution to the knowledge of the variety and extent of innovation in the tradition came from eighteen biographies of Andalusian singers from the courts of Al-Hakam and Abd-al-Rahman in Cordoba in the first half of the ninth century (ibid.).

Each of the twenty-four *nubat* supposedly corresponded in quality with an hour of the day, and with different temporal, seasonal and emotional characteristics. The performance of each *nubah* is also said to have served a therapeutic function by keeping various body humours in balance.

Although the *nubah* is the oldest and one of the most distinctive Andalusian musical structures, it is not the most geographically far-reaching. Al-Tifashi noted that by the eleventh century a new song form had emerged that 'combined Christian songs with those of the East' (Akbari and Mallette, eds 2013: 159). This new form was called the *muwashshah*, and its development is attributed to Ibn Bajja. The *muwashshah* was a musical form based on strophic poetry (alternating verse and chorus), which replaced the single-line rhyme schemes of the classical *qasida*. So popular was this new style that it bridged the gap between eastern and western musical forms of the time, and provided an Andalusian-derived style whose survival is not exclusive to the Maghreb. The *muwashshah* was incorporated into the eastern system of *maqām* when it travelled across North Africa into Egypt, where musicians, theorists and composers sought to analyse and emulate its form. From Egypt the *muwashshah* made its way to Syria, and it was not long before

Syrian composers adopted the style that is still used today.

A third popular song form called *zajal* developed in Andalusian Spain during the eleventh century. The *zajal* was similar to the *muwashshah* in form but was sung in colloquial languages as opposed to classical Arabic. It allowed more rhythmic freedom than the *muwashshah* but required that the song begin with the verse; in the *muwashshah*, the opening verse is optional. The song forms also differ in the number of times that verses are repeated throughout the song.

The literature on the music of al-Andalus is extensive, and in recent years, has also been a subject of computational musicology and analysis to identify what in contemporary performed music can be identified as Andalusian. Shannon (2007) points out the differences between the music found in Syria and in Morocco in terms of styles of performance, modes and vocal styles, but underlines the role that cultural memory plays in both countries in their common identification of the music as Andalusian. The suite form, referred to as *ala* in Syria and *nubah* in North Africa, is attributed to al-Andalus, even as Syrian Andalusian music is attributed with greater influences from Persian and Arabic poetic forms and modal music.

What is important to note is that this mapping of historical influences in the region of al-Andalus identifies continuity from Spain to Syria and North Africa, but falls short of connecting with another musical mapping exercise, from the Persian and Arabic world eastwards into India and China through Central Asia. Our contention is that a larger map of the extended territory from al-Andalus to Al-Hind has not yet been explored in as much detail and with as much care as the smaller stretches have been, and would yield precious information about the shaping of the AfroAsian musical imaginary. We saw earlier, in the section on China, that the *maqām*, the classificatory device employed in Persian, Arabic, Egyptian and Turkish classical musics, appeared as the twelve-*mukam* style in China and the *mugham* in Azerbaijan. The *qaul* was transformed into the *haul* in North Africa and became a progenitor for the *qawwali* in north India.

We now take up the case of India and the influences of long-term AfroAsian migrations on classical Indian music.

The Making of the Indian Classical Canon

In India, the wholesale destruction of ancient manuscripts from centuries before the first millennium CE meant that the *Natyasaastra*, the treatise on drama, dance and music compiled in the first few centuries CE, became the earliest surviving theoretical work on these art forms (Widdess 1979). As with the musics of China, Persia and Arabia that we dealt with earlier, from the sixth century onwards, Indian music theorists or compilers were collecting musics that reflected the interactions between the more rigidly codified 'ancient' music and the varied forms that came from different parts of the geographical region that became India. Two surviving records from the period, the seventh-century Kudumiyamalai inscription found on a rock in Tamil Nadu and the *Brhaddesi*, a musical chronicle compilation attributed to Matanga around the same time, point to specific aspects of music documentation. The inscription comprises seven extended melodies in the seven earliest known rāgas. Richard Widdess, who deciphered the inscription, says it is the first written example of musical notation in India. Indian music, like Persian and Arabic music, is dependent to a large extent on oral transmission, memorization and improvisation, and although these processes may be assisted by various systems of 'oral notation' for drums, dance and melody, these oral systems serve a mnemonic function, and are seldom written down (ibid.). Orally articulated symbols or spoken syllables thus come to constitute a sophisticated system for representing music, and can convey various kinds of information, including historical detail, about music. The following aspects of notation and transmission, as discussed in Widdess (1979), are interesting for our purpose. First, that notation itself could be a way of understanding oral transmission because of the necessary association between notation and performance practice variations. Second, that oral transmission could result in very long lines of reasonable continuity because of the principles that such transmission was founded on, which included specific kinds of recording of memories and actual events. To this day, whole musical repertoires for drums like the north Indian or the south Indian *mridangam* are encoded and memorized in syllables that can indicate not only the strokes to be played, but also, for example, whether the composition originated on the said drums or had been adapted from some other instrument, which has implications for the style in which the composition should be rendered. Notation syllables for rhythm or for melodic vocal improvisation using solmization syllables are also used orally in the teaching process, as a means of communication and an aid to memory.

From approximately the seventh to the thirteenth centuries, a number of treatises were written in Sanskrit in which the theory of music was further developed, focusing to a great extent on the definition and classification of melodic modes or rāgas, and with melodies illustrating them notated in a simple melodic solmization that has shown remarkable continuity down to modern times. Key among these texts is the *Brhaddesi*, attributed to the sage Matanga about whom there is no certainty as to when he lived. His work has been dated to as early as the fourth or as late as the seventh century CE. The revitalizing influence of new musical traditions or the 'infusion of various provincial musical traditions between 500 and 1000 AD . . . greatly expanded the boundaries of the ancient musical system and altered the future course of Indian music in far-reaching ways' (Rowell 2015: 7). This infusion was the acceptance of what were considered '*desi*' or 'provincial' or 'regional' traditions of music, along with the previously accepted '*marga*' or 'classical' traditions into the theorization of *sangita*, or music. This distinction, Rowell argues, is historical, and possibly indicative of major social changes occurring at the time. To a great extent, the manuscripts that were written on music reflected existing and past practices.

Marga traditions could be described as being associated with the classical Indian musical theatre, involving strict rules of composition, and having melodies using the *gramarāga*s and *jati*s which were ways of coding families of scales. *Desi* traditions were those employing relatively freer practices with greater improvisation, bringing in various 'little traditions', producing music for entertainment and having a melodic foundation based on later rāgas outside the old classical tradition. A small number of early scales based on seven *jati*s (constituting the superset) and eighteen *gramarāga*s (the sets formed out of the superset) of the ancient texts expanded, with the introduction of the *desi* traditions, into the vast system of 253 rāgas that were recorded in the *Sangita-Ratnakara* (Ocean of Music) of Sarangadeva in the thirteenth century, which provides a detailed description of the ancient and contemporary composition forms (Shringy and Prem, eds 1978: 15). Between the *Natyasastra*, said to have been written in the third century CE and which codified the 'science of *natya*' or theatre, and the *Sangita-Ratnakara* in the thirteenth century, the incorporation of the *desi* traditions and the expansion of the rāga system took place. Sarangadeva's *Sangita-Ratnakara* was a synthesis of musical doctrines of the previous millennium. He did not invent his own musical examples but copied them from pre-existing sources, some of which have been identified (ibid.). In his preface to the *Sangita-Ratnakara*, Sarangadeva claims to have consulted no fewer than forty earlier authorities on music, many of whose works are now lost or survive only in quotations.

As for the *Brhaddesi*, Rowell notes that songs from different languages spoken in Gujarat, Karnataka, Andhra, Bengal, Tamil Nadu and Kerala fell into the categories of *desi* songs, and that the text provided the most systematic and far-reaching attempt at cultural mapping found in early musical treatises in India (Rowell 2015: 287).

Widdess (1995) notes that the early treatises provide us with a surprisingly extensive body of notated music, but whether they represented musical practice or theoretical frameworks or whether they were the result of oral or literate processes of composition and adaptation, needs to be deduced. He notes that the standard practice was for each theorist to copy his examples from previously existing written sources in the surviving sources of the pre-Islamic period, and this suggests a close connection at source with a tradition of performance. We have seen that this was true for the Arabic as well as the Chinese systems of recording and codification, and in the same range of centuries. Clearly, the plenitude of styles that were being seen in actual performance, as well as the need to bring all of this into an orderly system, was being experienced across these various parts of the world.

The establishment of the Delhi Sultanate (at the beginning of the thirteenth century), also called the Slave Dynasty, changed both the cultural set-up and patterns of patronage in north India. From then on the assimilation of influences coming from the Turko-Persian traditions began, and as Rowell (2015) notes, the two streams of Indian classical music – north Indian and south Indian – appeared distinctly. Waves of Turko-Persian influence transformed the classical music of north India substantially. First, various categories of performance and performers that had existed prior to the influence of the Turko-Persian traditions underwent changes. For example, while *sangit* in the Indian context referred to composite performances encompassing music, dance and acting, theatre had no place in the Turko-Persian scheme, and this brought about a great decline in the status of theatre artists, especially that of the *nati* or actress. Catamites, who were as coveted in the Turko-Persian tradition as *ganika*s in the Indian one, became the subject of poetry and music, like the erotic *ghazal*s of Amir Khusrau (Khusrow) presented in the assemblies of Sultan Jalal al-Din Khalji (1290–1296) (Trivedi 2012). The *Tarikh-i Firuz Shahi* recorded that by the second quarter of the thirteenth century, professional groups from diverse places had made Delhi culturally rich enough to rival Baghdad, Cairo, Constantinople and Jerusalem (ibid.). By then the assimilation of existing traditions was also substantial.

Second, the transition involved a distinction being made between the different classes of performers within and outside courtly performance. The transition was more marked during the reign of Sultan Kaiqubad (1287–1290) who, Trivedi (2012) records, was an enthusiastic patron and participant in performance traditions that came from all classes of performers. It is said that his father, who disapproved of his mingling not only with performers who were part of court entertainment but also with 'lowlife' forms, forced him to abstain from the culture of musical soirées and entertainment. As in the Arabic, Persian and Andalusian courts, courtesans (*jalab*) and slave girls (*kaniz bachgans*) were selected and trained extensively, including in Persian music and language, in the sultan's courts in north India. Experts in Persian and Indian music composed eulogies to the sultan based on the *qaul* and *ghazal* forms.

There is a story about Kaiqubad that illustrates some of the social distinctions that were embedded in the music. When he was abstaining from art and music and was out hunting with his entourage, a courtesan, whom the group is said to have run into accidentally, demonstrated great prowess in music and wisdom that impressed him greatly. On being asked how she, as a performer of inferior status, showed such knowledge and skill, she replied that she was only one among many and that others in her company were equally wise and talented. The sultan reportedly immersed himself in entertainment once again after this episode (ibid.).

Third, even if some categories of entertainers, such as theatre artists, suffered a temporary setback, many of them, like the *nat*s, adapted themselves to the new artistic requirements and thus retained their status as instructors of musical arts till the end of the seventeenth century. The *nat*s, who were referred to as *gada-ghazigan* by the writer Al-Barani, became experts in the latest styles and techniques of the musical arts popularized by Central Asian and Khurasani musicians (ibid.).

Fourth, the development of music that could be distinguished into *marga* and *desi* types that was recorded from the time of the seventh-century *Brhaddesi* onwards continued with the same distinction into the period of the Turko-Persian assimilation. Various 'lighter' forms of music, such as the *jhombada*, *vartani*, *suryaprakash*, *chandraprakash* and *man*, as well as folk varieties like the *charchari*, were considered as essential knowledge for maestros, along with the rigorous classical forms, even as late as the nineteenth century (ibid.).

Fifth, the Sufi *sama*, which had developed roots in India possibly from the twelfth century, was reconceptualized with the incorporation of Indian performance forms. In north India, Amir Khusrau, the genius scholar, poet, prose writer and musician, had strong links with the Sufi circle. He was a devotee of Sheikh Nizam al-Din Auliya (d. 1324) of the Chisti order, and well versed in practices related to the *sama*. He had acquired knowledge of the Turko-Persian court traditions as well as Indian classical and folk traditions that were setting down roots in the *sama*, which he combined in the fashioning of the *qaul*, *tarana*, *naqsh*, *nigar*, *basit*, *tillana*, *farsi*, *fard* and *sohla* forms. In these musical forms, he blended Indian and Persian lyrics, genres and music techniques (for example, Indian rāgas and Persian *maqām*), composing in *desi* (the dialect of the Delhi region). The *sama* was thus Indianized and attained a status of its own through *qawwals*. *Qawwal* became a term for those who performed *qaul-tarana*. Other kinds of Sufi influences were to be similarly reworked in different parts of India, like the Sufi trance and healing traditions of the Sidis in Gujarat, Karnataka and Hyderabad, the specific Sufi influences of the Mappilas, and so on.

Sixth, indigenous devotional traditions like those of the Vaishnavite, Nath and Siddha were integrated within the practices of the Bhakti movement, which also assimilated some Sufi practices. Bhakti saints denounced the traditional *prabandh* form and adopted the *chhand*, *pad* and *doha* as poetic forms. They also began to compose in regional languages. It is in this scenario that musical forms such as the *shabd*, *dhrupad* and *bishnupad* took shape.

The specific kinds of music that came into existence in the court of the Delhi Sultanate are described in the seventeenth-century text by Faqirullah Saif Khan, *Raag Darpan*, and in Khusrau's *I'jaz-i Khusravi*. *Git*, which existed in India, was reworked in the form of the *qaul*. Khusraw writes about the *kalanvatan-i Hindi*, the only Indian instrumentalists (vina players) who found access to the assembly of royal performers, and about Nadima Turmati Khatun, who had master musicians of Isfahan and Iraq as her disciples and whose extraordinary talent made her the head musician of the royal court. It is also said that there was competition between Khurasani singers such as Daud-i Jabali, Shaban Qamri and flautist Abu-l Farrukhi and musicians from the Turko-Persian tradition. Trivedi (2012) argues that Khusrau encouraged young musicians to join hands with those who inherited and preserved the Turko-Persian traditions in order to surpass the handful of 'arrogant khurasani' musicians. Khusrau is said to have had intense interactions with Gopal Nayak, a distinguished musician from south India who is said to have inspired Khusrau to create the *qaul-tarana*, which consists of rhythmic syllables instead of words.

As with the Arabic and Persian systems, female musicians came from the lower strata of society. An important account by Shaikh Farid Bhakjari recorded that women from the Luli, Huruki, Domni, Kanchanu and

Kamachanu communities were the leading classes of female singers and dancers; another writer, Pelsaert, added Hentsinis (Hansini) and Lolonis to the list (Trivedi 2012). Lolonis were decendants of Persian courtesans and sang only in Persian, whereas Domnis sang in Hindustani (ibid.: 33; see also Bano 2011). The female musicians referred to here came from social groups at the lower levels of the hierarchy, and the names of some of the communities mentioned, like the Luli and Domni, resonate with those found along the north-western India, Baluchistan and Baghdad routes from the sixth century CE onwards, and who have been referred to in the first section of this chapter.

Even if the system of rāga-based music was bifurcated into the north Indian and south Indian systems from the thirteenth century, as Rowell (2015) states and as is commonly understood, the 'polyphonic pasts' (Soneji 2021) of south Indian rāga-based music need to be underscored despite very little research on this music being available. Brahaspati (1969), in studying the influence of music of Islamic origin and the *maqām* system on Venkatamakhi, the scribe whose text is considered canonical for the history and theory of south Indian rāga-based music, argues that the twelve-tone system that was adopted to define the *mela* classification (and the *that* classification in north Indian rāga-based music) was based on the tones of the *maqām* system. According to him, in south India, the names of the *svara*s or tones from earlier Hindu texts such as the *Sangita-Ratnakara* of Sarangadeva were superimposed onto the *maqām* tone names. Further, several important *mela*s that are found in Venkatamakhi's text cannot be derived from Vedic music principles but are reflective of the influence of the *maqām* system, like *Bhairava* and *Emana* or *Kalyani*, which he specifically described as *Turushkapriya* (a favourite of the Turushkas, a term presumably derived from Turk to denote Muslims and foreigners). At any rate, given the multiple channels through which Islam entered south India, it is highly improbable that the south Indian music system would not have absorbed Persian, Arabic and Turko-Persian influences. These channels included, for instance, the expansion of the Delhi Sultanate to Gujarat, Rajasthan and south India; the rise of the Muslim Bahmani kingdom in the Deccan in south India, in turn interacting with the Vijayanagara kingdom; the spread of north Indian Sufi philosophy and practices to south India; all these reflecting the developments from the thirteenth century onwards. It is also important to foreground the older links between the Arab and Persian worlds and the south-western coast, notably encompassing modern-day Tamil Nadu, Kerala and Lakshadweep, and stretching beyond India into Sri Lanka and the Maldives in the southern waters of the Arabian Sea and the Indian Ocean.

One crucial node that is missed out entirely in the analysis of musical traditions in India is the relationship of the Persian empires and the Arab world to the regions of Malabar and Kochi in Kerala on the south-western tip of the Indian peninsula. It is only in more recent times that actual networks of connections between the Sassanid empire, the Arab world, Africa and the western coast of India, particularly Malabar and Kochi, are beginning to be uncovered. As in the cases of Baghdad and Delhi, Kochi must have been an important cosmopolitan centre given these connections and the varied communities of people who lived there between the fifth and fourteenth centuries.

Pius Malekandathil, who has documented the Persian maritime links with India, particularly Kerala, notes that the Sassanid connection with India's western coast, through the ports of Gujarat, Konkan, South Canara, Malabar, Coromandel and Sri Lanka, was established from about the third century CE onwards (Malekandathil 2010: 34). As early as 345 CE, 72 mercantile families of Christians are said to have migrated from West Asia with Thomas of Cana and settled down in Cornelur (Cranganore) in Malabar, a small part of a wave of migrations into Kerala from West Asia.

Cosmas Indicopleustis (Winstedt 1910) attests to the sixth- and seventh-century maritime interconnections between Syriac Christendom, Ethiopia, the island world of the Indian Ocean, Kerala, Gujarat and Sri Lanka. By the sixth century CE, there were migrations of Nestorian Christians and Zoroastrians from Persia to Kerala as well, and in this period the politics of maritime trade between the Sassanids and the Byzantines unravelled. The Byzantine emperor Justinian roped in Ethiopian Christian traders to explore trading links with Kerala in an attempt to wrest control over the trade away from the Sassanids. This initiative, as Malekandathil has documented, was foiled during the reign of Khusrow II, who pioneered important human, material and cultural links with India and whose story is important for our narrative.

During his reign, as Shirin was sending her people to the Indian subcontinent, Khusrow was active in consolidating trade and cultural relations: the game of chess (*chaturanga* in India) is believed to have been introduced to Persia (where it was known as *shatranj*) at this time. Later, when Persia was conquered by the Arabs, the game quickly spread all over the Middle East and then to Europe.

Furthermore, under Khusrow, Jundishpur was developed as a leading centre of Persian medicine, in which the Indian Ayurvedic system was syncretized with the Greek system propagated there by the Nestorian Christians. In addition, the *Charaka Samhita*, the famous Indian medical text by the physician Charaka, was translated into Persian and then Arabic in the seventh century (Malekandathil 2010: 35).

Historiography of the region during the years that interest us is scant – there are passing references to the Dravidian/Tamil polities and a few musicological texts which we shall return to shortly, and there are histories of Kerala Christians and Jews (with scant references to Arabs and Persians/Parsis) with some reflection on the liturgical traditions. Work by Mark Aranha and George Pioustin on the RAA project are excellent contributions to the documentation and analysis of the music of the Jews and the Syrian Christians of Kerala (Aranha 2021; Pioustin 2019). However, the tracing of Indian Ocean connections or examining the traces of Persian influences, if they exist, are still at a nascent stage.

Leela Omchery's work (Omchery 1969) covers the period from when Hinduism asserted its dominance in the late seventh and eighth centuries CE, and it contains the most often-quoted paragraph in official Kerala documents:

> ... the early music of Kerala, with *natya* line at its helm, finds an eloquent expression in the contents of the chapter called *arangettru-kkadai* of *Chilappathikaram*, one of the five great epics of the ancient Dravida literature, for which an exhaustive commentary has been supplied by *Adivarkku-Nallar*, its leading commentator. This music had its heyday during the dominance of *Jainism* and *Buddhism* in South India, a few centuries before and after Christ. It is said to be the mirror of the music culture of the above sects, famous for their artistic achievements and organizations. As centuries moved on, these two religious systems were overpowered by Hinduism which came as a storm to uproot them. Yet, it took a few centuries for Hinduism to establish its supremacy. Though religion changed music and other arts they were not very much affected during these years except for the fact that from then onwards, the spiritual line became more prominent. (Ibid.: 36)

The epic *Chilappathikaram*, the subject of very serious musicological analysis by S. Ramanathan (1979) and by Lewis Rowell (2000), is a testimony to a remarkable performative and theoretical system. In the words of Rowell, 'their teachings are both a fossil record of the music from which they arose and a tribute to human ingenuity in formalizing the sensuous world of musical sound and translating it into concepts that can be taught, learned and remembered' (ibid.: 37). And according to Omchery, they are interrelated: 'in the case of Tamil music, there are probable connections to the rāgas of modern south India, as well as possible historical links with the music of neighbouring West Asia and the eastward spread of Indic culture throughout the Southeast Asian mainland and archipelago' (Omchery 1969: 38).

The work of Rowell is a theoretical *tour de force* in which he unpacks the historical layers of commentary to arrive at a clear description of the Tamil modal system, which, by the end of his analysis, he declares unique (Rowell 2000: 39). However, in his effort to define the *differentia specifica* of the Tamil system, he bends the stick too far in terms of uniqueness and distance from the Persian:

> . . . the Tamil scales were diatonic, with none of the chromatic tunings of the Persian scales to the west, and no hint of the equidistant scales and more restrictive sets of modal rotations heard today in various regions of Southeast Asia. For our purposes, the most appropriate comparisons are to the modes of the medieval Catholic Church and the scales of ancient Greece and India. (Ibid.: 40)

He goes on to state that there is no hint 'that these systems are the result of the spread of culture from one region to another' (ibid.: 41). He concedes, though, that the 'pattern of rotation reminds us of ancient Chinese practice in which the basic pentatonic scale was derived by ascending perfect fifths and then rearranged in consecutive steps within the compass of an octave' (ibid.: 43), and also that those Phrygian and Dorian resolutions in the Tamilian system might echo the ancient Greek system.

Our historical point is different, and always on the side of those who want to facilitate the opening of Lorca's 'hermetic flowers of semitones' (Lorca 1922: 4). South India and its Tamil world were not an insular or inert part of the world that received influences that in turn modified or rejected them; they were active parts of the whole world system of the time. If the music was discordant in relation to Persian chromatic scales, this might not have been because of distance or ignorance, but precisely because of a politics of differentiation.

In India, therefore, the AfroAsian musical landscape emerged from the seventh century, and even if the influences on music from outside the geographical region of India might have been recorded only from the thirteenth century or so, and only for north India, reading between the lines of texts such as the *Brhaddesi* and the *Sangita-Ratnakara*, and combining information available for the vast regions from north-western India into West Asia and then down to the eastern African coast or into North Africa, suggests possible explanations for several accommodations that were being recorded by the texts. The Islamic influences on Indian music, therefore, would have contained kernels from musical cultures that had spread across all these cultures. Further, as with the Arabic and Chinese systems, the emergence of classical music in both north and south India demonstrates the various impulses behind codification and the demarcation of the social status of performers in a highly dynamic social milieu.

Musical Routes and Imprints in AfroAsia: Summing Up

We began this chapter with examples of contemporary musical renderings that constituted the beginning of our enquiry into what might lie behind the close resemblances between melodies found across vast stretches of the globe. What might have been the factors that contributed to the similarity between the *heer* found in north-western India at one end, and the specific kinds of flamenco songs that we listened to at the other end in Cordoba, with several other examples that geographically are found in between? The said melodies are only one kind of example of the 'sounds like' that we have used as an important methodological tool in this work. There are perhaps many more such examples that can be excavated if we travel along the 'note-roads' that reflect long histories of interaction.

What has been done further is to employ the history of musical systems, related performance traditions, and stories about communities and their traditions, to tease out characteristics that reflect long-distance interactions as well as the influences of local dynamics across the AfroAsian landscape. We have extended the geographies of association, somewhat daringly, beyond what has been done in most research into music histories.

A major contention of this chapter is that if we listen carefully in AfroAsia for music and associated performance forms, although voice cultures, instrumentation, arrangements and notations differ, there are strong resemblances that are uncanny. Some of these resemblances are identified in musicological and ethnomusicological work, but what we are suggesting are resemblances and associations that go beyond the well-known routes. Thus, while the Turko-Persian influence on Indian music, mostly north Indian, or the music of al-Andalus, or the Persian, Arabic and North African *maqām* systems, or the musics of various Asian communities of African origin (say, the Sidis in Gujarat, the Kaffirinha music in Sri Lanka) are recognized, compared and documented, they remain limited in geographic scope. Our research into soundscapes and their *associational clusters* has led us to point out connections between communities and their social and ritual practices that have deep and long histories of migration and interconnectedness. We have argued that there appears to be a common *aesthetic constellation* that defined and defines musicality, linked to large-scale movements in society that created unique aesthetic acuities, which in turn allowed for aesthetic forms to travel and make themselves available to people who, deeply embedded in their own social spaces, could draw on these forms to innovate, imitate and create new constellations in turn. We focused on the period between the seventh century and the fifteenth century, ending just before colonialism, to trace the emergence of translocal yet deeply locally embedded musics that have also carried forward into the contemporary period.

Even examining one stretch of our geographical space demonstrates the traces of two or three routes: for example, if the exploration of musical connections begins from western and north-western India, as we did in chapter four, the route taken into parts of north-western India by communities from Sindh after the Arab invasion and the advent of Islam in the sixth century CE, the route taken by Luri/Luti musicians to Persia and then to various parts of the Roma route, and the travels of several of the communities to and from Greece/Syria into Sindh and north-western India can be traced. The research into the social practices of different communities in the different parts of this stretch have been studied in themselves, but the criss-crossing connections have often not been made. Our entry point of music leads us to understand the influence of these various migrations and routes and their interaction with local histories of state formation, and to point to connections that need to be explored across borders. Further, it is our belief that comparative musicology or organology will point us more substantially to the influences of both long-distance migrations as well as localized histories.

A second contention is that the circulation of musical traditions takes place very often through the motifs associated with archetypes. Contemporary renditions of love stories, praise poems and other historical forms deploy what A.K. Ramanujan called 'symbol pools' of oral narratives, music and visual representations that come down from centuries before (Ramanujan 1999). So, in north-western India, Heer becomes the archetypal woman yearning for her home, Marviis the archetypal one lamenting her loss of her desert home in large parts of West Asia, the archetypal Shirin is sung about in laments of various kinds, the 'blackbird' or the 'black crow' appears in Indian and Andalusian music, and so on. The archetypes are typically created around women, and the laments echo the conditions of separation, yearning, persecution and migration.

Third, whether it is the Luris of present-day Iran and Pakistan, the Uyghurs of China, the Sidis of India, or the Roma in Central Asia and Europe, their music has been imbued with notions of 'savageness', and is also in many cases linked with slavery and servitude. Further, to this date, the musics of many of these communities have their own versions of classification into systems that represent art music traditions from the regions or countries. The Jatts in India, for example, classify their music in terms of rāgas, the Uyghurs have *makams*, and West African communities in the Trabel Bidan have the *haul*. So, while the communities themselves might be among the lowliest in terms of social status, the amorphous boundaries between their musics and high-art music also point to continuities in systems of proliferation and dissemination. The distinctions that are clearly made, often to demonstrate civilizational prowess, between classical and non-classical or high and low forms of music thus tend to get disturbed with the uncovering of these histories.

Fourth, we can see a broad distinction between largely pentatonic and heptatonic musical systems in the AfroAsian world, and this often can prevent a comparison being made; but an extension of the geographies of association, as we have done, allows us to prise open the 'national' or 'regional' musical associations. For example, music from China is largely pentatonic, but heptatonic music is found in regions of Silk Route trade and migration. Pentatonicity also characterizes many musics from Africa, but the minor note-based inflections or heptatonic scales from parts of northern and western Africa echo Asian musical traditions in serious ways.

These points that we are making are guided by larger imperatives of understanding music histories, and, through them, understanding AfroAsian pasts in ways that are not apparent through known and well-practised methodologies of research. However, we are making these points with some hesitation as well. Not only is this 'work in progress', but there are many hypothetical and imaginary propositions that need further research. We hope, though, that after this the history of music will be told differently, and instead of the division between musicology and ethnomusicology, which separates what is considered 'core' music from the musics of communities that are embedded in social practices primarily from the non-west, something new will emerge. A broader canvas of its evolution is necessary, and a new challenge may emerge to how history has been dealt with in the past.

Notes

[1] Madan Gopal Singh, the Sufi musician and philosopher who has been one of the major resource persons in our project, stated in his interview with us that in his travels he has found around 56 versions of the *heer* of which he himself uses more than thirty in his music.

[2] The central element in both north Indian (Hindustani) and south Indian (Carnatic) classical music traditions is the rāga. A rāga, often defined as a melodic mode, is characterized by melodic features such as particular scales, treatment of individual notes, notes that are important and omitted, melodic phrases, etc. In addition, a rāga is also associated with extra-musical characteristics such as performance time, seasonal changes and aesthetic functions. Bhairavi (in the Hindustani tradition) or Sindhu Bhairavi (in the Carnatic tradition) is an example of a *sampoorna* (complete) rāga or heptatonic scale, employing seven notes in its melodic structure, with the second, third, sixth and seventh notes being lowered or being *komal swaras*. The Hindustani rāga classification system divides rāgas into categories called *thāt*, with each *thāt* having several rāgas under it.

[3] See https://youtu.be/0pCqb2XS0fg.

[4] See https://youtu.be/LaHejLDqXvY.

[5] See https://youtu.be/i_VRFwz3xTI.

[6] See https://youtu.be/E9ryYH_fVr4.

[7] See, for example, Ibrahim (2004) and Kothiyal (2016).

[8] Kathyayini Dash, a PhD scholar, travelled to thirteen villages in Kachchh in 2018 and 2019, and Sumangala Damodaran (with the research team of Abhishek Anid Dutta, Neelambari Bhattacharya and Akshita Bhat) travelled to Jodhpur and Bikaner in December 2019.

[9] See http//kabirproject.org.

[10] See http://kabirproject.org; https://www.dawn.com/news/643433/a-centuries-old-tradition-kept-alive-by-bhitais-faqirs.

[11] The Hudkal community is classified among the lower castes of western Rajasthan.

[12] We are basing our analysis of these two texts on secondary sources like G.D. Sawa (1985, 1989, 2019), and on a translation for this project of a small part of *Kitab-al-Musiqi al-Kabir* by Karen Press (Al-Farabi 2016).

[13] G.D. Sawa (1985, 1989, 2019), S.M. Sawa (2002), Farmer (1929) and Nielson (2012) are some of the works where details of these texts can be found.

[14] The discussion here is based on G.D. Sawa (1989).

References

Abu-Haidar, J. (1993), 'The Case for the Arabic Origins of the Muwashshahat: Court Poetry and Burlusque in Al Andalus', *Maghreb Review*, vol. 18, pp. 1–2.

Abu-Lughod, J.L. (1971), *Cairo: 1001 Years of the City*, Princeton: Princeton University Press.

—— (1991), *Before European Hegemony: The World System A.D. 1250–1350*, New York: Oxford University Press.

—— (2000), 'Review: *Re-Orient*', *Journal of World History*, vol. 11, no. 1, pp. 111-14.

Adorno, T.W. (2001), *Aesthetic Theory*, Minneapolis: University of Minnesota Press.

Akbari, S.C. and K. Mallette, eds (2013), *A Sea of Languages: Rethinking the Arabic Role in Medieval Literary History*, Toronto: University of Toronto Press.

Alam, M. and S. Subramaniam (2007), *Indo-Persian Travels in the Age of Discovery: 1400–1800*, Cambridge: Cambridge University Press.

Alatas, S.F. (2013), *Ibn Khaldun*, Oxford: Oxford University Press.

Al-Farabi, A.N. (2016), *Kitab al-Musiqi al-Kabir* (*Great Treatise on Music*), English translation by Karen Press of sections of the French translation, *La musique arabe, Tome I* by Rudolph D'Erlanger, first published in 1930 in Paris by Librairie Orientaliste Paul Geuthner, reissued in 2001 by Société Nouvelle Librairie Orientaliste Paul Geuthner, co-edited by the Institut du Monde Arabe, Paris, published with the support of Centre National du Livre.

Ali, O. (2011), *The African Diaspora in the Indian Ocean World*, Schomburg Center for Research in Black Culture and New York Public Library, http://exhibitions.nypl.org/africansindianocean/index2.php.

Ali, T. (1993), *In the Shadow of the Pomegranate Tree*, London: Verso.

—— (1998), *The Book of Saladin*, London: Verso.

Al-Tabari, A. (1992), *The History of Al-Tabari: The Revolt of the Zanj (A.D. 869–879/A.H. 255–265)*, vol. 36, translated and annotated by David Waines, Albany: State University of New York Press.

Amanolahi, S. and E. Norbeck (1975), 'The Luti, an Outcaste Group of Iran', *Rice Institute Pamphlet – Rice University Studies*, vol. 61, no. 2, https://hdl.handle.net/1911/63181.

Amin, S. (1971), *Accumulation on a World Scale*, New York: Monthly Review Press.

Amoros, L.G. (2012), 'Haul Music: Transnationalism and Musical Performance in the Saharaui Refugee Camps of Tindouf, Algeria', PhD dissertation, Rhodes University.

—— (2016), 'Music and Islam in the Saharawi Refugee Camps of the Hamada Desert, Algeria: The Practice of Medej as a Syncretic Musical Evolution', *Muziki*, vol. 13, no. 1, pp. 43–57.

Anfray, F. (1995), 'The Civilization of Aksum from the First to the Seventh Century', in G. Mokhtar, ed., *Ancient Civilizations of Africa*, General History of Africa, vol. 2, Paris: UNESCO, Berkeley: University of California Press, Oxford: James Currey.

Anonymous (2009), *Fetha Nagast: The Law of Kings*, translated from Ge'ez by A.T. Tzadua, Durham: North Carolina University Press.

Anonymous (2010), *The Harp of Glory – Enzira Sebhat: An Alphabetical Hymn of Praise for the Ever-Blessed Virgin Mary from the Ethiopian Orthodox Church*, New York: St Vladimir's Seminary Press.

Aranha, M. (2021), 'Jews and Mappilas of Kerala: A Study of Their History and Selected Song Traditions', Master's thesis, Faculty of Humanities, University of Cape Town.

Badalkhan, S. (2002), 'Coastal Makran as Corridor to the Indian Ocean World', *Euroasian Studies*, vol. 1, pp. 237–62.

—— (2005), 'The Lūṛīs: Artists and Artisans of Southwest Asia', in *Scritti in Onoredi Giovanni M. D'Erme, Saggi di Colleghie Amici in Occasionedel Suocompleanno*, Series Minor, vol. 48, Naples: Universitàdegli Studi di Napoli 'L'Orientale'.

Bagby, B. (2002a), 'Imagining the Early Medieval Harp', in R.W. Duffin, ed., *A Performer's Guide to Medieval Music*, Bloomington: Indiana University Press.

—— (2002b), 'Reflections on the Image of Musical Roots', *Sequentia*, https://www.sequentia.org/writings/musical_roots.html.

Bano, S. (2011), 'Women Performers and Prostitutes in Medieval India', *Studies in History*, vol. 27, no. 1, pp. 41–53.

Basu, H. (2008), 'Music and the Formation of Sidi Identity in Western India', *History Workshop Journal*, vol. 65, no. 1, pp. 161–78.

Bathily, A. (1988), 'Relations between the Different Regions of Africa', in M. El Fasi, ed., *Africa from the Seventh to the Eleventh Century*, General History of Africa, vol. 3, Paris: UNESCO, Berkeley: University of California Press, Oxford: James Currey.

Baum, W. (2004), *Shirin: Christian, Queen, Myth of Love, a Woman of Late Antiquity, Historical Reality and Literary Effect*, Piscataway: Gorgias Press.

Beaujard, P. (2007), 'East Africa, the Comoros Islands and Madagascar before the Sixteenth Century: On a Neglected Part of the World-System', *Azania: Archaeological Research in Africa*, vol. 42, no. 1, pp. 15–35.

—— (2011), 'The First Migrants to Madagascar and Their Introduction of Plants: Linguistic and Ethnological Evidence', *Azania: Archaeological Research in Africa*, vol. 46, no. 2, pp. 169–89.

Beeman, W.O. (2002), *Iranian Performance Traditions*, Biblioetica Iranica, Performing Arts Series, Costa Mesa, California: Mazda Publications.

Betreyohannes, S. (2010), 'Scholarship on Ethiopian Music: Past, Present and Future Prospects', *African Study Monographs* (Suppl. 41), pp. 19–34.

Bhambra, G.K. (2014), *Connected Sociologies*, London: Bloomsbury Press.

Blench, R. (2012a) 'Theory, Methods and Results in the Reconstruction of African Music History', mimeo.

—— (2012b), 'Using Diverse Sources of Evidence for Researching the Prehistory of Musical Exchange in the Indian Ocean and the Broader Significance for Cultural Prehistory', mimeo.

Brahaspati, K.C. (1969), *Muslim Influence on Venkatamakhi and His School*, New Delhi: Sangeet Natak Akademi.

Braun, J. and Y. Braun (2002), *Music in Ancient Israel/Palestine: Archaeological, Written, and Comparative Sources*, Grand Rapids: Eerdmans.

Brook, T. (1989), *The Asiatic Mode of Production in China*, New York: Armonk.

—— (1998), *The Confusions of Pleasure: Commerce and Culture in Ming China*, Berkeley: University of California Press.

—— (2010), *The Troubled Empire: China in the Yuan and the Ming Dynasties*, Cambridge, Mass.: Harvard University Press.

Bruinders, S. and V. Layne (2006), 'Our Language, Our Music, Our City?/Gold, Tears and Music/Scratch, mix and–? by Bridget Thompson and Abdulkadir Ahmed Said (producers and directors)', *Journal of the Musical Arts in Africa*, vol. 3, no. 1, pp. 119–22, doi: 10.2989/18121000609486717.

Buck, D.D. (1999), 'Was It Pluck or Luck that Made the West Grow Rich?', *Journal of World History*, no. 2, pp. 413–30.

Buzurg ibn Shariyār (n.d.), *Book of the Wonders of India*, English translation by K. Press of the French translation by L. Marcel Devic of the Arabic text *Kitāb ʿAjā'ib al-Hind*; prepared for the Recentring AfroAsia Project, University of Cape Town, University of the Western Cape, University of the Witwatersrand and Ambedkar University Delhi.

Byres, Terence J., K.N. Panikkar and Utsa Patnaik, eds (2000), *The Making of History: Essays presented to Irfan Habib*, Delhi: Tulika Books.

Camp, M. and B. Nettl (1955), 'The Musical Bow in Southern Africa', *Anthropos*, vol. 50, nos 1/3, pp. 65–80.

Caro Repetto, R., R. Gong, N. Kroher and X. Serra (2015), *Comparison of the Singing Style of Two Jingju Schools*, Proceedings of the 16th International Society for Music Information Retrieval Conference, Malaga, Spain, 26–30 October.

Caswell, F.M. (2011), *The Slave Girls of Baghdad: The Qiyan in the Early Abbasid Era*, London: I.B. Tauris.

Caitlin-Jairazbhoy, A. (2012), 'Sacred Pleasure, Pain and Transformation in African

Indian Sidi Sufi Ritual and Performance', *Performing Islam*, vol. 1, no. 1, pp. 73–101.

Chami, F.A. (1998), 'A Review of Swahili Archaeology', *African Archaeological Review*, vol. 15, no. 3, pp. 199–218.

Chandler, T. (1987), *Four Thousand Years of Urban Growth: An Historical Census*, Queenston: St David's University Press.

Charry, E. (1996), 'Plucked Lutes in West Africa: An Historical Overview', *The Galpin Society Journal*, vol. 49, pp. 3–37.

Chase-Dunn, C.K. (1991), *Global Formation: Structures of the World Economy*, London, Oxford and New York: Basil Blackwell.

—— (2000), 'Review of Andre Gunder Frank's *Reorient*: Global Economy in the Asian Age', *American Journal of Sociology*, vol. 105, no. 4, pp. xxix, 416.

Chaudhuri, K.N. (1991), *Asia Before Europe: Economy and Civilization of the Indian Ocean from the Rise of Islam to 1750*, Cambridge: Cambridge University Press.

Chejne, A.J. (1974), *Muslim Spain: Its History and Culture*, Minneapolis: University of Minnesota Press.

Chirikure, S. (2015), *Metals in Past Societies: A Global Perspective on Indigenous African Metallurgy*, New York: Springer.

—— (2020), *Great Zimbabwe: Reclaiming a 'Confiscated' Past*, London: Routledge.

Clot, A. (1989), *Harun Al-Rashid and the World of a Thousand and One Nights*, New York: New Amsterdam Books.

Connah, G. (2001), *African Civilizations: An Archaeological Perspective*, second edition, Cambridge: Cambridge University Press.

Cooper, P. (2018), 'The Ancient Poems that Explain Today', *BBC*, https://www.bbc.com/culture/article/20180820-the-6th-century-poems-making-a-comeback, accessed 5 September 2021.

Coquery-Vidrovich, C. and H. Moniot (1974), *A New Survey of Tropical Africa: L'Afrique Noire de 1800 à Nos Jours*, Paris: Presses Universitaires de France.

Crummy, D. (1999), *Land and Society in the Christian Kingdom of Ethiopia from the 13th to the 20th Century*, Oxford: James Currey.

Damodaran, S. and A. Sitas (2016), 'The Musical Journey: Re-Centring AfroAsia through an Arc of Musical Sorrow', *Critical Arts*, vol. 30, no. 2, pp. 252–68.

Dash, K. (2017), 'The Jatt Lament and Its Journeys', paper presented at Re-centring AfroAsia Conference, University of Cape Town.

Davila, C. (2009), 'Fixing a Misbegotten Biography: Ziryab in the Mediterranean World', *Al-Masaq: Journal of the Medieval Mediterranean*, vol. 21, no. 2, pp. 121–36.

Daymond, M.J., D. Driver, S. Meintjies, L. Molema, C. Musengezi, M. Orford and N. Rasebotsa, eds (2003), *Women Writing Africa: The Southern Region*, New York: The Feminist Press at the City University of New York.

Delius, P., ed. (2007), *Mapungubwe: History and Heritage*, Pietermaritzburg: UKZN Press.

Ducène, J.C. (2015), 'Une Nouvelle Source Arabesur L'océanindienau Xe Siècle', *Afriques*, vol. 6.

Dunn, R.E. (1986), *The Adventures of Ibn Battuta: A Muslim Traveler of the 14th Century*, Berkeley: University of California Press.

Duran, M.M.M.L. (2015), '"Soliyo" (Calling the Horses): Song and Memory in Mande Music', in R. Harris and R. Pease, eds, *Pieces of the Musical World: Sounds and Cultures*, London: Routledge, pp. 49–66.

Elvin, M. (2010), *The Retreat of the Elephant: An Environmental History of China*, New Haven: Yale University Press.

Ertman, T.C., ed. (2017), *Max Weber's Economic Ethic of the World Religions*, Cambridge: Cambridge University Press.

Esteban, J.A. Rodriguez, ed. (2011), *Espanaen Africa: La cienciaespanolaen el Sahara Occidental, 1884–1976*, Madrid: Calamar Ediciones.

Fabrizi, M. (2015), 'The Round City of Baghdad', https://socks-studio.com/2015/10/06/the-round-city-of-baghdad/, accessed 15 April 2019.

Fagan, B.M. (1984), 'The Zambezi and Limpopo Basins: 1100–1500', in D.T. Niane, ed., *General History of Africa IV: Africa from the Twelfth to the Sixteenth Century*, Paris: UNESCO, Berkeley: University of California Press, Oxford: James Currey.

Fagan, B.M. and J. Kirkman (1967), 'An Ivory Trumpet from Sofala, Mozambique', *Ethnomusicology*, vol. 11, no. 3, pp. 368–74.

Farhat, H. (1990), *The Dastgah Concept in Persian Music*, Cambridge: Cambridge University Press.

Farmer, H.G. (1925a), *The Arabian Influence on Musical Theory*, London: Reeve.

—— (1925b), 'The Influence of Music: From Arabic Sources', *Proceedings of the Musical Association*, vol. 52, no. 1, pp. 89–124.

—— (1929), *A History of Arabian Music to the XIIIth Century*, London: Luzac.

Ferdowsi, A. (2007), *The Shahnameh: The Persian Book of Kings*, translated by D. Dicks, Harmondsworth: Penguin.

Ferreira, M.P. (2000), 'Andalusian Music and the Cantigas de Santa Maria', in S. Parkinson, ed., *Cobras e Son: Papers on the Text, Music and Manuscripts of the Cantigas de Santa Maria*, Oxford: European Humanities Research Centre of the University of Oxford, pp. 7–19

Finnegan, R. (1976), *Oral Literature in Africa*, Nairobi: Oxford University Press.

Frank, A.G. (1998), *Reorient: Global Economy in the Asian Age*, Berkeley: University of California Press.

Ghosh, A. (1992), *In an Antique Land*, London: Vintage.

Gordon, M.S. (2004), 'The Place of Competition: The Careers of 'A Rib Alma'muniya and 'Ula Yy A Bint Almahdi: Sisters in Song', in J.E. Montgomery, ed., *'Abbasid Studies: Occasional Papers of the School of 'Abbasid Studies, Cambridge, 6–10 July 2002*, Leuven: Peeters, pp. 61–82.

—— (2009), 'Yearning and Disquiet: Al-Jahiz and the Risalat Al-Qiyan', in A. Heinemann, M. Kropp, T. Khalidi and J.L. Meloy, eds, *Al-Jahiz: a Muslim Humanist for our Time*, Wurzburg: Ergon, pp. 253–68.

Gordon, M.S. and K.A. Hain, eds (2017), *Concubines and Courtesans: Women and Slavery in Islamic History*, Oxford: Oxford University Press.

Habib, I. (1995), *Essays in Indian History: Towards a Marxist Perception*, Delhi: Tulika Books.

Hall, M. (1987), *The Changing Past: Farmers, Kings and Traders in Southern Africa 200–1860*, Cape Town: David Philip.

Hall, R. (1998), *Empires of the Monsoon: A History of the Indian Ocean and Its Invaders*, London: Harper Collins.

Hamilton, C. (2002), '"Living by Fluidity": Oral Histories, Material Custodies and the Politics of Archiving', in *Refiguring the Archive*, Dordrecht: Springer, pp. 209–28.

Harris, E. (1992), 'The African Diaspora in the Old and the New Worlds', in B.A. Ogot, ed., *General History of Africa V: Africa from the Sixteenth to the Eighteenth Century*, Paris: UNESCO, Berkeley: University of California Press, Oxford: James Currey, pp. 113–36.

Harris, R. (2008), *The Making of a Musical Canon in Chinese Central Asia: The Uyghur Twelve Muqam*, Aldershot: Ashgate.

Huan, M. ([1433] 1970), *Ying-Ya: Sheng-Lan; The Overall Survey of the Ocean's Shores*, Cambridge: Cambridge University Press.

Hung, H.F. (2008), 'Agricultural Revolution and Elite Reproduction in Qing China: The Transition to Capitalism Debate Revisited', *American Sociological Review*, vol. 73, no. 4, pp. 569–88.

Huffman, T.N. (1988), 'Southern Africa to the South of the Zambezi', in M. Elfasi, ed., *Africa from the Seventh to the Eleventh Century*, General History of Africa, vol. 3, Chapter 24, Berkeley: Heinemann and UNESCO, pp. 664–80.

—— (2000), 'Mapungubwe and the Origins of the Zimbabwe Culture', in M. Leslie and T. Maggs, eds, *African Naissance: The Limpopo Valley 1000 Years Ago*, The South African Archaeological Society Goodwin Series, no. 8, pp. 14–29.

—— (2005), *Mapungubwe: Ancient African Civilization on the Limpopo*, Johannesburg: Wits University Press.

—— (2007), *Handbook to the Iron Age: The Archaeology of Pre-Colonial Farming Societies in Southern Africa*, Scottsville: University of KwaZulu–Natal Press.

Ibn Battuta (1958–1994), *The Travels of Ibn Battuta*, vols 1–4, Cambridge: Hakluyt Society.

Ibn Khaldun (2004), *The Muqaddimah: An Introduction to History*, translated by F. Rosenthal, Princeton: Princeton University Press.

Ibn Majid (1470), *First Navigational Poem (As Sufaliyya – The Poem of Sofala)*, available at http://www.geocities.ws/derideauxp/madjid_sofali yya.html, accessed 2 October 2018.

Ibrahim, F. (2004), 'No Place Like Home: History, Politics and Mobility Among a Pastoral Nomadic Community in Western India', *Nomadic Peoples*, vol. 8, no. 2, pp. 168–90.

Janzen, J.M. (1992), *Ngoma*, Berkeley: University of California Press.

—— (2017), 'Theories of Music in African Ngoma Healing', in P. Gouk, ed., *Musical Healing in Cultural Contexts*, London: Routledge, pp. 46–66.

Jayasuriya, S. de Silva and J.P. Angenot, eds (2008), *Uncovering the History of Africans in Asia*, Leiden: Brill.

Jenkins, J. and P.R. Olsen, (1976), *Music and Musical Instruments in the World of Islam*, London: World of Islam Festival Publishing Company.

Jeyachandran, N. (2014), 'Memory, Heritage, and Cultural Display in the Former Colonial Port Cities of Elmina (Ghana) and Fort Kochi (India)', PhD thesis, University of California Los Angeles.

Joris, P. and H. Tengour, eds (2012), *Poems for the Millennium*, vol. 4, Berkeley: University of California Press.

Kalu, A. ed. (2007), *The Rienner Anthology of African Literature*, Boulder: Lynne Rienner.

Kennedy, H. (2004), *The Court of the Caliphs: The Rise and Fall of Islam's Greatest Dynasty*, London: Weidenfeld and Nicolson.

Kenrick, D. (2004), *Gypsies: From the Ganges to the Thames*, Hatfield: University of Hertfordshire Press.

Kilpatrick, H. (2003), *Making the Great Book of Songs: Compilation and the Author's Craft in Abu l-Faraj Al-Isbahani's Kitab al-Aghani*, London: Routledge.

Koela, E.N. (2019), '"Seeds of the Braced Bow" (The Flower, the Seed and the Bee)', Master's thesis, Faculty of Humanities, College of Music, University of Cape Town.

Kothiyal, T. (2016), *Nomadic Narratives: A History of Mobility and Identity in the Great Indian Desert*, Cambridge: Cambridge University Press.

Kroher, N., A. Chaachoo, J.M. Díaz-Báñez, E. Gómez, F. Gómez-Martín, J. Mora and M. Sordo (2018), 'Computational Ethnomusicology: A Study of Flamenco and Arab-Andalusian Vocal Music', in R. Bader, ed. *Springer Handbook of Systematic Musicology*, Berlin: Springer, pp. 885–97.

Kusimba, C.M. (2004), 'Archaeology of Slavery in East Africa', *African Archaeological Review*, vol. 21, no. 2, pp. 59–88.

Lach, D. and Van Kley (1993), *Asia in the Making of Europe, Volume III: A Century of Advance*, Chicago: Chicago University Press.

LaViolette, A. (2008), 'Swahili Cosmopolitanism in Africa and the Indian Ocean World, A.D. 600–1500', *Archaeologies: Journal of the World Archaeological Congress*, vol. 4, no. 1, pp. 24–49.

Lawergren, B. (2010), 'Harps on the Ancient Silk Road', in *Conservation of Ancient Sites on the Silk Road*, Los Angeles, CA: The Getty Conservation Institute, pp. 117–24.

Layne, V. (2019), 'Goema's Refrain: Sonic Anticipation and the Musicking Cape', submitted for the Degree of Doctor of Philosophy in History, Faculty of Arts, University of the Western Cape.

Le Strange, G. (1983), *Baghdad during the Abbasid Caliphate: From Contemporary Arabic and Persian Sources*, Westport: Greenwood Press.

Levin, T. (2002), 'Music and Musicians Along the Silk Road', *Smithsonian Folklife Festival*, available at https://festival.si.edu/2002/the-silk-road/music-and-musicians-along-the-silk-road/smithsonian, accessed 25 February 2019.

Lihamba, A., F.L. Moyo, M.M. Mulokozi, N.L. Shitemi and S. Yahya-Othman, eds (2007), *Women Writing Africa: The Eastern Region*, New York: The Feminist Press at the City University of New York.

Liu, X. (2011), 'A Silk Road Legacy: The Spread of Buddhism and Islam', *Journal of World History*, vol. 22, no. 1, pp. 55–81.

Lodhi, A.Y. (2008), 'Bantu Origins of the Sidis of India', *Pambazuka News*, 29 October, available at https://www.pambazuka.org/global-south/bantu-origins-sidis-india, accessed 28 March 2019.

Loomba, A. (1987), *Gender, Race, Renaissance Drama*, Oxford: Oxford University Press.

Lorca, F.G. (1922), 'Deep Song' (*Importancia Histórica y Artística del Primitivo Canto Andaluz Llamado 'Cante Jondo'*), prose translation by A.S. Kline (2008), available at http://www.poetryintranslation.com/klineasdeepsong.htm, accessed 4 April 2016.

Ma, H. (1970), *The Overall Survey of the Ocean's Shores*, Cambridge: Cambridge University Press.

Mafeje, A. (1991), *The Theory of Ethnography of African Social Formations: The Case of the Interlacustrine Kingdoms*, Dakar: CODESRIA.

Mahalingam, T.V. (1951), *Economic Life in Vijaynagar Empire*, Madras: Madras University Press.

Mahfouz, N. (1959), *Children of Gebelawi*, London: Heinemann.

Malekandathil, P. (2010), *Maritime India: Trade, Religion and Polity in the Indian Ocean*, New Delhi: Primus Books.

Manuel, P. (1989), 'Andalusian, Gypsy, and Class Identity in the Contemporary Flamenco Complex', *Ethnomusicology*, vol. 33, no. 1, pp. 47–65.

—— (2008), 'North Indian Sufi Popular Music in the Age of Hindu and Muslim Fundamentalism', *Ethnomusicology*, vol. 52, no. 3, pp. 378–400.

Marouf, N. (1995), 'Structure de Répertoire Andalou: Quelques Problemes de Méthode', in N. Marouf, ed., *Le Chant Arabo-Andalou: Essai sur le Rurbainou la Topique de la Norme et de la Marge dans le Patrimonie Musical Arabe*, Paris: Harmattan, pp. 11–22.

Marx, K. (1974), *Grundrisse*, Harmondsworth: Penguin.

—— (1976), *Capital*, vol. I, Harmondsworth: Penguin.

Masao, F.T. and H.W. Mutoro (1988), 'The East African Coast and the Comoro Islands', in M. El Fasi, ed., *Africa from the Seventh to the Eleventh Century*, General History of Africa, vol. 3, Paris: UNESCO, Berkeley: University of California Press, Oxford: James Currey.

Massey, R. and S. Massey (1993), *The Music of India*, London: Kahn and Averill.

Matveiev, V.V. (1984), 'The Development of Swahili civilization', in D.T. Niane, ed., *General History of Africa IV: Africa from the Twelfth to the Sixteenth Century*, Paris: UNESCO; Berkeley: University of California Press; Oxford: James Currey.

McGee, T.J. (1998), *The Sound of Medieval Song: Ornamentation and Vocal Style According to the Treatises*, Oxford: Clarendon Press.

Mda, Z. (2013), *The Sculptors of Mapungubwe*, Cape Town: Kwela Books.

Mhlambi, T. (2017), 'The Meanings of Izinyanga in Ngini Traditions', paper presented at the Re-Centring AfroAsia Conference, Cape Town.

Millward, J. (n.d.), 'Uyghur Art Music and the Ambiguities of Chinese Silk Roadism in Xinjiang', *Silk Road Foundation Newsletter*, vol. 3, no. 1, available at http://www.silkroadfoundation.org/newsletter/vol3num1/3_uyghur.php

Mirelman, S. (2009), 'New Developments in the Social History of Music and Musicians in Ancient Iraq, Syria, and Turkey', *Yearbook for Traditional Music*, vol. 41, pp. 12–22.

Moorjani, P., N. Patterson, P.R. Loh, M. Lipson, P. Kisfali, B.I. Melegh, M. Bonin, L. Kádaši, O. Rieß, B. Berger, D. Reich and B. Melegh (2013), 'Reconstructing Roma History from Genome-Wide Data', *PloS One*, vol. 8, no. 3, e58633, doi: 10.1371/journal.pone.0058633.

Moss, J. and R. Rahman (2013), *The Sahmat Collective: Art and Activism in India since 1989*, Chicago: Smart Museum of Art, University of Chicago.

Mu, Y. (1994), 'On the Hua'er Songs of North-Western China', *Yearbook for Traditional Music*, vol. 26, pp. 100–16.

Muyanga, N. (2020), 'Decomposing Aria: The Work Voice Performs in Opera and Music Theatre in the Black Community in South Africa', Master's thesis submitted to the Faculty of Humanities, University of Cape Town.

Myrne, P. (2010), *Narrative, Gender and Authority in 'Abbāsid Literature on Women*, Orientalia et Africana Gothoburgensia 22, Göteborg: Department of Oriental and African Languages, University of Gothenburg.

Nettl, B. (1992), *The Radif of Persian Music*, Champaign: Elephant and Cats.

Neubauer, E. (2001), 'Ziryab', *Grove Music Online*, doi: 10.1093/gmo/9781561592630.article.31002.

Neuman, D.M., S. Chaudhuri and K. Kothari (2006), *Bards, Ballads and Boundaries: An Ethnographic Atlas of Music Traditions in West Rajasthan*, Calcutta: Seagull Books.

Newitt, M. (2017), *A Short History of Mozambique*, Oxford: Oxford University Press.

Ngcongco, L.D. (1984), 'Southern Africa: Its Peoples and Social Structures', in D.T. Niane, ed., *General History of Africa IV: Africa from the Twelfth to the Sixteenth Century*, Paris: UNESCO, Berkeley: University of California Press, Oxford: James Currey.

Nielson, L. (2012), 'Gender and the Politics of Music in the Early Islamic Courts', *Early Music History*, vol. 31, pp. 235-61.

Nizami (2012), *Selected Poems*, translated and introduced by Paul Smith, CreateSpace Independent Publishing Platform, Amazon.

Norris, H.T. (1962), 'Yemenis in the Western Sahara', *The Journal of African History*, vol. 3, no. 2, pp. 317–22.

Nyamushosho, T.R. and S. Chirikure (2019), 'Regional and Global Networking in Precolonial Southern Zambezia: Re-Examining the Archaeology of Chumnungwa', mimeo.

Odhiambo-Owuor, Y. (2019), *Dragonfly Sea*, London: Vintage.

Omchery, L. (1969), *Music of Kerala: A Study*, New Delhi: Sangeet Natak Akademi.

Opland, J. (1998), *Xhosa Poets and Poetry*, Cape Town: David Philip.
Opland, J. ed., (1992), *Words That Circle Words: A Choice of South African Oral Poetry*, Johannesburg: Donker Paper Books.
Orringer, N. (2016), *Lorca in Tune with Falla*, Toronto: University of Toronto Press.
Oxby, C. (1998), 'The Manipulation of Time: Calendars and Power in the Sahara', *Nomadic Peoples*, vol. 2, nos 1 and 2, pp. 137–49.
Pankhurst, R. (1992), *A Social History of Ethiopia: The Northern and Central Highlands from Early Medieval Times to the Rise of Emperor Tewordos II*, Trenton: Red Sea Press.
—— (1998), *The Ethiopians: A History*, Oxford: Blackwell.
Parvulescu, A. and M. Boatcă (2020), 'The Longue Durée of Enslavement: Extracting Labor from Romani Music in Liviu Rebreanu's Ion', *Literature Compass*, vol. 17, nos 1 and 2.
Pearson, M.N. (1998), *Port Cities and Intruders: The Swahili Coast, India and Portugal in the Early Modern Era*, Baltimore: Johns Hopkins University Press.
Peterson, W.J. (2002), *The Cambridge History of China*, vol. 9, Cambridge: Cambridge University Press.
Picken, L.E. and N.J. Nickson, eds (1997), *Music from the Tang Court*, vol. 6, Cambridge: Cambridge University Press.
—— (2006), *Music from the Tang Court*, vol. 7, Cambridge: Cambridge University Press.
Pioustin, G. (2019), 'Towards a New Shabd aur Sangeet: A Study on the Politics of Vernacularizing the Liturgical Music of the Syrian Christians of Malabar', in S. Mudgal, A. Pradhan and Kunal Ray, eds, *Shabd aur Sangeet: Unravelling Song-text in India*, Gurgaon: Three Essays Collective, pp. 119–45.
Pollock, S. (2006), *The Language of the Gods in the World of Men: Sanskrit, Culture and Power in Premodern India*, Berkeley: University of California Press.
Pollock, S., ed. (2003), *Literary Cultures in History: Reconstructions from South Asia*, Berkeley: University of California Press.
Pomeranz, K. (2000), *The Great Divergence: China, Europe and the Making of the Modern World Economy*, Princeton: Princeton University Press.
Pomeranz, K. and S. Topik (2012), *The World that Trade Created: Society, Culture and the World Economy, 1400 to the Present*, 3rd edition, London: Routledge.
Prabhu, M.M. (1996), 'Some Thoughts on the Bhuta Worship in South Kanara', in U. Padmanabha Upadhyaya, ed., *Coastal Karnataka: Studies in Folkloristic and Linguistic Traditions of Dakshina Kannada Region of the Western Coast of India*, Udupi: Rastrakavi Govind Pai Research Institute, pp. 43–65.
Radkau, J. (2008), *Nature and Power: A Global History of the Environment*, Cambridge: Cambridge University Press.
Ramanathan, S. (1979), 'Music in Cilappathikaaram', PhD dissertation, Madurai Kamaraj University, Madurai.
Ramanujan, A.K. (1999), 'Who Needs Folklore?', in V. Dharwadker, ed., *The Collected Essays of A.K. Ramanujan*. New Delhi: Oxford University Press, pp. 532–52.
Randel, D.M. (1976), 'Al-Farabi and the Role of Arabic Music Theory in the Latin

Middle Ages', *Journal of the American Musicological Society*, vol. 29, no. 2, pp. 173–88.

Reimer, M. (2020), 'Music for One World: Moroccan Musical Experience of Diversity, Fusion, Happiness, Healing, and Peace', *Journal of Global Awareness*, vol. 1, no. 1, Article 4, available at https://scholar.stjohns.edu/jga/vol1/iss1/4, accessed 15 July 2019.

Reynolds, D. (2009), 'The Re-Creation of Medieval Arabo-Andalusian Music in Modern Performance', *Al-Masaq: Journal of the Medieval Mediterranean*, vol. 21, no. 2, pp. 175–89.

Richards, J. (2005), *The Unending Frontier: An Environmental History of the Early Modern World*, Berkeley: University of California Press.

Richardson, K. (2009), 'Singing Slave Girls (Qiyan) of the Abbasid Court in the Ninth and Tenth Centuries', in G. Campbell, S. Miers and J.C. Miller, eds, *Children in Slavery through the Ages*, Athens: Ohio University Press, pp. 105–17.

Rowell, L. (2000), 'Scale and Mode in the Music of the Early Tamils of South India', *Theory Spectrum*, vol. 22, no. 2, pp. 35–156.

—— (2015), *Music and Musical Thought in Early India*, Chicago: University of Chicago Press.

Sadiqi, F., A. Nowaira, A. El Kholy and M. Ennaji, eds (2009), *Women Writing Africa: The Northern Region*, Johannesburg: Wits University Press.

Saitowitz, S. (1996), 'Glass Beads as Indicators of Contact and Trade in Southern Africa ca. AD 900–AD 1250', PhD dissertation, University of Cape Town.

Sarangadeva (1951), *Sangita Ratnakara (Ocean of Music)*, Madras: Adyar Library.

Sastry, N.K.A. (1955), *A History of South India, from Prehistoric Times to the Fall of Vijayanagar*, Oxford: Oxford University Press

Sawa, G.D. (1985), 'The Status and Roles of the Secular Musicians in the *Kitab al-Aghani* (Book of Songs) of Abu al-Faraj al-Isbahani (D. 356 A.H./967 A.D.)', *Asian Music*, vol. 17, no. 1, pp. 69–82.

—— (1989), *Music Performance Practice in the Early 'Abbasid Era 132–320 A.H/750–932*, Toronto: Pontifical Institute of Mediaeval Studies.

—— (2019), *Musical and Socio-Cultural Anecdotes from Kitāb al-Aghānī al-Kabīr: Annotated Translations and Commentaries*, Leiden: Brill.

Sawa, S.M. (1987), 'The Role of Women in Musical Life: The Medieval Arabo-Islamic Courts', *Canadian Woman Studies – Les Cahiers de la Femme*, vol. 8, no. 2, pp. 93–95.

—— (2002), 'Historical Issues of Gender and Music', in V. Danielson, D. Reynolds and S. Marcus, eds, *The Garland Encyclopedia of World Music*, vol. 6, London: Routledge, pp. 293–98.

Schwengel, H. (2006), 'World Systems, Cities and Elites: An Archaeological-Sociological Intervention', mimeo, Institute of Sociology, Freiburg.

Segal, R. (2003), *Islam's Black Slaves: A History of Africa's Other Black Diaspora*, London: Atlantic Books.

Sells, M.A., trans. (1989), *Desert Tracings: Six Classic Arabian Odes by Alqama, Shan-*

fara, Labid, 'Antara, Al-A'sha, and Dhu al-Rumma, Middletown: Wesleyan University Press.
Serra, X. (2014) 'Creating Research Corpora for the Computational Study of Music: The Case of the Compmusic Project', *Audio Engineering Society Conference: 53rd International Conference: Semantic Audio*, New York: Audio Engineering Society.
—— (2017), 'The Computational Study of a Musical Culture through its Digital Traces', *Acta Musicologica* vol. 89, no. 1, pp. 24–44.
Shamsie, K. (2014), *A God under Every Stone*, London: Bloomsbury.
Shannon, J.H. (2007), 'Performing al-Andalus, Remembering al-Andalus: Mediterranean Soundings from Mashriq to Maghrib', *Journal of American Folklore*, vol. 120, no. 477, pp. 308–34.
Shehadi, F. (1995), *Philosophies of Music in Medieval Islam*, Leiden: Brill.
Sheng, B. (1999), 'Interview with Bright Sheng', *Journal of the International Institute*, vol. 7, no. 1, available at http://hdl.handle.net/2027/spo.4750978.0007.103, accessed 10 November 2019.
—— (2000), 'Melodic Migration of the Silk Road: Music Samplings of Northwest China', http://brightsheng.com/articles/essayfilesbybs/MELODIES%20OF%20THE%20SILK%20ROAD%20.pdf.
—— (n.d.), 'Hua'er Folksongs of Qinghai', http://brightsheng.com/articles/essayfilesbybs/Huaer.pdf.
Sheriff, A. (2010), *Dhow Cultures of the Indian Ocean: Cosmopolitanism, Commerce and Islam*, London: C. Hurst and Co.
Sherratt, A. (1981), 'Plough and Pastoralism: Aspects of the Secondary Products Revolution', in I. Hodder, G. Isaac and N. Hammond, eds, *Pattern of the Past: Studies in Honour of David Clarke*, Cambridge: Cambridge University Press, pp. 261–75.
—— (2000), 'Envisioning Global Change: A Long-Term Perspective', in R.A. Denemark, J. Friedman, B.K. Gills and G. Modelski, eds, *World System History*, London: Routledge.
—— (2004), 'Themes – Routes, Trade and Exchange', *ArchAtlas*, University of Sheffield, available at https://www.archatlas.org/themes/trade/, accessed 20 June 2016.
Sheth, A. (2017), 'Traveling Tunes: The Story of Zangula', paper presented at Re-Centring AfroAsia Project, University of Cape Town.
Shiloah, A. (1991), 'The Meeting of Christian, Jewish and Muslim Musical Cultures on the Iberian Peninsula (before 1492)', *Acta Musicologica*, vol. 63, fasc. 1, pp. 14–20.
—— (2000), *Music in the World of Islam: A Socio-Cultural Study*, Detroit: Wayne State University Press.
Shringy, R.K. and L.S. Prem, eds (1978), *Saṅgīta-ratnākara of Śāraṅgadeva: Sanskrit Text and English Translation with Comments and Notes, Vol. 1: Treatment of Svara*, Delhi: Motilal Banarsidass.
Simpson, E. (2007), *Muslim Society and the Western Indian Ocean: The Seafarers of Kachchh*, London: Routledge.

Sitas, A., W. Keim, S. Damodaran, N. Trimikiniotis and F. Garba (2014), *Gauging and Engaging Deviance, 1600–2000*, Delhi: Tulika Books.

Soneji, D. (2021), 'Resounding Islam: Occluded Muslim Histories of Modern South Indian Rāga-Based Music', talk given at British Library, London, available at https://www.bl.uk/events/occluded-muslim-histories-of-modern-south-indian-rga-based-music, accessed 30 December 2022.

Staniforth, M. (1996), 'Tracing Artefact Trajectories: Following Chinese Export Porcelain', *Bulletin of the Australian Institute for Maritime Archaeology*, vol. 20, no. 1, pp. 13–18.

Stone, R.M., ed. (2017), *The Garland Encyclopedia of World Music: Africa*, London: Routledge.

Strayer, H.R. (2013), 'From Neumes to Notes: The Evolution of Music Notation', *Musical Offerings*, vol. 4, no. 1, Article 1, available at https://digitalcommons.cedarville.edu/musicalofferings/vol4/iss1/1, accessed 18 November 2019.

Subramaniam, S. (1990a), *The Political Economy of Commerce in South India, 1500–1650*, Cambridge: Cambridge University Press.

—— (1990b), *Improvising Empire: Portuguese Trade and Settlement in the Bay of Bengal, 1500–1700*, Delhi: Oxford University Press.

—— (1993), *The Portuguese Empire in Asia, 1500–1700: A Political and Economic History*, London and New York: Longman.

Sutherland-Addy, E. and A. Diaw, eds (2005), *Women Writing Africa: West Africa and the Sahel*, Johannesburg: Wits University Press.

Sutton, J.E.G. (2002), 'The Southern Swahili Harbour and Town on Kilwa Island, 800–1800AD: A Chronology of Booms and Slumps', Uppsala University, available at https://www.yumpu.com/s/YJiI3p2tIIIwMJAIA, accessed 4 December 2019.

Sykes, P. (1921), 'South Persia and the Great War', *The Geographical Journal*, vol. 58, no. 2, pp. 101–16.

Talbi, M. (1988), 'The Independence of the Maghrib', in M. El Fasi, ed., *Africa from the Seventh to the Eleventh Century*, General History of Africa, vol. 3, Paris: UNESCO, Berkeley: University of California Press, Oxford: James Currey.

Talengala, S. (2017), 'Bobbare: A Spirit that Straddles the Sea', paper presented at Re-centring AfroAsia Conference, University of Cape Town.

Talhami, G.H. (1977), 'The Zanj Rebellion Reconsidered', *International Journal of African Historical Studies*, vol. 10, no. 3, pp. 443–61.

Talib, Y. and F. Samir (1988), 'The African Diaspora in Asia', in M. El Fasi, ed., *Africa from the Seventh to the Eleventh Century*, General History of Africa, vol. 3, Paris: UNESCO, Berkeley: University of California Press, Oxford: James Currey, pp. 704–33.

Tibbets, G.R. (1971), *Arab Navigation in the Indian Ocean before the Coming of the Portuguese*, London: Royal Asiatic Society.

Tiley-Nel, S., ed. (2011), 'Sermons in Stones, Poetry in Potsherds: The History of the Mapungubwe Collection at the University of Pretoria', in *Mapungubwe Remembered*, pp. 173–92. Johannesburg: Chris Van Rensburg Publishing.

Tolmacheva, M. (1980), 'On the Arab System of Nautical Orientation', *Arabica*, vol. 27, no. 2, pp. 180–92.

Trivedi, M. (2012), *The Emergence of the Hindustani Tradition*, New Delhi: Three Essays Collective.

Van Khê, T. (1985), 'Chinese Music and Musical Traditions of Eastern Asia', *World of Music*, vol. 27, no. 1, pp. 78–90.

Vansina, J. (1985), *Oral Tradition as History*, Madison, Wisconsin: University of Wisconsin Press.

—— (1990), *Paths in the Rainforests: Toward a History of Political Tradition in Equatorial Africa*, Michigan: University of Wisconsin Press.

—— (2003), *How Societies Are Born*, Philadelphia: University of Virginia Press.

Villiers, A. (1969), *Sons of Sinbad*, New York: Charles Scribner's Sons.

Virmani, S. and V. Rikhi (2019), *I Saw Myself: Journeys With Shah Abdul Latif Bhitai*, Gurgaon: Penguin Random House India.

Wallerstein, I. (1974), *The Modern World System: Capitalist Agriculture and the Origins of the European World Economy in the Sixteenth Century*, New York: Academic Press.

—— (2000), *The Wallerstein Reader*, New Haven: Yale University Press.

Waterson, J. (2007), *The Knights of Islam: The Wars of the Mamluks*, London: Greenhill Books.

Weber, M. (1969), *The Rational Foundations of Western Music*, Carbondale: Southern Illinois University Press.

Whitfield, S. (2004), 'The Silk Road: Trade, Travel, War and Faith', *History Today*, vol. 54, no. 5, pp. 2–3.

Widdess, R. (1979), 'The Kuḍumiyāmalai Inscription: A Source of Early Indian Music in Notation', *Musica Asiatica*, vol. 2, pp. 115–50.

—— (1995), *The Ragas of Early Indian Music*, Oxford: Clarendon Press.

Wilkinson, J.C. (1981), 'Oman and East Africa: New Light on Early Kilwan History from the Omani Sources', *International Journal of African Historical Studies*, vol. 14, no. 2, pp. 272–305.

Williams, M. (2007), 'The Role of Deforestation in Earth and World-System Integration', in A. Hornborg, J.R. McNeill and J. Martinez-Alier, eds, *Rethinking Environmental History: World-System History and Global Environmental Change*, Lanham, MD: AltaMira Press, pp. 101–23.

Winstedt, E.O. (1910), 'The Christian Topography of Cosmas Indicopleustes', *Nature*, vol. 84, pp. 133–34.

Wong, R.B. (1997), *China Transformed: Historical Change and the Limits of European Experience*, Ithaca: Cornell University Press.

Wood, F. (2002), *The Silk Road: Two Thousand Years in the Heart of Asia*, Berkeley: University of California Press.

Wood, M. (2011), 'A Glass Bead Sequence for Southern Africa from the 8th to the 16th Century AD', *Journal of African Archaeology*, vol. 9, no. 1, pp. 67–68.

Wright, O. (1978), *The Modal System of Arab and Persian Music, AD 1250–1350*, London: Oxford University Press.

—— (1992), 'Music in Muslim Spain', in S.K. Jayyusi, ed., *The Legacy of Muslim Spain*, Leiden: Brill, pp. 555–79.

Xiaodun, W. and S. Xiaohui. (2004), 'Yuebu of the Tang Dynasty: Musical Transmission from the Han to the Early Tang Dynasty', *Yearbook for Traditional Music*, vol. 36, pp. 50–64.

Yoffee, N. (2012), 'Deep Pasts: Interconnections and Comparative History in the Ancient World', in D. Northrop, ed., *A Companion to World History*, Malden, MA: Wiley-Blackwell, pp. 156–70.

Zemedu, G. and Y. Assabie (2014), 'Concatenative Hymn Synthesis from Yared Notations', in A. Przepiórkowski and M. Ogrodniczuk, eds, *Advances in Natural Language Processing: Lecture Notes in Computer Science*, vol. 8686, Cham: Springer, pp. 400–11, doi: 10.1007/978-3-319-10888-9_40.

Zhang, H. (2015), 'Property of the State, Prisoners of Music: Identity of the Song Drama Players and Their Roles in the Washi Pleasure Precincts', *Journal of the Chinese Academy of Sciences*, pp. 277–326.

Zonis, E. (1973), *Classical Persian Music: An Introduction*, Cambridge, Mass.: Harvard University Press.

Discography

Bakewell, A. (2000), *Music of Makran: Traditional Fusion from Coastal Balochistan*, recordings, text and photographs recorded and annotated by Anderson Bakewell, International Music Collection of the British Library National Sound Archive, World Series, TSCD 916.

Diabate, T. (2008), *The Mande Variations*, Nonesuch/Warner Records.

Dun, T. (2020), *Budhha Passion: The Hearts Sutra*, https://youtu.be/KuAZOvEhQ0M.

Lorca, F.G. and LaArgentinita (1994), *Colecciónde Canciones Populares Espanolas*, Madrid: Sonifolk.

Savall, J. (2008), *Jerusalem*, Alia Vox.

—— (2009), *Hesperion XXI – Istanbul*, Alia Vox.

—— (2010), *The Forgotten Kingdom – The Cathar Tragedy*, Alia Vox.

—— (2016), *Granada*, Alia Vox.

—— (2017), *Venizia Millenaria*, Alia Vox.

—— (2018), *Venezia Millenaria*, Barcelona: Alia Vox.

Filmography

Gatlif, T. (1993), *Latcho Drom*, France: K.G. Productions.

Neville, M. (2015), *The Music of Strangers: Yo-Yo Ma and the Silk Road Ensemble*, HBO Documentary Films, https://youtu.be/qvFjOw9K8eo.